Harper's New American Bible Study Program

Resource Book

Harper's New American Bible Study Program

Resource Book

General Editor: James P. Campbell

1817

Harper & Row, Publishers, San Francisco
1-800-328-5125
P.O. Box 1630
Hagerstown, MD 21741

New York, Grand Rapids, Philadelphia, St. Louis
London, Singapore, Sydney, Tokyo, Toronto

Acknowledgments

All scripture selections from *The New American Bible with Revised New Testament,* copyright © 1986 by the Confraternity of Christian Doctrine, Washington, D.C., are used with permission of copyright owner. All rights reserved.

All selections from Vatican II documents, copyright © 1987 by Austin Flannery O.P., ed. are reprinted with permission of Costello Publishing Co.

Selections from *On Genesis,* by Bruce Vawter, copyright © 1977, are used with permission of Doubleday, a division of Bantam, Doubleday, Dell Publishing Group, Inc.

Selections from the following titles are reprinted with permission of Harper & Row Publishers, Inc.: *Harper's Bible Commentary,* ed. James L. Mays, copyright © 1988 by the Society of Biblical Literature; *Harper's Bible Dictionary,* ed. Paul Achtemeier, copyright © 1984 by the Society of Biblical Literature; *The People Called,* by Paul D. Hanson, copyright © 1986 by Paul D. Hanson.

Selections from *The Collegeville Bible Commentary,* copyright © 1988 by the Order of St. Benedict, Inc., published by The Liturgical Press, Collegeville, Minnesota, are used with permission.

Text Design by R. Kharibian & Associates
Cover Design by Casandra Chu

Nihil Obstat
Reverend Ronald D. Witherup, S.S.
Censor Librorum

Imprimatur
✠ Most Reverend John R. Quinn
Archbishop of San Francisco
November 13, 1989

Harper's New American Bible Study Program is adapted from *Kerygma: The Bible in Depth, Resource Book* and *Leader's Guide,* published by The Kerygma Program, Pittsburgh, PA. The *Kerygma: The Bible in Depth Resource Book* was written by Dr. James A. Walther, Sr. to whom grateful acknowledgment is made. Copyright © 1984 James A. Walther.

FIRST HARPER & ROW EDITION

ISBN 0-06-253858-6

90 91 92 93 94 RRD 10 9 8 7 6 5 4 3 2 1

General Editor

James P. Campbell. D. Min.
author of *Christ, Yesterday and Today*
adjunct faculty member of Chapman College, Orange, CA,
past instructor at the Orange Catechetical Institute, Diocese of Orange, CA, specializing in Church history
 and New Testament studies
past Director of the Orange Catechetical Institute
past co-Chairman of the California Catholic Conference of Catechetical Ministers

Advisory Board

Carol Cowgill, D. Min.
Director of Adult Faith Development,
 Santa Paula, CA
past Diocesan Director of Religious Education,
 Orange, CA
past instructor of theology at Mt. St. Mary's College
 and Loyola Marymount University, Los Angeles,
 CA

Gerald Darring, M.A.
author of books on the theological themes of
 peace and justice
teacher of scripture and theology at McGill-Toolen
 High School and Springfield College, Mobile, AL
Chairman of the Peace and Justice Commission,
 Diocese of Mobile

Sister **Paule Freeburg,** D.C., M. Th.
author of diocesan adult education programs,
 San Jose, CA
contributing author of *A Lectionary for Children*
Pastoral Care Minister, Oakland, CA
speaker and lecturer on Scripture and the
 sacraments
past Director of Religious Education, Denver, CO

Reverend **Eugene LaVerdiere,** S.T.L., S.S.L.
author of *Luke* and other biblical texts and articles
Senior Editor, *Emmanuel Magazine*
adjunct professor of New Testament Studies at
 Catholic Theological Union, Chicago, IL
national educational consultant to the Society for
 the Propagation of the Faith
international speaker, lecturer, and leader of
 workshops and retreats

Marianne Sawicki, Ph. D.
author of many books, articles, and reviews on
 religious education, theology, and biblical studies
guest professor of Christian Education at Princeton
 Theological Seminary, Princeton, NJ
past professor of Religious Education at Loyola
 Marymount University, Los Angeles, CA, and at
 Lexington Theological Seminary, Lexington, KY
past consultant to the United States Catholic
 Conference for *The New American Bible* Revision

Most Reverend **John F. Whealon,** D.D., S.T.L., S.S.L.
Archbishop of Hartford
Chairman of the Liturgy Sub-Committee, National
 Conference of Catholic Bishops
co-Chairman of the Anglican-Roman Catholic
 Dialogue in the United States
past Vice-President of the Catholic Biblical
 Association
past Chairman of the National Catechetical Director,
 New American Bible Revision
past Chairman of the Committee on Doctrine and
 the Committee on Ecumenism, National
 Conference of Catholic Bishops

Contents

Preface

Harper's New American Bible Study Program

By undertaking this in-depth program of Bible study, you are acknowledging both the importance of the Bible in the Church and also in each person's life. You are joining a great company of people who have responded to the call of the Church to explore the Bible, with guidance from Catholic scholars and educators.

Biblical Foundations

This program focuses on the biblical material in three ways. One has to do with the method by which we organize our study. A second involves the learning goals we set. A third focuses on how we find lasting significance in what we have studied and learned.

Harper's New American Bible Study Program uses a thematic approach to the Bible. This is one of its most distinctive features. The special value of this is that it presents a grasp of the Bible as a whole with material that is most often studied piecemeal. The Church affirms that the Bible is one sacred book; so it is appropriate to approach it as a whole in order to learn a framework by which we can organize and keep together further study of parts of the Bible. The themes in this program help achieve this goal.

The themes come from the biblical material. Each theme title in this program states something about the interaction between God and God's people. Experienced Bible scholars have developed the ten themes used here to organize and simplify your study. Many people who have used this method of study have testified that it produces an effective grasp of the Bible as a whole.

The value of this program will become increasingly apparent as you proceed. Gradually, as you work through the Bible in the different themes, think of them as more or less parallel tracks, you will broaden and deepen your grasp of the material part by part and as a whole. One day you will realize that the Bible has become new and exciting for you. You will have a fresh understanding of what "inspiration" means, for it will be an experience that has come alive through your Bible study.

As we move through the Bible again and again, we shall emphasize some parts of the Bible more than others. There is precedent for this in the Bible itself. For example, New Testament authors use five books of the Old Testament far more than all the rest of it. Before completing this study, you will have an organized picture of the contents of much of the Bible and you will be able to move easily among the biblical books. Of course, this calls for serious study, but you will have help along the way and the rewards are great.

Unless this program is to be little more than an intellectual exercise, there must be a further focus. Inevitably, we must ask what significance this study has for believing and living today. The answers to such questions will emerge in ongoing dialogue with the living Body of Christ—the Church.

Our aim, therefore, is not just to master a quantity of biblical details. Although the Bible is full of intriguing data, the book was never intended to be used as an almanac or encyclopedia. It is a book with a purpose. The Gospel of John makes a clear statement of such a purpose: "these [signs] are written that you may [come to] believe that Jesus is the Messiah, the Son of God, and through that belief you may have life in his name (Jn 20:31)." We shall try to determine what this purpose, for example, meant for the writers, for the initial hearers, and finally for us.

Biblical interpreters and theologians often distinguish between what a text meant at the time it was written and what it means today. Our first task is to become so familiar with the biblical texts that we can learn what they meant in their original settings. Unless we do that, what we think the text means today may be only a projection of our own ideas. To take the Bible seriously requires that it be studied with the best available resources and diligent applica-tion. Thus we can deal responsibly with personal application only if we have made the writer's intent sharp and clear.

About the Resource Book

Each session begins with a *Session Overview* that provides a brief summary of the material to be studied. Then follows a list of *Key Bible Readings* that will be treated in the text. This list is the minimum scripture that you should read in preparing for the session. The references occur again at the appropriate places in the text. There is also a list of *Key Words* with which you should become familiar.

Each session also includes additional Bible readings that enhance the study of the subject being discussed. For example, in Theme 3, Session 4, complete biblical references for Paul's mission travels are given, but the text focuses only on selected incidents. You will find that reading the additional references is helpful and informative. If time is limited, you may find it difficult to study all of them. In any case, read through the text for the session itself early in the time you allot for study, as this helps tie together the scripture passages.

No simple guideline can be offered regarding the relative importance of the additional passages. With experience in studying the materials, you will become skilled in sorting the levels of value for your own study. Obviously, the more of the Bible passages you read, the better you will grasp the material and the Bible itself.

As a partial aid for those who must trim their study to fit a time limitation, each session includes built-in aids to help in setting a schedule. The following terms, symbols, and signs are used with the scripture references:

- **Boldface type.** Some Bible references included in the text are basic and are printed in **boldface** so you can't miss them. They are also the ones that are listed entirely or in part at the beginning of the session.

- *"Read."* These references are also very important and you should read as many of these passages as possible. You may find some of the passages are already familiar, so you can go through these very quickly.

- *"Scan," "skim,"* or *"read quickly."* This is enrichment material that may be skipped if time is limited.

- *"Note"* or *"See."* These references, usually enclosed in parentheses, are the evidence for, or the explanation of, statements or resource material in the text. You can probably follow the ideas presented without reading the passages, but they provide the backup support for the subject at hand.

- ( ). Parentheses that enclose Bible references are supportive or illustrative of the related text. You may skip these references if you trust the authors! When you can, go back later and check such passages for a more complete grasp of the subject.

- *Footnotes.* Found at the end of each session, the footnotes provide further references or documentation to the points made in the text.

At the end of each session are *Suggestions for Further Study.* Listed first are suggestions for research activities, which provide opportunities for more in-depth study of issues raised in the themes. These will enrich your understanding of the theme, but are not essential to it. Suggestions for activities that provide for personal reflection offer leads to help you find contemporary meaning and application to your study. You will also find passages listed that you may wish to master word for word.

Four points should be observed about how you relate the study material to group time:

- Prime time should be reserved for consideration of the principal theme material.

- The leader's judgment should usually have priority in distributing group time.

- The individual rights of each group member must be respected (see 1 Cor 14:29–33).

- It is not fair to use group time to make up for missed personal study time.

Anticipating the Introduction

Before starting the study of the contents of the Bible, the three sessions of the Introduction will help you consider the Bible as a book made up of many books. This is an important introduction to the study of the themes that follow. Treat it as you would an introduction to a person you very much want to know better. This not only involves absorbing as much as you can about your new acquaintance, but also being as conscientiously open and friendly as you can manage! It is essential to begin in this way.

Since there is much to master in Harper's New American Bible Study Program, make an appropriate start by preparing for the first session well. Some group time will be spent in organization and arrangements. It is vitally important, however, that you grasp at the outset the details that are offered as basic tools for further progress. Consider carefully your personal response to questions that are raised in the material. Analyze what you think and know at the outset so you can gauge your growth in understanding during the progress of the program.

Editorial Note

The authors and editors of this program have made every attempt to use inclusive language throughout both the *Resource Book* and the *Leader's Guide*. They have not, however, felt at liberty to change the language of the translations of the Bible, Church documents, or other material that has been excerpted in text.

INTRODUCTION

The Bible as a Whole

SESSION 1

What Is the Bible?

Session Overview

Our study begins with two questions: What is the Bible? Why do we study it as a whole? The first exercises work with how the names of the books of the Bible are grouped, and provide us with a kind of table of contents. This is followed by a look at how these books were selected to comprise the Bible, a process known as the development of the canon.

Key Bible Readings

Matthew 5:17; 7:12
Luke 16:29; 31; 24:44
John 1:45
Acts 28:23

Key Words

Pentateuch
Torah
canon
Septuagint
Writings
deuterocanonical
Revelation

A Difficult Question

When we ask people, "What is the Bible?" we will get almost as many different answers as there are people. This is not surprising, for the Bible is many things. The Bible has been called God's love letters to us. It has also been called our instruction book for living. Which definition do you think is the best? Why?

What is the Bible? Write your answer in your own words and file it away. Later in the program, you will be asked to compare this answer with your growing understanding of the Bible. The better you know the Bible, the more you will appreciate how difficult it is to describe it in a brief yet adequate statement. As you grow in your understanding, you will discover that your answer to the question is likely to change.

The Bible presents us with a vast amount of material to read. That is one reason why some people never read it at all, and it certainly adds to the difficulty of understanding it as a whole. The division of the Bible into many parts or "books," some of them with formidable names, adds to the complication.

The faith communities who accept the Bible as the inspired word of God differ about which books to include. For Jews, the sacred scripture consists of what Christians call the Old Testament. Some writers call these the "Hebrew Scriptures," and call the New Testament the "Christian Scriptures." This program will use the standard designations Old Testament and New Testament.

How many books are in the Bible? In the Jewish scriptures, the books of the Old Testament are arranged in a different order from that in Christian Bibles. Roman Catholic versions of the Bible contain forty-six books in the Old Testament, as compared to thirty-nine in Protestant versions. These additional books in the Catholic editions of the Bible are called apocrypha when they are added to Protestant editions, or deuterocanonical in Catholic editions. The additional books come from the Septuagint, the Greek version of the Old Testament, which was in use in most of the New Testament Christian communities.

Learning the Contents of the Bible

Our first task is to become familiar with the names of the seventy-three books in the Bible. The names of the books are a road map we can follow to discover the path through the Word of God. Learning what is in the Bible is an aid to using it effectively.

Try the following exercise to see how efficiently you can use the Bible: Open the Bible at random and note what book is named at the top of the page. Then see if you can name the preceding book and the following book. After doing this a few times, you will have a better idea of how well you can locate books in the Bible.

It is helpful and appropriate to learn the books in groups. Scripture study materials sometimes picture the Bible books arranged in sections on a bookshelf. This is a useful idea.

In Appendix 4 of this book there is a summary of several different groupings of the books. Refer to this now, for it will be useful later. For our purposes, we will follow the order of the seventy-three books that are in the New American Bible (NAB).

Books of the Old Testament

The first five books of the Old Testament are called the *Pentateuch*. They are also called the *Torah* (meaning "instruction" or "teaching") by the Jews. The New Testament refers to them as "the Law," because they contain legal prescriptions and regulations. The first five books of the Bible are: Genesis, Exodus, Leviticus, Numbers, and Deuteronomy.

In the NAB, Joshua, Judges, and Ruth are gathered with the first five books. In other editions of the Bible, such as the New Jerusalem Bible (NJB), these are listed under the Historical Books.

Under the heading of Historical Books in the NAB are: First and Second Samuel, First and Second Kings, First and Second Chronicles.

Here "first" and "second" indicate merely that in the days when scripture was handwritten on scrolls, the books of Samuel, Kings, and Chronicles were so long that each required two scrolls. In later writings, "first" and "second" can refer to two distinct pieces of writing. For example, "first" and "second" Corinthians are two separate letters.

Other Historical Books include: Ezra, Nehemiah, Tobit, Judith, Esther, First and Second Maccabees.

The books of Tobit, Judith, parts of Esther, and First and Second Maccabees are among those called deuterocanonical in Catholic versions and apocrypha in Protestant versions of the Bible. This means that they are considered canonical by the Catholic Church but secondary to the canon by Protestant churches.

The next grouping contains Wisdom Books: Job, Psalms, Proverbs, Ecclesiastes, Song of Songs, Wisdom, and Sirach (Ecclesiasticus).

The Book of Wisdom and the Book of Sirach are among the deuterocanonical books.

The Prophetic Books include: Isaiah, Jeremiah, Lamentations, Baruch, Ezekiel, Daniel, Hosea, Joel, Amos, Obadiah, Jonah, Micah, Nahum, Habakkuk, Zephaniah, Haggai, Zechariah, and Malachi.

Books of the New Testament

In the New Testament, the four gospels come first: Matthew, Mark, Luke, and John. These are followed by a book about people and events in the early Church: Acts of the Apostles.

Then follow the letters traditionally attributed to Paul, called the New Testament Letters: Romans, First and Second Corinthians, Galatians, Ephesians, Philippians, Colossians, First and Second Thessalonians, First and Second Timothy, Titus, and Philemon. (Here "first" and "second" actually refer to different letters.)

The letter to the Hebrews is grouped with Paul's letters, but it is not one of the letters traditionally attributed to Paul.

The next group is called the Catholic Letters, meaning that they were intended for the whole Church: James, First and Second Peter, First, Second, and Third John, and Jude.

Finally, there is the book entitled Revelation. Be careful not to refer to this book in the plural, as "Revelations." Read what the writer calls the book in the first verse (Rv 1:1). It is also referred to as the "Apocalypse," from the Greek word for revelation.

The groupings summarized above show that these books are part of two distinct religious traditions, Jewish and Christian. The persons, events, and ideas dealt with in these books have exceptional significance for each one of those historic traditions. The Old Testament has a thread of continuity. It deals with the story of the Jewish people, who had a very strong sense that they had experienced God in their history. The writings of the New Testament evolve within the context of the Jewish faith. The New Testament deals with the early Christian community: the gathering of believers in Jesus Christ, who sensed that they had experienced God's presence in the person, life, death, resurrection, and ongoing Spirit of Jesus Christ. The Church shares the conviction found in the Old Testament that God is intimately involved in human history and especially concerned with the needs of the poor and the oppressed.

Why These Books?

The lists and groupings in Catholic editions of the Bible assume the collection of seventy-three books. It is reasonable to ask why the collection contains precisely these books. During both the period covered by the Old Testament and the first century of the Christian era, other writings were produced in Jewish and Christian communities that are not included among the seventy-three. One example is Enoch, two quotations from which are found in Jude, verses 14 and 15.

The process by which Judaism and the Christian Church finally decided which books belonged among the scriptures inspired by God is referred to as selecting and closing the canon. *Canon* is a Greek word that means "rule" or "standard." It is the list of books officially accepted as inspired sacred scripture. This final selection, or closing of the canon, was not reached all at once.

The Old Testament Canon

In Jesus' day, the sacred Jewish scriptures consisted of the Torah or Pentateuch, the Prophets, plus the Psalms and most of the other Writings. Note how this is reflected in these New Testament passages: **Matthew 5:17; 7:12; Luke 16:29; 31; 24:44; John 1:45; Acts 28:23.** How does each passage refer to canonical scripture?

Sometimes in these references, "scriptures" are mentioned without specifically naming a book or group of books (see Mt 21:42; Lk 4:21; Rom 4:3, 6; Jas 2:8). These are references to what might be called the Bible of the first Christian century. The early Church, of course, did not call it the Old Testament. After the destruction of the Second Temple in 70 AD, Judaism was in chaos. In the late 80s and 90s a group of rabbis met in a town called Jamnia, and in council developed the spirit of modern Judaism. It is they who selected the books of inspired literature that comprise the Hebrew writings of the Old Testament. This "Palestinian Canon" consists of twenty-four books (thirty-nine as we count them today, according to different divisions).

A somewhat different list of books became accepted by the large colony of expatriate Jews who lived in Alexandria, Egypt. Since Alexandria was a Greek-speaking city, it was inevitable that Hebrew scriptures would be translated into Greek. This collection eventually included some writings written in Greek that were never accepted into the Palestinian canon. This Greek Bible became known as the Septuagint, from the Greek work for "seventy." It was so named because an early legend attributed the translation to seventy men. The additional books written in Greek were accepted by the early Church and continue to be accepted by Catholics today as canonical. Protestants, who follow the Palestinian decision to accept only Old Testament books written in Hebrew as canonical, called the Greek books apocrypha (from a Greek word meaning "hidden," referring to their questioned authority). More recently, a number of those books have been known as deuterocanonical (a term indicating a later inclusion in the canon).

The New Testament Canon

The first collection of Christian books was probably a group of Paul's letters (see 2 Pt 3:15, 16). The process by which books written in the early Church came to be accepted as uniquely inspired was affected by several factors. One was the reading of these books during the celebration of the Eucharist. Connection with an apostle was also important. At the close of the apostolic age, the Church was spurred on to sort out and judge the growing body of literature. The spread of the Church beyond Palestine brought a need for authoritative, written guidance for the new congregations. More and more writings (gospels, "acts," epistles, apocalypses) were produced, some of which contained false or nonauthoritative teaching. Decisions had to be made.

The need for a decision on which books of the Bible were to be judged inspired became especially important with the publication of a canon of scripture in the middle of the second century by an early Christian named Marcion. In his canon, Marcion excluded the Old Testament entirely and included only the Gospel of Luke and some of Paul's letters.

In response, bishops such as St. Irenaeus began to gather collections of books they considered inspired. Their collections included the Old Testament and the great majority of the New Testament books universally accepted today. Late in the fourth century, a canon consisting of the Old Testament and the twenty-seven books now recognized as the New Testament was approved by a Church council in Carthage. The Catholic Church finally issued a listing of the books of the canon in 1547, at the Council of Trent.

The development of the canon shows clearly the role of the Church in confirming which books were accepted as the inspired word of God. The Bible does not stand in isolation. It is the reflection of the faith and teachings of the Church. The process of selection of the canon shows the continuing discerning presence of the Holy Spirit in the life of the Church.

So what is the Bible? Some of the pieces to answer this question are now in place. In the next session, we will trace the history of how the canonical collections reached the order of the present day.

The actual writing of the books of the Bible occurred during a period of about a thousand years. The Church has faithfully preserved this great collection of literature for some two thousand years more. Along with the work of Jewish scribes, Christian monks and nuns copied the scriptures by hand to preserve the Word of God. The Bible has been cherished by the Church because it records the revelation of God as experienced by the people of God. This record of their experience is the measure by which the people of God today understand the call of God in their own lives.

Suggestions for Further Study

Research

1. Review your answer to the question, "What is the Bible?" which you formulated at the beginning of this session. Then answer the question again, drawing from your newly acquired knowledge.

2. Ask several friends whose judgment you respect to give you their answers to the question above.

Reflection

1. How important has the Bible been in helping you to become a better Christian? How do you think the study of the Bible can help you to grow in your personal spirituality?

2. Do you think the Church can open the canon to add books to the Bible? Why or why not?

3. You may want to memorize the names of the seventy-three books of the Bible.

SESSION 2

How Did We Get the Bible?

Session Overview

This session discusses the history of the Bible from the formation of the canon to the present day. We will trace the path to the New American Bible that began in the 1500s. Early translations of the Bible into English were produced in the period of the late Middle Ages and the Reformation (1380–1648). The controversy between Catholics and Protestants over the choice of translations comes from this tragic time in Church history. Catholics today can be assured of an accurate translation of the Bible with the *imprimatur*.

Key Bible Readings	Key Words
Genesis 1:1–8	translation
Psalm 23	revision
Matthew 5:1–12	version
1 Corinthians 13	edition
	paraphrase
	Aramaic

A Unique History

Wherever missionaries of the Church have taken the Christian message, they have brought the Bible. The role of the Bible in communicating and nurturing the Christian faith has made it the best-selling book of all time. When the American Bible Society issued *Good News for Modern Man: The New Testament in Today's English Version* in 1966, it sold 10 million copies in less than ten years!

This large distribution of Bibles is not just something that happened after printing from movable type was invented in the 1450s. Over five thousand manuscripts from the Middle Ages and ancient times still exist—a concrete illustration of people's continuous interest in the word of God. A visit to a religious bookstore will show you that a number of English translations, versions, and paraphrases are readily available.

An English Tradition

The first major translation of the Bible into English to be fully approved by the Catholic Church was the Rheims-Douay translation

(1582–1609), written by a group of Catholic exiles from England on the European continent. The New Testament appeared in Rheims in 1582; the Old Testament in Douay in 1609. The English translation was from the Latin Vulgate translation of St. Jerome, the standard Bible at that time.

The Rheims-Douay Version of the Bible was revised by Bishop Richard Challoner, who produced the Challoner revision (1749–1763). In this revision, the style of the Rheims-Douay was considerably modernized. For two centuries, the Challoner revision was universally used by English-speaking Catholics. (1st version)

Further revisions based on the Latin Vulgate include the Confraternity Revision of the New Testament (1941), and finally the Knox Bible (1944–1950).

In 1943, Pope Pius XII issued his famous encyclical on biblical studies, *Divino Afflante Spiritu*. He wrote:

> We ought to explain the original text which was written by the inspired author himself and has more authority and greater weight than any, even the very best, translation whether ancient or modern. This can be done all the more easily and fruitfully if to the knowledge of languages can be joined a real skill in literary criticism of the same text.

Responding to the Pope's call to translate the Bible from the original Greek, Hebrew, and Aramaic languages, the Bishops' Committee of the Confraternity of Christian Doctrine in 1944 requested the Catholic Biblical Association of America "to translate the sacred scriptures from the original languages or from the oldest extant form of the text, and to present the sense of the biblical text in as correct a form as possible."[1]

The New American Bible (NAB), published in 1970, was the first translation prepared to respond to the needs of the Church in America.

This edition contains extensive footnotes and cross-references. Portions of the Old Testament were produced on a trial basis and published between 1948 and 1969. These earlier collections were known as the Confraternity Version. The New Testament of the NAB, a fresh translation of the Greek text, was completed in 1970. This translation has taken its place among the standard contemporary translations of the New Testament, respected for its fidelity to the original and its attempt to render this into current American English.

A thorough revision of the New Testament of the NAB was begun in 1978 and published in 1986. This edition, like the 1970 edition, was prepared by members of the Catholic Biblical Association of America and accomplished with the collaboration of scholars from other Christian Churches. The revised edition contains explanatory materials more abundantly than in the first edition. In most cases, the introductions and notes have been entirely rewritten and expanded, and the cross-references checked and revised. The revision was undertaken to produce a text more closely equivalent to the Greek original, and one that uses inclusive language wherever possible. This newly revised translation and the 1970 Old Testament are the principal references for this program.

A second major modern translation of the Bible into English for Catholics was the Jerusalem Bible (JB) (1966). This translation was based on La Sainte Bible, published in France between 1948 and 1954 under the editorship of the Dominicans at L'École Biblique in Jerusalem. The English edition was a translation from the French, with reference to the original languages. The JB was particularly valuable for the inclusion of the elaborate introductions and footnotes in the original French edition; in spite of some inaccuracies, this is recognized as one of the greatest achievements of Catholic biblical scholarship.

The JB, however, is now revised and updated. The New Jerusalem Bible (NJB), published in 1985, takes advantage of and goes beyond the updated and corrected notes of the 1973 French edition. (These notes are not included in most paperback editions.) In the NJB, the English translation is now made from the original Hebrew, Greek, and Aramaic.

The longest connected piece in the history of the Bible in English concerns the Revised Standard Version (RSV), the most widely accepted English Bible today. The RSV traces its lineage through the King James Version (KJV) of 1611, to earlier versions stemming from the first printed English Bible in 1535. The RSV New Testament appeared first in 1946, the complete Bible in 1952. This edition was issued with a few changes in 1972. In 1990 a completely revised edition was published and includes the deuterocanonical books. The "Revised" in RSV is evidence that this version has attempted to keep alive a tradition that is over 450 years old. The RSV exists in a Catholic edition with the *imprimatur,* which was published in 1966.

All of these modern versions and translations are revised as the English language changes in time. They are based on what the latest scholarship has discovered about the ancient Hebrew, Greek, and Aramaic.

Back through the Middle Ages

The first complete English translation of the Bible from Latin was completed by John Wycliffe (1384–1395). Many handwritten ("manuscript") copies were produced during this time period. Wycliffe's translation was marred by a prologue in which he criticized the Church's teaching on the Eucharist. In the early 1500s, English translations were made by William Tyndale and Miles Coverdale. Again, attacks on the Catholic Church in the prologues and notes led to the condemnation of these editions. The first book printed by Johann Gutenberg was a Latin Bible (1456). Martin Luther translated the Bible into German (1522–1534). The great Dutch scholar Erasmus published a Greek New Testament in 1516.

Before the age of print the Bible was copied by hand from generation to generation. This was the work of Jewish scribes, monastic communities, and convents. It is because of the diligence and faith of these unknown men and women that thousands of manuscripts exist and form a firm foundation for today's translations. Scrolls are still hand-copied by Jewish scribes for use in synagogues.

The Vulgate Latin translation, the source of the earliest English translations of the Bible, was done by St. Jerome (384–404). (Vulgate comes from the Latin word *vulgus,* which means "people," "crowd.") St. Jerome, a careful scholar, was asked by Pope Damasus to provide the Western Church with a reliable translation of the Bible into vulgate Latin, the everyday language of the people of the Western Roman empire. St. Jerome's Vulgate Bible replaced a number of earlier inferior Latin versions and provided a reliable translation for study and prayer.

The Earliest Times

The Septuagint version of the Old Testament canon, the Greek translation produced by the Jewish community in Egypt, was completed about 132 BC. This was a widely accepted version used by Jews outside of Palestine, and is the version St. Paul and the gospel writers use in references to the Old Testament. This canon is the basis of the Old Testament canon for the Catholic Church.

The Hellenistic (Greek) world of cities like Antioch, Corinth, and Ephesus was the home of the Church by the time the early scriptures were taking shape. Even in Rome, Greek was the language of the educated people and the language of business. So when the early evangelists wrote the epistles and gospels, they wrote in Greek. The early Church made every effort to make the scriptures accessible to the common person. That is why there is presently an ongoing effort to revise the translations of the Bible.

Which Versions Today?

Translations of the Bible today are based on the original Greek and Hebrew languages. Wherever the Church preaches God's Word, the Bible is translated into the modern language of the people. Keeping the Bible current is the ongoing responsibility of the Church.

In light of all this, consider the following recommendations concerning the choice of Bibles for serious Bible study.

The New American Bible (NAB) with revised New Testament is the Bible of reference for this program. It not only provides a clear, modern English translation but also provides up-to-date notes on the major points that will be studied and discussed. The New Jerusalem Bible (NJB) may also be mentioned for the same reason. Both of these translations have an *imprimatur*.

Special mention must also be made of the Revised Standard Version (RSV) of the Bible, especially in the Oxford Annotated Bible edition published in 1966. This edition includes the deuterocanonical books in Catholic order. Explanatory notes were included in accordance to Canon Law and an *imprimatur* was given. Some passages omitted in the RSV were restored. The publication of this Bible is a great step forward toward the ideal of a common Bible.

The *Good News Bible: Today's English Version* (TEV), published in 1976, is intended particularly for persons who want an accurate translation into everyday speech. The expertness and experience of the American Bible Society translators commends this as a reliable version for Americans.

The New International Version (NIV) is a recent translation from the original languages done by an international committee of conservative Protestant scholars.

Paraphrases such as *The Living Bible* (or *The Word*) contain a greater element of interpretation than is employed in responsible translations. Paraphrases are more open to the inclusion of editorial biases in the work and may dilute the meaning of God's Word. For this reason, they are not used in serious Bible study.

Secure several different versions of the Bible (including especially some of those mentioned in this section), and compare the following well-known passages: **Genesis 1:1–8, Psalm 23, Matthew 5:1–12,** and **1 Corinthians 13.**

Make note of some of the differences that are particularly striking. These may be discussed in group time.

Suggestions for Further Study

Research

To understand the difficulty of manuscript writing in the days before printing, copy by hand (preferably with pen and ink) the first chapter of the Gospel of John without any punctuation or separation of words. Then have someone else copy your copy. Compare the copies with the original. (To match conditions in the Middle Ages, you should not wear eyeglasses or use electric light!)

Reflection

1. What are the advantages and the problems of using modern translations or versions?

2. How has this session affected your appreciation and understanding of the Bible?

3. Identify the following terms in one or two
   sentences:

   Jerome   NAB
   Vulgate   RSV
   Rheims-Douay   NIV
   Challoner   NJB

Notes

1. **From the Preface to the New American Bible.**

SESSION 3

How to Study the Bible

Session Overview

The purpose of Harper's New American Bible Study Program is to study the Bible as a whole. Themes in this program are drawn from the Bible itself. They deal with God's interaction with the people of God in the Old Testament and New Testament. Bible dictionaries, commentaries, concordances, and a Bible atlas are among the tools helpful in studying the Bible.

Key Bible Readings

Jeremiah 31:31–34
Matthew 14:13–21
Mark 6:30–44
Luke 9:10–17
John 6:1–13

Key Words

themes
concordance

Ways and Means

We have many reasons for studying the Bible. There are also many ways to study the Bible, and certain ways are especially suited to particular reasons. Many Christians, however, are likely to focus their interest on those parts of the Bible that seem to relate most easily to their situation and understanding. As a result, they often become familiar with a limited range of biblical material and the potential impact of the Word of God in their lives is limited.

Review your own experiences in Bible study. What courses have you taken? How many books of the Bible have you read? How many have you studied? With which ones are you really familiar? Can you relate these books with the Bible as a whole? Make some notes to compare with others in your group so you can arrive at a composite picture of your common Bible knowledge.

This program gives the opportunity to study the Bible as a whole. Knowing the general themes of the Bible will help you to understand specific passages within the complete context of the Bible. In that way, the reader will be able to make connections from particular passages in a way that will enrich the entire study.

The Unity of the Bible

The Bible forms a unified whole. In the *Constitution on Divine Revelation,* the Church affirms "that the Old and New Testaments in their entirety, with all their parts, are sacred and canonical because, written under the inspiration of the Holy Spirit, they have God as their author and have been handed on as such to the Church herself." The unity of the Bible reflects the one God whom it reveals over time. The more we are acquainted with the whole of the Bible, the more we are able to know about ourselves and our own relationship with God.

Jesus' ministry was lived out against a background of Old Testament tradition, and New Testament writers regularly found in the Old Testament vital clues for understanding the mission and message of Jesus. One particular instance is the use by New Testament writers of the images of the suffering servant in Isaiah (Is 52:13–53:12) to help Christians understand the meaning of Jesus' suffering and death. For Christians, the New Testament provides an extension and outcome of many Old Testament themes and a fulfillment of many Old Testament hopes.

In Judaism, the Hebrew scriptures are revered, studied, and commented upon. The deep awareness of the continuing and abiding presence of God in their lives is reflected in the writings of such Jewish theologians as Abraham Heschel. Heschel's works on prayer, *Man's Quest for God* and *God in Search of Man*, and his classic study *The Prophets*, are profound meditations showing how God's Word in the biblical tradition continues to influence human life.

A Common Approach

One common procedure for trying to acquire a knowledge of the whole Bible is to begin with Genesis and read, book by book, to the end of Revelation. This method is sometimes undertaken by an individual in private study, sometimes even without reference to study tools. It requires a great deal of perseverance, and many well-meaning persons have bogged down in such an attempt. There are enough stories in Genesis to carry one through the book; but the difficult details of Exodus, Leviticus, and Numbers are discouraging, to say the least. A greater problem is that the books of the Bible are not ordered chronologically or sequentially. The beginning of Matthew, with its extended genealogy, may be baffling. A student using this method is likely to lose the main point of the materials.

A Thematic Approach

Harper's New American Bible Study Program follows a thematic approach. Each of the ten themes is focused on the action of God in the lives of the people. These themes will be the main highways, crossing and recrossing the biblical landscape. By following them, we become familiar with the historical landmarks and the related scenes.

This approach involves three fundamental presuppositions:

- The themes give practical, usable clues to the unity of the Bible, and their recurrence throughout both Testaments provides ties for the various parts of the Bible.

- The heritage of Jews and Christians is rooted in history, which constantly shows the interrelationship between God and the people.

• The Church's confession that Jesus is the Messiah inescapably links Christian and Hebrew experience, history, and literature.

The Bible is an experience-centered book rooted in history. The Bible records the ongoing revelation of God to the people as experienced in the eastern Mediterranean world. The Bible does not contain the abstract religious thinking prevalent in the world today. The themes, then, develop directly from the biblical texts reflecting the concrete experience of the people involved.

The Ten Themes

The themes that have been developed for this program are the result of a great deal of reflection in recent biblical scholarship. In the course of this study, the themes will help us to trace a path through the Bible.

The experiences that first gathered and consolidated the people of God were events of deliverance; so the first theme is "God Saves the People." In the Old Testament, the critical moment of salvation is the Exodus from Egypt, which is memorialized in the Passover celebration. The Exodus event becomes a focal point for the continuing relationship between God and the Hebrew people. In the New Testament, the mission of Jesus culminating in his death and resurrection is identified as the crucial experience that establishes a new relationship between God and a new people of God, the Church.

The Exodus event provided evidence that God kept the promise made long before in a covenant with the Hebrew ancestor Abraham. God's people occasionally fail to be faithful, but they discover that always "God Is Faithful to the People" (Theme 2). This is profoundly demonstrated in the new covenant established through Jesus.

The Bible rarely presents theoretical discussion about God. Rather, as a consequence of deliverance and faithfulness, "God's People Reflect on God" (Theme 3). They declare God's creative power. They wrestle with good and evil, with God's justice and love. Ultimately, they claim to know God through the revelation in Jesus Christ.

The land where the Hebrews settled was an ancient, international crossroad, and they could not escape experiencing that "People Live in God's World" (Theme 4). Their relationship to the surrounding world was often ambiguous as they tried unsuccessfully to avoid involvements. The Christian Church, however, very early moved into the surrounding world with a profound sense of mission and tried, with varying degrees of success, to maintain a distinctive separation from that world.

All through the Bible, "God's People Have Leaders" (Theme 5). Most of the sustained narratives are carried along by these persons, who are appointed by God for particular tasks. These leaders are patriarchs, judges, prophets, priests, kings, seers, apostles, courageous men and women, and ordinary people who do extraordinary things.

A king in the Old Testament is a special kind of leader. Kings were anointed to rule as God's special representatives, as the Hebrews thought of God as their supreme ruler. A time came when there was no longer a Hebrew king. Later, Jesus taught about the reign of God, and the Christian Church saw Jesus as the fulfillment of expectations of an anointed savior and ruler. Thus there is the double truth that "God's People Have Kings and a King" (Theme 6).

From their earliest perceptions, God's people understood that the divine rule imposes requirements. The Bible regularly presents these as Law, and the appropriate life response is always righteous living. Put simply, "God's Law Demands a Righteous People" (Theme 7). The new revelation in Jesus Christ brings new perceptions of this double emphasis, especially as a law of love.

God's people share areas of knowledge and understanding with the wise and the moral people around them. The Bible includes portions, even books, of wisdom literature, for "God's People Learn Wisdom" (Theme 8). Hebrew wisdom, however, has a special quality rooted in the Hebrews' unique relation to God. The New Testament also has some examples of wisdom literature, but the Church's confrontation with Western thought brings new dimensions. Jesus Christ becomes the focus of wisdom.

The relationship between God and the people takes on special qualities as "God's People Worship" (Theme 9). The Bible offers rich resources for expressing and celebrating this worship: ritual, psalms, hymns, prayer, and sacraments, especially the Eucharist. Continuity between the Testaments broadens and deepens this theme.

From earliest times, God's people believed in a divine guarantee of their future. When exile brought despair, they found renewed courage in new kinds of expectation. Jesus' death dashed his disciples' faith for the future, but his resurrection became a new guarantee of ultimate victory. The Book of Revelation provides a final proclamation that "God's People Have Hope" (Theme 10)

Some Observations

The biblical emphasis on history is important. Some attention to dates is instructive. For example, the last days of the Judean monarchy (587 BC) were roughly contemporary with the rise of Greece in the eastern Mediterranean; and Confucius was teaching in China (551–479 BC) when Nehemiah was rebuilding Jerusalem after the Babylonian exile. Occasionally, other literature from antiquity and the results of archeological research provide insights on the biblical texts. For example, in 1 Samuel 4, we have the story of how the Philistines captured the Ark of the Covenant from Israel in battle near the town of Shiloh, where the Ark was kept. Readers of the Bible have often surmised that Shiloh itself must have been destroyed at the same time, for when Israel recovered the Ark, it was not returned there. Recent excavation has shown that Shiloh was indeed destroyed at the time of this incident in the eleventh century BC (IOT 34). This was a real world with real people.

The ten themes presented here do not exhaust the thematic possibilities of the Bible. Careful study of these, however, will give us a grasp of the whole and so prepare us for further productive study.

Some Tools to Use in Study

Several tools for Bible study are indispensable. Learn how to use them, and have your own copies if at all possible.

Almost every edition of the Bible has some study helps. Editions called Study Bibles contain extensive helps. The one we will be using for reference is the New American Bible (NAB) with the revised New Testament. The NAB provides outlines for each book that are very helpful. The cross-references in the margins or footnotes of most Bibles are essential resources to identifying relationships between verses; they are particularly useful for moving back and forth between the Testaments. Other notes provide information necessary for understanding the text.

Let's look at several examples. A glance at 2 Samuel 22:1–51 will call attention to the fact that the poem there is repeated in Psalm 18. You may also learn that 2 Samuel 23:8–39 is repeated in 1 Chronicles 11:11–47. **Jeremiah 31:31–34** should have a note helping you to find out more about the idea of "covenant," and indicating that this passage is quoted in the New Testament entirely in Hebrews 8:8–12 and again in part at 10:16, 17. Mark 9:42–48 shows four footnotes in the NAB; note the variety. **Matthew 14:13–21** indicates that the story of the feeding of the five thousand is paralleled in **Mark 6:30–44, Luke 9:10–17,** and **John 6:1–13.**

A concordance has several important uses. It lists occurrences of Bible words by books, chapters, and verses, and gives enough of each particular verse to identify the usage. A complete concordance lists every occurrence of each word. There are also abridged versions. Each concordance is based on a particular translation (for example, the RSV or NIV), though some give limited reference to other versions. A concordance enables you to locate any verse in the Bible if you remember one key word. You can also trace the use of a given word in various books of the Bible, which is helpful when you are following themes or other ideas in scripture.

Again, check some examples. You might have found the relationship between Jeremiah and Hebrews by looking at the entries for the word "covenant." You would also have found the four stories of the feeding of the five thousand if you had been hunting for one of them under the words "thousand" or "loaves" or "baskets." You might also have found that Mark 8:1–10 and Matthew 15:32–39 give another narrative in which four thousand are fed.

Harper's Bible Dictionary (HBD) (or another Bible dictionary, such as McKenzie's *Dictionary of the Bible*) lists the most important word-subjects in the Bible and provides extensive articles explaining the subjects. These articles often include the language background of the word and a survey of its use and importance throughout the Bible. Historical, geographical, and archeological data are mentioned as appropriate.

Harper's Bible Commentary (HBC) contains in-depth articles on the background to the Bible. It also contains extended commentary on all the books of the Bible. HBC is designed to be used in tandem with *Harper's Bible Dictionary*. A standard Catholic commentary of the Bible for the past twenty-five years has been the *Jerome Biblical Commentary,* which may be available in many parish libraries and Catholic homes; a revised edition, *The New Jerome Biblical Commentary,* is now available. Recently, Liturgical Press published the *Collegeville Bible Commentary,* which also contains articles that reflect the most recent research on the books of the Bible. Any of these resources may be used to follow up any questions that may arise in the course of this study. Quick references to the Harper & Row materials will be included in the text.

The *Harper Atlas of the Bible* (HAB) provides maps and articles that vividly portray the land, events, and people in the Bible. It (or one like it) should be available in your parish or public library. A good study Bible also contains maps and atlas material. There also are a number of paperback atlases of the Bible, which can be used for easy reference.

Each of these resources supplements the others. For example, you might be studying the Passover. You would probably begin reading Exodus 12 in a study Bible with introductory notes. *Harper's Bible Commentary, The New Jerome Biblical Commentary,* or the *Collegeville Bible Commentary* would then offer extended commentary on the whole chapter. *Harper's Bible Dictionary* or McKenzie's *Dictionary of the Bible* will expand upon the meaning of the word Passover and will give you examples of other Passovers mentioned in the Bible. A concordance will enable you to pursue the study another way by checking all of the references to "Passover" in the whole Bible.

Some study Bibles have abridged concordances and dictionaries. These are useful for quick reference and for learning to use these tools. They will probably whet your appetite for more complete editions. It is important to learn to use every tool available now, as you begin your study. Remember that your group leader is also an important resource and will help you become familiar with your learning tools.

Suggestions for Further Study

Research

1. What are the areas of the Bible about which you know the least? What do you think are the main reasons why these are unfamiliar?

2. On a list of the books of the Bible, note which themes you think will relate to the re-spective books. Set this aside for checking later.

3. Study the charts in Appendix 7 that present a time comparison of biblical and secular events. Can you add any other data?

Reflection

1. The text above states, "The more we are acquainted with the whole of the Bible, the more we are able to know about ourselves and our own relationship to God." Do you think this is true? In what ways would you like the study of the Bible to influence your relationship with God?

2. Are some parts of the Bible more important than others? Think of reasons for answering both "yes" and "no." How can you account for the fact that the New Testament quotes some Old Testament books far more than it does others?

THEME 1

God Saves the People

SESSION 1

The Exodus: Pattern of Freedom Offered by God

Session Overview

The central theme running through the Old and New Testaments is that God saves the people. The Book of Exodus describes the pivotal events that reveal Yahweh as the God who saves. The first lesson begins with the story of the Exodus, the liberation of the Hebrew people from slavery in Egypt.

The central figure in the Book of Exodus is Moses. Through Moses, God's Word is mediated to the people. Moses is credited with giving the people the Law, and establishing the celebration of Passover, the holiest festival in the Hebrew religious calendar.

There is a great deal of material to be studied in this session. Be assured that its importance in helping you to understand the whole Bible justifies extra effort on your part now. Organize your study time. The Bible passages are much more extensive than the *Resource Book* text, so emphasize the Bible reading. Use the material in this book to help you relate the texts to each other. Finally, go on to Suggestions for Further Study, and work through as much of it as you can.

Key Bible Readings	Key Words
Exodus 1–4; 12; 14; 15:1–21; 20:2	manna
	Passover
Deuteronomy 6:20–23	Pentateuch
Psalm 78:12–16	Sea of Reeds
	Yahweh

Background of the Exodus

In the Exodus event, the Hebrew people began a conscious existence as the people of God. Earlier stories in the Book of Genesis about Abraham, Isaac, Jacob, and Joseph, the ancestors of Israel, show an awareness of divine destiny, but they really are used as an introduction to the story of God's people. The Genesis materials concern a family or tribe that had a special relationship with God. (These materials will be covered in Theme 2.) With the events in the Book of Exodus, however, a continuous story begins as God leads to freedom the oppressed Hebrew people. In this way, God shows special concern for social justice as the liberator of the poor and the needy. This concern is still reflected today in the social teaching of the Church on the need to take responsibility for meeting the needs of the poor.[1]

The *Pastoral Constitution on the Church in the Modern World* 69 states:

> Faced with a world today where so many peoples are suffering from want, the Council asks individuals and governments to remember the saying of the Fathers: "Feed the man dying of hunger, because if you don't feed him you are killing him," and it urges them according to their ability to share and dispose of their goods to help others, above all by giving them aid which will enable them to help and develop themselves.

Social concern is also seen in the work for political justice for the oppressed, and in the work of Mother Teresa and her community with those abandoned by society throughout the world.

According to Jewish biblical tradition, Moses assembled, edited, and handed down the first five books of the Bible, which are often referred to as the Pentateuch. Modern scholarship has shown that the Pentateuch is the result of centuries of gathering materials, reflecting on them, and interpreting them in the light of the continuing presence of God in the life of the people. In the New Testament, the Mosaic tradition is reflected in the reference to "the law of Moses" in Luke 24:27, 44. Abraham, forefather of the twelve tribes of Israel, is honored in various ways and degrees; but it is Moses who is the pivotal figure in the formation of the Hebrew people and their primary traditions.

When the Hebrew people began their experience as a cultural entity, they did not have an organized religious faith. The development of their relationship with God begins with the story of their journey to freedom from Egypt. Moses becomes the interpreter of the event. Through Moses, the people learn of their call to enter into a special relationship with God. God is revealed to Moses as being concerned and compassionate for the needs of the people. Moses in turn teaches the Israelite people the name of this God. The formative experience in this part of the Old Testament begins with a recognition that God saves the people.

Moses' Early Years

At this point read **Exodus 1–4.** Even if some parts of the narrative are familiar, read it all.

After you have read these chapters, work on answers to the following questions. If you are uncertain about your answers, read the passage again.

- What brings on the crisis for the Israelites in Egypt?

- What influenced the courageous stand of the midwives against the Egyptians?

- How does Moses' background particularly equip him for leadership?

- Why is Moses in the solitary territory of Midian?

- When God calls Moses, what is Moses' response?

- How does God validate Moses' commission?
- Who is Aaron and what is his ministry?

The God Moses Met

Among people of the Bible, the name of an individual was of great significance. Nothing existed unless it had a name. A person's name revealed the person's reality. Thus, according to Mark 3:16, Jesus changed Simon's name to Peter (*Cephas*, meaning "rock") to signify Peter's role as the foundation of the Church. The cultures surrounding the Hebrews knew the names of their gods, and by using their names called them down and sought control over them.

In the Book of Exodus, Moses asks God's name. God's answer, according to Exodus 3:14, is translated "I am who am." Elsewhere the form of the sacred name is *Yahweh,* which can mean something like "He who is" or "He who causes what is" or "I am the one who is with you."

Yahweh is the Hebrew language-form of four consonants: YHWH. Although this is rendered "Jehovah" in the American Standard Version and the New English Bible, scholars generally agree that the English equivalent of the ancient pronunciation would be Yahweh. The Jews' great respect for the power of the name of God led them to substitute the word "Lord" for YHWH, and the Greek translation of the Old Testament usually followed this substitution. Yahweh is the form used in the NJB. In the NAB and the RSV, the name is rendered "Lord." The Lord is also revealed as the God of the Hebrew ancestors, the God of Abraham and Sarah, the God of Isaac and Rebekah, and the God of Jacob and Rachel.

The sense of the whole Exodus passage is that the Lord has always been present to the people, is present to the people today, and will be present to the people forever. The name Yahweh also reveals a God who is a mystery, who is beyond the power of Moses and the people to control. God's freedom in relation to the people is reiterated in Exodus 33:19, "I who show favors to whom I will, I who grant mercy on whom I will."

The Lord's message to Moses is that God's presence is revealed in the events of history. There are many places for the people to look for God: in their memories, reflecting on the God of their ancestors; in the present, in the midst of their suffering; and in the events to come.

Preparation for the Exodus: The Passover

Now read Exodus 5–11. The events described there show a dramatic escalation of tensions among Pharaoh, the gods of Egypt, and the Lord. The Lord is described as making Pharaoh "obstinate" (NAB; "hardening his heart" in other translations). The writers of the Old Testament did not think in the philosophical language of free will that people do today. They were recording the fact of Pharaoh's refusal to obey God and they attributed everything that happened in the world to God. The sense of the passage makes it clear that it is Pharaoh's pride and his desire to keep the Hebrews in slavery that leads him to reject Moses' demands. Pharaoh's persistent refusal to release the Hebrews increases the dramatic tension leading up to the Passover, the death of the firstborn of the Egyptians, and the Hebrews' flight from Egypt.

Read **Exodus 12.** The Passover event became the central symbol of freedom from oppression for the Hebrews. The yearly celebration of the Passover, event is the principal festival of the Jewish people today. Celebrating the Passover, they remember the astonishing intervention of God in their lives. From their hopeless situation in Egypt they were led into the desert, bound into a covenant with God, and led to the promised land.

In remembering, the Hebrew people were not simply recalling a past event. In the theology of the Old Testament, the call to remember means that they are called to make a new decision for God today. In the Passover Seder, the meal Jews today celebrate to remember the Passover, God's people still say:

> In every generation let everyone realize that it is ourselves whom God has brought forth from Egypt. It is not only our ancestors that the Holy One, whose name we bless, redeemed, but redeemed us with them. But he led us out from there to bring us unto the land and gave it to us as he had promised it to our forefathers.

Celebrating Passover means making the same decision for God today as was made centuries ago, in the faith that God's commitment remains alive and well.

The book of Deuteronomy contains theological reflections upon these early events. **Deuteronomy 6:20–23** retells the significance of Passover.

The Exodus Event

Now comes the second act of the drama, in which God saves the people. Although the record is sketchy, its purpose is to declare God's saving action, by which God's people begin their long trek to nationhood. Read the story in **Exodus 14.**

Traditionally, English translations have associated the place where God intervened to save the people with the Red Sea, but the etymology of the Hebrew name and geographical hints in the text suggest that the crossing was north of the Red Sea at what is more appropriately called the Sea of Reeds.[2] This was a miraculous intervention by God: God's mighty arm reached out to deliver them. The gift of freedom given by the Lord is the kernel of the passage.

Israel remembered these events in liturgical celebrations such as Passover, the Feast of Booths, and the Feast of Weeks. **Exodus 15:1–21** recalls such a celebration. Through the centuries, the story of the events were kept alive by their inclusion in the worship of the Hebrews.

From the Exodus Onward

From Exodus 15:22 through chapter 18, there are stories of what took place on the journey to Mount Sinai. Scan these quickly. Several of the events are recalled in the New Testament. You will read about manna and about water from the rock. Remember both these incidents among God's saving acts for the people.

The Selection of Texts

The selection of texts to be studied in this program is necessarily limited. The choice of texts is determined by the ability of the text to clarify the theme, the use of the text in the New Testament, and the importance of the texts in gaining a working knowledge of the Bible. This last category includes traditionally well-known stories and frequently quoted passages that contribute to biblical literacy. Some of the narratives about Sinai and the further wanderings in the wilderness will be examined under later themes. For the rest of this session, however, references to the Passover and Exodus from other books of the Old Testament will be considered.

Passover and Exodus Elsewhere in the Old Testament

References to the Passover occur in the rest of the Pentateuch among various regulations for the religious and civil life of Israel. See Leviticus 23:4–8 and Deuteronomy 16:1–8 for directives concerning the regular observance of Passover. Numbers 9:1–14 records the first anniversary observance of liberation from Egypt. There are also rules for handling problems that might arise, such as the right of a stranger to join in the festival. These regulations were concerned with activating the meaning of the covenant Israel made with God in daily life.

Much later, a particularly impressive Passover was celebrated in Jerusalem under King Josiah, one of David's successors. The record is found in 2 Kings 23:21–23 and 2 Chronicles 35:11–19.

God is frequently referred to in the Old Testament as the one who led Israel from Egypt to freedom. For example, see Deuteronomy 6:12; Judges 6:8–9; 1 Samuel 10:18; 12:6; and Psalm 81:11. Notice that the preface to the Ten Commandments reads: "I, the LORD, am your God, who brought you out of the land of Egypt, that place of slavery" (**Ex 20:2** and Dt 5:6). In the deuteronomic form of the Ten Commandments, the reason for keeping the Sabbath is associated with the remembrance of Israel's slavery in Egypt (Dt 5:15).

When the Israelite people were at the threshold of the promised land, they took an oath of allegiance to the Lord, basing it on the gift of freedom from Egypt (Jos 24:16, 17). When Jeremiah wanted to mark the authoritative beginning of God's dealing with Israel, he pointed to that same gift of freedom (Jer 7:22; 11:7; 34:13). The theme is also common in the Psalms. In **Psalm 78:12–16,** several events are mentioned. Psalm 135:8–9 contains more allusions; Psalm 136:10–16 retells such events in an antiphonal form.

The prophet Hosea appeals to the people on the basis of God's actions in Egypt (see Hos 11:1; 12:14; 13:4–6). Isaiah offers encouragement on a similar basis (see Is 11:16). In the midst of national disaster, other prophets look for national restoration in the light of the first experience of liberation (see Ez 45:21; Hg 2:5; Zec 10:10–11). When the Jews returned to their homeland after exile in Babylon, they kept the Passover (see Ezr 6:19).

God's people gradually came to understand that it was "in character" for the God who had liberated them from Egypt to save them again and again. It is a central insight around which their understanding of their existence and destiny is set. In the next session of this theme, other experiences of God's intervention to help the Hebrew nation are studied. You will see that in those texts the Exodus event is often recalled.

Suggestions for Further Study

Research

1. Examine the word "Jehovah" in a Bible dictionary. How was this term derived from YHWH?

2. Review Exodus 1–18. List the major events of the Hebrews' journey out of Egypt.

Reflection

1. Some of the issues raised in this first session may sound strange. Keep a record of your questions. Raise them in the session if there is time. Not all issues can be covered in the first session, so patience is needed as you continue through the program.

2. How do you think God is involved in the interactions of people and the world today? What are some possible modern parallels to the Exodus experience? How do you think Mother Teresa would answer the question, "Where does a person find God?"

3. Where do you look for God in your own life? How is the liberating power of God revealed to you? Where does the Book of Exodus suggest that you look?

4. You may wish to master the following text word for word: Deuteronomy 6:20–23.

5. Many of the Bible passages referred to in this session will be important for later reference. It will be helpful to keep some kind of a listing with notes of the contexts. This is especially true of the basic Bible references. Experiment to find what helps your memory most.

Notes

1. See U.S. Bishop's *Economic Justice for All*, 1986.

2. On the map of Egypt and Sinai in Appendix 8, this area is in the region marked "Bitter Lakes."

SESSION 2

God's Intervention after the Exodus

Session Overview

The experiences of the Exodus provide a pattern for viewing the subsequent saving relationship between God and the people. In the following years, God intervened repeatedly to save Israel from desperate situations.

Under the rule of kings, God was still the power behind the most notable events in which Israel was saved. The prophets became the chief interpreters of this understanding. When the Hebrew national destiny deteriorated into exile, a new exodus became the hope. Still later, after that exodus, when the Hebrews were again under repressive foreign domination in the period "between the Testaments," God helped them into a period of political freedom.

Key Bible Readings

Numbers 20:1–13;
  21:4–9
Deuteronomy 1:1–8
Joshua 4
Judges 6, 7
1 Kings 18
2 Kings 5
Ezekiel 37:1–14
1 Maccabees 1:1–2:48

Key Words

Ark of the Covenant
Baal
Ebenezer
exile and restoration
intertestamental period
Israel and Judah
judge
messiah

From Sinai to the Promised Land

After the experience of the Exodus, the Hebrews spent a generation in the desert. The wilderness experiences were extremely difficult for the unorganized host of people led by Moses and Aaron. Various events and the divine instructions given at Sinai are recounted in the later part of Exodus and Leviticus and provide structure for the would-be nation; but they were still far from being a settled people in a defined land. This session details some of the occasions of God's continuing intervention to save the people.

The Book of Numbers tells the story of the transition from the generation that had left Egypt with Moses to the next generation, which will enter the promised land. Numbers records the continuing rebelliousness of the Israelites against God that results in this period of exile.

Numbers 10 records the Israelites' departure from Sinai. The Israelites were led by a pillar of cloud in daylight and a pillar of fire at night (Ex 13:22). They survived fearful experiences in the wilderness and were saved repeatedly by God's action. The following instances are noteworthy and are recalled later.

Exodus 17:2–7 tells the story of how the Lord supplied water by instructing Moses to strike a rock. A similar story occurs in **Numbers 20:1–13,** where God is angry because

Moses and Aaron are not obedient. The fact that the two leaders of the people, especially Moses, are disobedient shows the depths of the rebelliousness and lack of faith of the whole generation, who had so soon forgotten how God had freed them from Egypt. For their lack of faith, both Moses and Aaron are forbidden to enter the promised land. In **Numbers 21:4–9,** another complaint of the people is met by deadly serpents sent by the Lord. When Moses prays that the people be freed from this affliction, the Lord commands him to erect on a pole a bronze model of the serpents. Those who are bitten are saved from death by looking at this figure. Still later, the military defeat of Sihon, king of the Amorites, and Og, king of Bashan (Nm 21:21–35), is credited to the Lord's intervention. These events are repeatedly remembered as symbols of God's continuing gift of freedom (as in Jos 9:10).

In Numbers 22, the Hebrew people reach the east bank of the Jordan River, the threshold of the promised land, approximately opposite Jericho. There the king of Moab enlists Balaam to put a curse on Israel. At the end of a rather long ordeal (through chapter 24), Balaam gives Israel a blessing rather than the expected curse. The event is referred to in various later biblical writings.

Read **Deuteronomy 1:1–8,** which gives the literary setting for the whole book. Most of Deuteronomy is in the form of an oral recounting of Israel's history up to the threshold of the promised land. This is attributed to Moses and offers a theological interpretation of those events (note verse 5). This book will be discussed in a later theme.

Invasion and Settlement of Canaan

After Moses' death, Joshua assumes leadership and the people of Israel cross the Jordan River (Jos 3:7–17). At a location called Gilgal, a memorial is erected consisting of twelve stones from the eastern side of the Jordan. Read **Joshua 4.** Notice especially verses 20–24 and recall the role played by the Passover in Israel's remembrance of God's gift of freedom. Joshua 5:10–12 tells how the first Passover in the promised land was observed. From that time on, the miraculous manna was no longer provided. Most of the rest of the narrative about the settlement of the new land recounts military offensives by Israel.

After Joshua's death, the period of settlement led the people to live in the manner of their pagan neighbors. Little by little, the people ignored the covenant and matters went badly for Israel. Judges 2:16 affirms that the Lord intervenes on behalf of the people again and again through the agency of "judges." The pattern of the Book of Judges is the continuing rebelliousness of the people, their defeats at the hands of their enemies, their plea to God for a savior, and God's gracious response raising up a hero. The Hebrew word for "judge" does not simply mean an officer of the court, but one who is also called on to defend and govern. In most of these stories, the focus is on the human leader. They will be discussed in Theme 5. For now, read the story of Gideon, **Judges 6, 7.**

God's Intervention in Samuel's Time

Samuel is sometimes referred to as the last of the judges and the first of the prophets. His career marks a transition in the national life of the Israelites. Their enemies in this period are the Philistines. Early in 1 Samuel, the Philistines capture Israel's sacred Ark of the Covenant (see Theme 3, Session 1); but it brings them such bad fortune that they return it. In 1 Samuel 7, Israel gathers with Samuel for national penitence and renewal. When the Philistines make a military move against them, the Lord liberates them. Samuel celebrates the occasion by setting up a memorial stone, an *Ebenezer,* which means "stone of help."

How Saul rose to be king of Israel is recounted in 1 Samuel 9 and 10. The kings are studied particularly in Theme 6. For now, notice Samuel's words in 10:1: "You are to govern the Lord's people Israel, and to save them from the grasp of their enemies roundabout." The subsequent narratives make it clear that it is the Lord who saves the people through the agency of the kings. After a victory over the Ammonites, Saul declares, "No man is to be put to death this day, for today the LORD has saved Israel" (11:13).

The same theme persists when David becomes king after Saul. 2 Samuel 22:1 contains "The words of this song to the LORD when the Lord had rescued him from the grasp of all his enemies and from the hand of Saul." The words of the song are almost identical with Psalm 18. (For general reference, the time of David's reign is around 1000 BC. See the chronology chart in Appendix 7.)

Elijah and Elisha

The action of God to save Israel is not always prompted by an external threat. Under a later king named Ahab, worship of the pagan god Baal threatened the national faith. Ahab's queen was Jezebel from Sidon. Jezebel worshiped Baal and fostered that cult in Israel. Consequently, her name became a synonym for a wicked woman. The prophet Elijah confronted the prophets of Baal on Mount Carmel in the presence of a great assembly. They vied to see whose god would respond by consuming with fire an animal sacrifice on an altar. Read the story in **1 Kings 18.**

Other stories about Elijah's conflict with Ahab and Jezebel illustrate how God saves individual people. The individual is never forgotten, but in the Bible God's care occurs in a community setting. For example, the story of David's rescue from Saul is associated directly with his becoming leader of the nation. In 1 Kings 17, Elijah is on the run from Ahab, and God saves the prophet in the wilderness by sending ravens to feed him. Then Elijah is directed to stay with a widow in the village Zarephath, near the seacoast outside Israelite territory, and her oil and meal are providentially extended during the ensuing famine. After Elijah's victory on Carmel, he is divinely preserved again. The story of his flight and meeting with the Lord is in 1 Kings 19.

Dramatic stories of the Lord's power to save continue with Elisha, successor to Elijah. One such incident is in 2 Kings 6:8–23. On occasion, God aids even those outside the formal bounds of the Hebrew people. The widow of Zarephath is one illustration, and the story of Elisha and Naaman, a Syrian army officer, is another. Read **2 Kings 5.**

Into Bondage

Theme 6 surveys the period of the kings. After the reign of Solomon, David's son, the kingdom became divided into two kingdoms, usually referred to as Israel in the north and Judah in the south. The final fall of the northern kingdom of Israel (721 BC) and its subjugation under Assyria is told in 2 Kings 17:1–6. Notice also the interpretation by the narrator in verses 7–8 and the striking reference to the story of the journey to freedom from Egypt. The story continues in 2 Kings 18:9–12.

The demise of the southern kingdom of Judah came more than a century later (587 BC). During the intervening years, the saving action of the Lord is emphasized; and when the king and people rely upon God, they are rescued from danger. One notable occasion that happened under King Hezekiah is recorded three times: 2 Kings 18:1 to 19:37; 2 Chronicles 32:1–23; Isaiah 36:1 to 37:38. This freedom, however, is short-lived. The beginning of Judah's Exile to Babylon is recounted in 2 Kings 24 and 2 Chronicles 36. The name of the Jews has its origins as the national name for the citizens of Judah. After the Babylonian Exile it becomes the religious name of the Hebrew people.

As Isaiah is related to earlier events in the southern kingdom of Judah, particularly under Hezekiah (716–687 BC), Jeremiah appears somewhat later (687–580 BC). Jeremiah got into serious trouble for prophesying doom (Jer 37 and 38), but his warning too soon became reality. See particularly chapters 39 and 52.

When they encounter trouble, the people cry out for God to rescue them. This ancient cycle is repeated during the Babylonian Exile (586–538 BC). A noteworthy illustration is Psalm 137 (note the setting in Babylon). Several other prophets, particularly second Isaiah (Is 40–55), also reflect the despair and hope that mark this period.

Ezekiel spans the beginning of the Exile in a remarkable way. The first half of the book contains the prophet's words and symbolic actions directed against the nation for its wickedness before Exile. The second half starts with prophecies against other nations but soon turns to hopes and visions of Jewish restoration from the Exile. The most memorable vision concerns a valley full of dry bones; read **Ezekiel 37:1–14.** God promises Ezekiel that the people will surely have new life in their homeland.

Hosea, perhaps more than any other Old Testament writer, expresses the conviction that God will save the people, even in the face of deepest despair. Read Hosea 11:1–11; note also 13:4. Another prophetic passage to be noted at this point is Joel 2:12–3:5.

Liberation from Exile

This second most noteworthy story of an Old Testament journey to freedom for God's people is comparable in ways to the Exodus. It occurs near the end of the Old Testament story. Details of this new exodus from this captivity experience are not easily recovered. The historical allusions in the biblical records are sketchy. The release became possible after the Persian conquest of Babylon by Cyrus. In Isaiah 45:1, Cyrus is referred to as the Lord's "anointed," or "messiah." The title shows how strong was the hope of liberation, and the conviction that history is moved by God's purpose for the people.

The amnesty and repatriation decreed by Cyrus are the topic in Ezra 1. The Book of Nehemiah also is concerned with these events, but the exact relationship to the material in Ezra is not made clear. Details are skimpy in these records, but the rebuilding of the Jerusalem wall and Temple is very important. The wall protected the Jews from their local enemies, and the Temple was the center of their national life. The Book of Haggai and part of Zechariah are also concerned with the new Temple.

Two Later Resources

The narrative portions of the Book of Daniel are set in the Exile years, but the writing itself is later. Daniel is a nonhistorical reflection of the need for freedom for the Jews suffering from Greek oppression (c. 164 BC). It may indeed be the latest literary record of God's intervention in the Old Testament. It tells how the Lord saved Daniel and his friends in the rigors of Exile, and it is intended to encourage God's people to the same kind of faithfulness. Two legendary stories have had particular appeal to readers: the rescue from the fiery furnace (chapter 3) and from the den of lions (chapter 6). Daniel 13 tells the story of Daniel's rescue of a young and beautiful woman condemned to death for adultery as a consequence of a plot by two magistrates to blackmail her into having intercourse with them. It is this case which establishes Daniel's reputation as a wise man among the Jewish people.

The First and Second Books of Maccabees recount how the Jews were beset by the Hellenistic world and its culture after the conquests of Alexander the Great. This new kind of paganism threatened those who were trying to be faithful to the Torah and the Jewish way of life. Antiochus IV ("Epiphanes"), king of Syria, tried to force Hellenistic culture upon Judah. He meddled in the appointment of high priests, looted the Temple, defiled the altar, and persecuted Jews who wished to follow their religious customs. A pious Jew named Mattathias launched a sort of holy war using guerilla methods. Under his son Judas, who was given the nickname Maccabaeus ("the hammer"), the resistance was successful. The Temple was purified from pagan defilement, and for about a hundred years the Jews had a semblance of self-rule. This period extended from 165 BC to 63 BC when the Roman general Pompey took Jerusalem. Read the story in **1 Maccabees 1:1–2:48.** The fleeting period of freedom under the Maccabees was surely not forgotten when Jesus' contemporaries were assessing the nature and goal of his leadership.

Suggestions for Further Study

Research

1. Consult a Bible atlas and other sources for information about the "wilderness" between Egypt and Palestine.

2. Gather information about "manna" from a Bible dictionary.

3. Investigate the history and culture of the Philistines.

4. Review the story about Sennacherib's siege of Jerusalem in a Bible history or resource book. Study the politics, the role of Isaiah, any extrabiblical evidence about the event, and the significance of the reference to the Aramaic language.

5. Try to find New Testament references to:

   water from the rock
   the serpent on the pole
   Elijah and the widow
   Elisha and Namaan
   Joel's prophecy about the pouring out of God's spirit

6. You may want to make a simple outline or timeline of events covered in this session. Keep it for reference. We shall see some of this material again in other contexts.

Reflection

1. In what ways have you experienced being rescued from the plight your lack of faith got you into? How have you responded to the God who has freed you?

2. What kind of liberation may a nation today expect from God? Under what circumstances?

3. You may want to retell in your own words the story of

   Gideon
   Elijah at Carmel
   Ezekiel's vision of the dry bones
   Nehemiah
   Judas Maccabaeus

SESSION 3

Liberation Through Jesus Christ

Session Overview

The New Testament centers on the unique event of salvation through the resurrection of Jesus Christ. Jesus' followers interpreted this in various ways, often in continuity with Old Testament traditions, particularly the Exodus. In this process, a unique community, the Church, emerged. Its emphasis was on calling all to a new relationship with God through Jesus Christ. This generated a mission to the world. The focus throughout the New Testament is on Jesus Christ as the source of salvation.

Key Bible Readings

Luke 24
Acts 2:14–40
Romans 6:1–11
Luke 4:16–30
Matthew 28:18–20
Acts 1:8

Key Words

transfiguration
Samaritan
Pentecost

How the Good News Started

The first Exodus had vividly demonstrated to the Hebrews that they were entering a new life of freedom, experienced physically and corporately under a human leader, Moses. The freedom was tangible. In the Exodus, God created a people, giving them an identity, a land, and the commandments so they could worship the true God and live in justice with one another. The Jews returning from the Exile in Babylon saw their journey as an exodus.

The New Testament exodus was not immediately so obvious. There was no physical rescue of a social group, no politically independent nation, no geographical promised land. The early Christians were convinced that God, through the resurrection of Jesus Christ and the sending of the Holy Spirit, had saved them decisively from a bondage that was marked by sin and death. This experience called them to dream of a society in which the barriers of race and social divisions would be broken down. All would now live in a society of mutual support, with special care given to those most in need. The New Testament is the reflection of the teaching of the early Christian Church, using the models of God's interaction with humanity found in the Jewish traditions.

Read **Luke 24** and Acts 1:1–14. Note especially Luke 24:8, 32, and 45. These passages show that the experience of resurrection illuminated the gospel writer's understanding of what God had revealed in the scriptures. Paul highlights the importance of the teaching he received from the Church in 1 Corinthians 15:1–11. Now read **Acts 2:14–40.** During the Jewish festival at Pentecost, seven weeks after the resurrection, the Holy Spirit came upon Jesus' followers. Peter, the rock, is the spokesman, the interpreter of the occasion. In his sermon, Peter quotes Joel 3:1–5. Who does Peter see as the inheritor of Joel's promise? In Acts 2:22–38, "Jesus-events" are summarized. What point do you see in this?

Continuity with the Old Testament

In recounting the transfiguration of Jesus (Lk 9:28–36), the author writes in verse 31 that Moses and Elijah were speaking with Jesus about his "exodus." It is clear that this refers to the death, resurrection, and ascension of Jesus that will take place in Jerusalem. It also echoes the Old Testament journey of the Hebrew people. The reader who was (or is) steeped in traditions of the Old Testament, where the Exodus is a principal pattern of God's saving acts, would readily be able to understand Jesus' career and its climax in these terms.

Jesus is presented as interpreting his life and mission in terms of the saving event of the Passover. The Passover season seems deliberately chosen as the time for confrontation that leads to Jesus' death. Mark emphasizes that Jesus foresaw and accepted the passion events (8:31; 9:30–32; 10:32–34). All four gospels clearly place the events of Jesus' last week in Jerusalem in a Passover setting (Mt 26:1–2, 17–19; Mk 14:1–2, 12–16; Lk 22:1, 7–13; Jn 13:1, 19:14). In the dis-

course on the bread of life (Jn 6:31–35, 49–51), Jesus contrasts the manna of Moses' lifetime with himself: "I am the bread of life; whoever comes to me will never hunger, and whoever believes in me will never thirst" (Jn 6:35).

The Church saw the connection in other contexts. The wilderness stories after the Exodus form the background of John 3:14–15. The mountain setting of Jesus' sermon in Matthew 5–7 echoes the giving of law of Moses that came from "the mountain of God."

The Awareness of God's Presence in Jesus Christ

The early Church experienced the liberation of Jesus as physical healing (Acts 3:1–10), freedom from destructive legalism (Gal 5:16–26), and as a new ordering of social relationships (Gal 3:27–29). This liberation was associated with the freedom from "sin" and its disastrous social consequences. Look again at Acts 2:37–40. Those who answer the call to repent and be baptized in the name of Jesus Christ for the forgiveness of their sins are promised the gift of the Holy Spirit. Paul develops and emphasizes this insight. See, for example, Romans 3:9–18, which includes a composite quotation, mostly from Psalms 14 and 53. Paul declares that slavery to sin is a universal problem. He has already outlined the frightful consequences of sin in Romans 1:24–32. In **Romans 6:1–11,** freedom from slavery to sin is related explicitly to the death of Jesus. Freedom from sin and life in God is promised to those who commit themselves to Jesus by becoming members of the Church. Much of the letter to the Romans deals with this theme. It occurs also in the gospel traditions (see particularly Jn 8:34–36).

What Jesus accomplished was overwhelming to the early Church. The New Testament writers described and explained the experience in a variety of ways. The dominating event, however, was the resurrection. The experience of the resurrection and the pouring out of the Spirit impelled the early Church to spread the good news throughout their world. They proclaimed that salvation had come in the crucified Christ. They interpreted the experience of Christ through the prism of the Old Testament that was immediately accepted by the early Church as God's inspired word.

The complexity of detail that developed from interpreting the New Testament in light of the Old may be illustrated by Matthew's story about the flight of the holy family to Egypt (Mt 2:13–15). This tale about Jesus' babyhood is identified with Hosea 11:1, suggesting that the journey Jesus makes is an exodus from Egypt as the representative of God's people. In Matthew 4:2, the temptation of Jesus is preceded by "forty days and forty nights" in the wilderness, a period of time reminiscent of Moses' stay on Mt. Sinai (Ex 24:18) and the forty years of wilderness wandering (Jos 5:6). In Acts 7:17–38, Stephen, an early Church leader chosen to minister to Greek-speaking members of the Jerusalem Church, retells the Exodus story to show its connections with Jesus.

The early chapters of Acts make it clear that the existence of the Church was seen by Christians as evidence that a unique society had come into being (see, for example, 2:39–41, 47; 4:4, 32–35; 6:7). The later chapters tell about Paul's extensive travels in the Mediterranean world as he spread the good news. Paul's letters are also a valuable record of the numerical and geographical expansion of the Church.

The people of the first Exodus were conscious of a special relationship with God. Their relationship with the Lord set them apart. Many within the Jewish community were not particularly disposed to bring outsiders into their company. However, extreme attitudes of exclusivity were criticized and satirized in the Book of Jonah. In the Greek cities, pagans, attracted by the strong ethical values of the Jews, were associated with synagogue worship.

In **Luke 4:16–30,** Jesus is presented as being aware of a universal purpose for his preaching. The Book of Isaiah was to be read that day and Jesus selected 61:1–2, the classic description of the work of the expected messiah. This was a message of release for oppressed people. Jesus' interpretative comments turned his hearers against him, and they ejected him from the village. The Old Testament illustrations he used, such as the example of Naaman (Lk 4:27), angered them. The passages told of salvation for Gentiles, and this implication was unpopular with the listeners in Nazareth.

Jesus' good news was for all who would listen. The gospels present him showing concern for the Samaritans. For a detailed study about how Jesus treated Samaritans, read John 4. One of Jesus' best-known stories is about the good Samaritan (see Lk 10:30–37). This attitude led Jesus' critics to label him scornfully "a Samaritan" (Jn 8:48). John 3:16 expresses the conviction that God's love, in Jesus, is the dynamic principle of world salvation. Here "everyone" is a key word.

Paul and Salvation in Jesus Christ

The implications of this open offer critically affected Paul's life and thought. He saw how far-reaching was the liberation made possible by Jesus. The most extended discussion of the matter is Romans 9–11, an important but difficult passage. Here Paul explores the relationship between Jews and Gentiles. Note especially 9:22–24. To the surprise of God's people in Israel (Jews), a host of people outside Israel (non-Jews) flocks to accept God's saving offer (see also Acts 2:9–11). Paul thinks that this illustrates concretely the statement in Hosea 2:25.

The people saved by God in Jesus Christ is a body united by the Holy Spirit, not a national nor an ethnic group. Therefore they recalled the saving event in terms of what Jesus did. Instead of referring to the God who liberated the Israelites from slavery, Paul writes of liberation "through Jesus Christ and God the Father who raised him from the dead" (Gal 1:1). Since this event has the power to bring new life to anyone who is willing (1 Cor 6:14; 2 Cor 4:14), it continues to be good news that offers salvation. See how Paul uses these words in Romans 1:16. Compare this with John 3:16.

Salvation and Mission

The Church came to understand that this salvation, which has been made available for all humanity, led to the sending out of missions to proclaim good news to all the world. A succinct statement of this is the "great commission," **Matthew 28:18–20.** Another summary is **Acts 1:8.** Paul relates his unique sense of mission in Galatians 1:11–17 (see also 1 Cor 9:16 and 2 Tm 1:8–12).

Suggestions for Further Study

Research

1. Review Luke 24. List the steps the disciples experienced as they came to recognize the presence of the risen Jesus. What was their reaction?

2. Review Romans 6:1–11. What is the nature of the bondage Jesus liberates humanity from?

3. Read Luke 10:30–37; Matthew 28:18–20; Acts 1:8; Acts 2:14–40. What do these texts reveal about the nature and purpose of the Church?

Reflection

1. What destructive behaviors exist in your own life that need the healing grace of Jesus Christ? What social needs are you aware of that need healing? In what ways have you prayed for yourself and others who are in bondage to sin?

2. There are many references in this section that should be remembered. Either memorize or identify the major details in each passage, as indicated.

Matthew 28:18–20	The "great commission" (memorize)
Luke 4	Jesus' sermon in the Nazareth synagogue (identify)
Luke 10:30–37	The good Samaritan (identify)
Luke 24	The Emmaus road encounter (identify)
John 6:35	Jesus the bread of life (memorize)
John 4	Jesus and the Samaritan woman at Jacob's well (identify)
Acts 1:8	Summary of Acts (identify)
Acts 2	Pentecost and Peter's sermon (identify)
Acts 7	Stephen's speech (identify)
Luke 22:14–20	Jesus' desire to eat the Passover with his disciples (identify)
Romans 9–11	Jews and Gentiles (identify)
1 Corinthians 15	Paul's thoughts on the resurrection (identify)

SESSION 4

Salvation of the Church

Session Overview

As the liberation experienced in the Exodus is replicated repeatedly in Israel's later history, so salvation in Jesus Christ is the repeated experience of the early Church. The Book of Acts gives many illustrative instances of liberation. Paul's career and letters make salvation a principal focus. The scope of the salvation thus broadens to encompass both individuals and the world. Ultimately, confrontation with Roman power is seen as the occasion of victory for the exalted Christ in the Book of Revelation.

Key Bible Readings
Mark 2:1–12
Acts 4:1–22; 12:1–19
1 Peter 4:12–19
Mark 13:1–13
Revelation 1; 4; 5

Key Words
apocalyptic writings

A Liberation Model in Jesus' Ministry

In exilic and post-exilic literature, Israel is conceived as a vehicle by which other nations would come to recognize and acknowledge the greatness of God. The restoration of the Jews would lead other nations to recognize the unique character of God.

The early Christian community perceived itself as a community that crossed national and racial boundaries (Gal 3:28). The corporate nature of salvation is emphatically related to the developing Church. The salvation offered through the Church involved dramatic escapes from danger on the part of the early disciples. The link between "physical" and "spiritual" salvation has already been seen in the ministry of Jesus.

Jesus emphasizes the physical and spiritual dimensions of salvation in the story of the paralytic man in **Mark 2:1–12.** The paralytic man is brought to Jesus for healing. At this stage in his public career, Jesus is regarded as a charismatic healer, a prophet-figure who aroused popular enthusiasm. Jesus' first words to the infirm man are a declaration that his sins are forgiven! Then, after a heated discussion with unfriendly critics in the crowd, Jesus heals the man's paralysis.

By healing the man's body and spirit, Jesus clearly reflects the Hebrew understanding of the unitary nature of human life; body and spirit are not to be treated in isolation from one another. For further examples in the gospels, see Matthew 8:16, 12:28; Luke 8:2; John 5:2–14, 9:1–41.

First Years of the Church

Read **Acts 4:1–22** and chapter 5. Try to sense the excitement in the Church at that time. Acts presents a picture of the Church in conflict with local Jewish authorities over the correct interpretation of the meaning of Jesus. (This could also reflect the situation of the Church at the time of the writing of Acts, about 80–85 AD, when the conflict between the Church and some Jewish authorities was more pronounced.) Here are some details to consider in these two chapters. What caused the first clash (4:1–2)? What would be the special concern of the Sadducees in the matter (compare Mk 12:18)? Note the cross-victory theme (4:10). Identify the Old Testament quotation from Psalm 118:22 (used in Mk 12:10 and several other times in the New Testament). In Acts 4:12, we have a succinct statement of the good news about Jesus' saving actions. Verses 24–30 accent the salvation theme.

The Church is also saved from danger perceived within its own membership. The story in 5:1–11 is startling; the consequence of Ananias and Sapphira's action seem terribly severe. The essential point of the punishment is that Ananias and Sapphira lied to the Church. How may it be understood as a liberation of the Church? Consider how the impact of their discovered guilt may have affected the persons involved.

Acts 5:29–32 is loaded with important details. Note how the freedom effected by Jesus

becomes the basis of the apostle's obedience. (A less explicit statement of the same relationship occurs in 4:19–20.) Gamaliel, a teacher of Paul, makes a wise, prophetic judgment in 5:33–39.

Acts 12:1–19 recounts how Peter is again rescued from prison. Observe several details. The first martyrdom of an apostle, James, the brother of John, is recorded in 12:2. Notice the solidarity between Peter and the local Church. See Acts 12:5, 12. Verse 11 emphasizes the role of the Lord in the rescue of Peter. The humorous detail in Acts 12:13–16 suggests how vivid was the recollection in the Church tradition.

Acts 16:16–40 tells about still another rescue from prison. Paul and his mission-companion Silas are engaged in Paul's second "missionary journey" in the Macedonian city of Philippi. The jailer was absolutely distraught thinking his prisoners had escaped.

The most ironic drama of all is that the Church was, in a way, saved by Paul, a former persecutor of Jesus' followers. The story is in Acts 8:1–3, 9:1–22. (The importance of this event is emphasized also in 22:3–16 and 26:9–19.) Paul had witnessed the stoning of Stephen, whose defense speech included detailed references to Israel's journey to freedom. For the whole story, see Acts 6:8 to 8:1.

Paul as Interpreter of Salvation in Christ

In Paul's letters, God's salvation in Jesus Christ is prominent. The death of Jesus might seem to be a strange way to effect salvation. The apostle repeatedly explains to the Church how this is precisely the case. Sometimes Paul's explanation is pointedly related to this theme; sometimes it is indirect or implied.

Consider the application of the word "Christ" to Jesus. The Hebrew language equivalent is "messiah," and this is used of Jesus sparingly outside of Pauline writings, where it occurs some 72 percent of the time. A suffering, dying messiah was a contradiction in terms for Jewish traditions. In some Jewish circles, the messiah was seen as an "ideal king," a human ruler who would be endowed with special gifts of wisdom and righteousness. The Qumran communities in the area of the Dead Sea apparently were not looking for a single messiah, but thought the ideals of the future messiah could be experienced as part of the daily life of the community. The term "messiah" had no fixed, technical meaning in Jesus' time. It appears to be Paul who made the usage common in applying it to Jesus' victory over death.

Any description of the salvation process always falls short of being adequate. The whole truth is greater than any one metaphor to describe it and greater than the sum of all descriptions. Paul addresses this problem in 1 Corinthians 1:17–25. Note especially verse 18. A major part of 1 Corinthians is directed toward local Church problems, which Paul tries to correct. The Corinthians need to be saved from themselves! In 1 Corinthians 5:1–13, Paul deals with a situation of a man living with his stepmother. The purge he calls for is set in Passover language (verses 7–8).

Since the New Testament situation does not have to do with a homogeneous people in one land, the balance between individual and corporate salvation must always be kept in view. In 1 Timothy 1.15, for example, salvation is related to individuals; but in Ephesians 2:8 and 5:25 salvation appears to be corporate.

Salvation, the Church, and the World

The full scope of the salvation effected by Jesus Christ was not immediately clear. The good news was preached first in the synagogues of the cities the first apostles and disciples visited.

A pivotal story in the conversion of the Gentiles is the experience of Peter in the household of Cornelius (Acts 10:1–11:18). Cornelius was a Roman centurion stationed in Caesarea who was associated with the synagogue as a "god-fearer." While he and his household listened to Peter proclaim the gospel, the Holy Spirit came upon them. For the writer of Acts, this was divine attestation that Gentiles should be accepted into the Christian community on the same basis of faith in Jesus as Jewish converts were. It is significant for the author of Acts that it is Peter who opens the door of faith to the Gentiles in response to the vision he had received.

Paul was called to be the evangelizer of the Gentiles. He further broke the limits and extended the good news to the Gentile world around present-day Lebanon, Turkey, and Greece.

Paul still did not envisage a situation in which the Church or even its individual members would confront the Roman world in a life-and-death struggle. In Romans 13, Paul expresses support for the Roman government. He was proud of his citizenship, or at least he did not hesitate to utilize its privileges. For examples, see Acts 16:37–38 and 22:25–29 and also 1 Timothy 2:1–2.

Another kind of situation is implied in **1 Peter 4:12–19,** where it appears that God's people risk punishment by Rome simply because of professing their faith. Warning of just such a danger is included in **Mark 13:1–13.**

The Book of Revelation

Complete disruption of the Church's life is anticipated in the last book of the Bible. Read **Revelation 1:1–11.** Revelation is a carefully and impressively drawn message of assurance to the Church in the terribly threatening situation in which it was actually confronted by a Roman government gone demonic. "Revelation" is a

Latin-derived word of which the Greek equivalent is "apocalypse," a term by which this book is known. Apocalyptic writing is deliberately obscure in style and written in symbolic imagery to fool the Roman authorities. Revelation is studied in later themes (particularly Theme 10). The reason for its inclusion here is to note its message of salvation.

John, the mystic and pastor, who is described as the author of the Revelation, was in exile because of his Christian witness (1:9). The message of his book is directed to be read (1:3) to seven churches in the "circuit" probably anchored at Ephesus. Read **Revelation 1:12–20.** The seven churches are given to understand that they have heavenly "connections" guaranteed by the Lord. It is clear from verse 18 that the divine figure is none other than the exalted Jesus Christ. Jesus' death and resurrection give assurance that he has control over all destiny. This initial vision is basic to all the rest of the book.

Chapters 2 and 3 contain a series of messages to each of the seven churches. Each message is addressed "to the angel of the Church," which may be taken as allusion to a sort of "guardian angel" (a similar idea occurs in Psalms 91:11). Each little letter concludes with a promise of a gift for those who "conquer." The seventh letter reminds the people of the Church that the Lord, standing at the door and knocking, is the victor (Rev 3:20–21).

Read **Revelation 4.** The details of heavenly scenery are very strange. The writer is recounting a vision (4:2), an attempt to describe what is indescribable. Try to decide what this vision of heaven is attempting to convey. Are the short "hymns" perhaps a key? If so, is the writer trying to declare how great the Creator God is?

Now read **Revelation 5.** Here a figure known as the "lamb" is introduced, a startling reversal from the anticipated "lion" in verse 5. The lamb alone is able to open the seven-sealed scroll, which, one may infer, holds the knowledge of the future history John so desperately wants to know. The role of the lamb in the Passover-Exodus story has already been mentioned. John the Baptist also applied the term to Jesus (John 1:29, 36), and Paul alludes to the identification in 1 Corinthians 5:7. Notice that in Revelation 5:6, the lamb "seemed to have been slain." Study carefully the hymn in verses 9–10. The death of the lamb has been effective for the salvation and victory of God's people. The lamb is the one who can reveal the destiny of all creation (that is, "open the scroll"). Thus chapter 4 tells of the power of the Creator God and chapter 5 reveals the power of the Redeemer God.

It would require a separate course to study all the details of Revelation, but consider here several more illustrations of the theme that God saves the people. In chapter 7, God guarantees to save a "great multitude." Since the people traditionally and symbolically consist of twelve tribes, the number is first given as $12 \times 12 \times 1000$ (1000 is the largest counting unit in the first-century Greek alphabet). The author thus describes a throng too great to count. The white robes symbolize victory—God saved them—and this is related to the death of Jesus Christ by the eucharistic metaphor of washing in the lamb's blood. In a striking role-change, the lamb becomes the shepherd. (There is a similar exchange in Jn 10.) In a montage of Old Testament phrases and allusions that is typical of Revelation, God's people are guaranteed a blessed future. Again and again, hymns and messages from heaven are heard, and always their theme is the sure salvation of God's people, "sealed" by the victory of the lamb. (The impression of a signet ring made in wax by an important person to seal a letter was evidence of the authority and power of the person.)[1]

Read Revelation 11:15–19. Seven is the "complete" number (for example, seven days of creation; here seven churches),[2] so when the seventh trumpet sounds, we hear the word of total victory. Revelation 11:19 is reminiscent of events at Sinai and later moments in Israel's history. Read 15:2–4. Note "the song of Moses" (see Ex 15:1–18). Again, Old Testament phrases are prominent.

In 19:10, note the statement "Witness to Jesus is the spirit of prophecy." This means that the Christian is called to give witness to the Word of God made flesh. This is the declaration of Revelation: All Christian expectation is already secured by the victory of Jesus Christ. The wonderful images in 21:9 through 22:5 put this in words the Church has always treasured.

Suggestions for Further Study

Research

1. Review the material in Acts. In what ways were the disciples rescued by God?

2. In Mark 2:1–12 is an example of physical healing performed by Christ. What instances of physical healing can you find in Acts? What do these examples tell us about the Church's mission of healing the sick?

3. In a Bible dictionary, look up the term "apocalyptic" or "apocalyptic literature." What kind of literature is it? What are the social circumstances of the people who wrote it?

Reflection

1. In what ways are you called to participate in Christ's healing ministry in your community?

2. Where and how do the biblical insights in this theme affect the life of God's people today?

Notes

1. See Seal, HBD 918–19.

2. See also Genesis 33:3; Leviticus 4:6, 8:11, 14:7, 16:14; Joshua 6:15; 2 Kings 5:14; and so on. See also Numbers, HBD 711–12.

THEME 2

God Is Faithful to the People

SESSION 1

Promise and Covenant: The Old Testament

Session Overview

Before the Exodus, there were traditions that told how God had established a relationship with Abraham and his descendants. At Sinai, this covenant promise was formalized and the responsibilities of Israel were developed. God also made a particular agreement with David and his descendants, including the promise of a perpetual dynasty. The prophets became the interpreters of Israel's covenant obligations, and they denounced the unfaithfulness of leaders and people. In spite of these failures and the Exile, however, some prophets spoke of a time of a new covenant yet to come.

Key Bible Readings

Genesis 12:1–7; 15;
   17:1–14; 28:10–22
Exodus 6:2–8; 24:3–8
Numbers 14:18–19
Deuteronomy 26:5–9
2 Samuel 7:1–17
Amos 3:1–2
Micah 4:1–8
Hosea 11
Jeremiah 31:31–34
Isaiah 55:1–5

Key Words

circumcision
covenant
cubit

Long Before the Exodus

In Theme 1, we looked at the Bible from the perspective of the Hebrew people, who were convinced that God delivered them from bondage, danger, and despair. The Hebrews saw the Passover-Exodus experience as the foundation of their national identity and destiny. That experience was not, of course, the first time the Hebrew people became aware of God. They already possessed stories and traditions that were later recorded in the Old Testament. Moses built upon the memory of these stories to convince the Israelites that his leadership and call were indeed God's will for them.

Several of these very ancient stories assured the people that God would be faithful in acting on their behalf even if they were unfaithful in return. Genesis 6–9 tells the renowned story of Noah and the ark. Several details are important. Read Genesis 8:15–22 and 9:1–17. The text tells of the covenant (Gn 9:9) God unilaterally establishes with humanity, promising never again to destroy life on earth with a flood. Covenant is a key term in this theme.

Abraham and His Family

Genesis 12 through 25 contains the saga of Abraham, or Abram, as he was called at first (see 17:5). Chapters 26 through 50 tell about his immediate descendants. The story of Abraham and Sarah tells of the establishment of a covenant with a mutual relationship between God and the people. Read **Genesis 12:1–7;** 13:14–17; **15:1–21; 17:1–14,** 15–21. The promise to Abraham that he would be the father of a great nation was remembered and repeated through all subsequent generations of Israel. It helped to explain and justify the Hebrews' journey to the promised land (see Dt 1:8). Circumcision, an ancient custom thought to ward off evil, is reinterpreted as a covenant sign (Gn 17:11) or symbol. It has survived to the present as a distinctive mark of Jewish faith.

The Lord is also shown as the God who vindicates the oppressed in the stories of the women of patriarchal times. Women in this time had no individual rights and were at the mercy of their fathers, husbands, and sons. In the stories of Hagar, Sarah, Rebekah, and Leah, we see God on the side of those who were helpless. Hagar is rejected by Abraham, but becomes the mother of a great nation (Gn 16:10, 15). Sarah, who was barren for most of her life, is vindicated by God (Gn 21:1) with the birth of Isaac in her old age. Rebekah sees to it that the covenant with Abraham is passed on through her favorite son, Jacob. Leah is vindicated in her son Judah, who is the ancestor of King David (Gn 49:8–12).[1]

The covenant promise is renewed with Abraham and Sarah's son Isaac in Genesis 26:1–5, and again with Isaac's son Jacob through the influence of Rebekah in 27:1–19. **Genesis 28:10–22** tells of Jacob's well-known vision at Bethel, which means "house of God." On a somewhat later occasion, God renews this promise and gives Jacob a new name, Israel, which becomes the family and national name of his descendants (see Gn 35:9–15).

The story of Jacob's family revolves around the career of Joseph, who became a slave in Egypt, and later a very high-ranking official. (Joseph's saga is found in Genesis 37–50.) This story provides the background to the enslavement of the Hebrews in Egypt. The narrative of Jacob's journey to join Joseph in Egypt, however, includes God's promise that Jacob's family, under the leadership of Leah's son Judah, will become great and will eventually leave Egypt (Gn 46:1–4).

The promise to Abraham and the covenant that certified it became the ground of assurance for the Exodus. At the burning bush in Midian, the Lord is identified to Moses as "the God of your fathers, the God of Abraham, the God of Isaac, and the God of Jacob" (Ex 3:15). The promise of a homeland, Exodus 3:17, is elaborated in **Exodus 6:2–8,** where the covenant with the Hebrew ancestors is reiterated. In Exodus 13:5, the promise is made even more emphatic, for it is said that the Lord "swore" to give the land to the people. Oath-taking, often invoking God as guarantor, is common in the biblical world. An oath made by God is the ultimate certainty.

The People's Covenant Obligation

A covenant usually implies two consenting parties. So far, the Lord's part has been studied. What might the people's part be? When Israel camps at Mount Sinai, the Lord gives Moses commandments for the regulation of Israel's life, and these are treated as a covenant. Read **Exodus 24:3–8.**

There is a further development, however. While Moses is conferring with the Lord on the mountain, the people make a golden calf as an object for worship, and God threatens to destroy them. In response, Moses cites the covenant oath made to the patriarchs, thereby averting God's wrath (see the story in Ex 32; note verses 13 and 14). It begins to appear that although there are covenant requirements for the people to fulfill, the Lord is faithful beyond the requirements set by mutual obligation and keeps the covenanted promises even in the face of Israel's unfaithfulness.

Another story illustrative of this aspect of the divine covenant is found in Numbers 13. During the wilderness wandering after Sinai, spies are sent into Canaan, the "promised land," to see whether it would be safe to move in. After forty days, the spies bring back a very pessimistic report—except for the minority opinion of Caleb. In Numbers 14, the people raise an outcry against what seems too great a risk of failure. The Lord threatens to destroy the people, but again the intercession of Moses modifies the outcome. Note especially **Numbers 14:18–19.** The promise of the land remains, but not for the people who murmured about the danger. They will not be allowed to enter the promised land.

Deuteronomy contains a review of Israel's experiences in the wilderness and a restatement of the people's obligations to God. Chapter 26 has an important summary. Sometimes **Deuteronomy 26:5–9** is referred to as a "little creed" because it expresses so neatly Israel's self-understanding. Notice how the ritual is a reminder of God's promise. The people's response includes harvest offerings reflecting the agricultural life of the later period, when Deuteronomy was written. Joshua 24 recounts the promises and covenant in somewhat broadened terms. Just before his death, Joshua challenges the people to serve the Lord. He bases his appeal upon God's past faithfulness, and the covenant relationship is renewed.

In the discussion to this point, note again that God's covenant promises are focused on children (family) and the land (nation). The Hebrew people thought in concrete terms. Circumcision, the covenant sign given to Abraham, was physical. Only later are there abstract or "spiritual" promises.

The Covenant with David

When Israelite national life stabilizes under a monarchy, a special covenant promise is made to David the king: God assures David that his royal line will continue as a perpetual dynasty. Read **2 Samuel 7:1–17.** Also look at 23:1–7, which contains a little psalm that is called "the last words of David." Verse 5 refers to the covenant God made with David. When David's son Solomon becomes king, he builds a great temple and moves Israel's sacred symbols into it. At the dedication of the temple, Solomon makes a public address in which he repeatedly refers to God's faithfulness to the promise and covenant. Read 1 Kings 8:14–26. In a subsequent response, God renews the covenant promise but adds a warning that the king and people must keep God's commandments and statutes. Read 1 Kings 9:1–9.

Several psalms reflect this view of the relationship between God and the king. Because of this connection, students usually refer to these as the "royal" psalms. Psalm 2 is a notable example. (See also Ps 18:50–51; 23:5–6; 27:4–6; 69:36–37; 89:20–38; 108:6–10; and 144:9–10.)

The Prophets and Human Failure

A covenant is between two parties. The Lord will be the faithful God of the people. The people are called to remember God's faithfulness in leading them out of slavery and into freedom in the new land. They, in turn, promise to worship the true God and to live in justice and compassion with one another. The destruction of the nation forged by God is the result of the infidelity and apostasy of the people. God's faithfulness never fails, yet the people ignore their covenant obligations. Unfaithfulness and rebellion, often called simply "sin," led to oppression and grief for Israel. The prophets are called as God's witnesses of the consequences of failure to live up to the promises made by the people. The prophets are the voice on behalf of those who have no voice. The message of the prophets has important consequences for Christians today. They still witness to the importance of hearing the concerns of the helpless in today's world and to the responsibility of Christians to respond to the call of justice.

The prophet Amos is notable for his denunciation of Israel's sins. Amos begins his prophecies or messages (the Hebrew text calls them "words") by denouncing the sins of neighboring peoples. In Amos 2:6, however, he makes a dramatic switch by accusing Israel itself. In later chapters the prophet's charges become graphic and vehement. Amos especially denounces the exploitation of the poor. In **Amos 3:1–2,** Amos declares that it is precisely because of the Lord's intimate relationship with Israel that punishment is coming; in 9:11–15, a note of hope is sounded.

The prophet Micah also denounces the wickedness of God's people and predicts punishment, but he concludes with a hymn on the faithfulness of the Lord (7:18–20). He also looks to a time when Jerusalem will become the center of the world's longing for peace. Read **Micah 4:1–8.** Christians have noted that in 5:1–3 Micah looks for a future deliverer of God's people to come from Bethlehem. This was probably an extension of the promise to David, for Bethlehem was David's hometown.[2]

The Prophets and God's Faithfulness

The Book of Hosea focuses with unique intensity upon God's determined, faithful love for Israel, even in the face of rejection that might warrant divine judgment. Like many of the biblical prophets, Hosea makes his message graphically explicit by symbolic actions. At God's bidding, Hosea marries an unfaithful wife, and the children subsequently born are given symbolic names (Hos 1; see also Is 8:4). Interspersed with dire prophecies in later chapters are promises that indicate God's struggle to supplant judgment with forgiving, faithful love. Thus even when Hosea's wife is completely unfaithful to him, he takes her back and declares that this is a sign of what God's mercy is like. **Hosea 11** was mentioned twice in Theme 1, and now the significance of the whole chapter can be appreciated. Chapter 14 is a good summary of the major emphasis of the whole book.

In the face of disaster and exile, the kingdoms of Israel and Judah are reminded of the covenant promises of God as the prophets in various ways emphasize God's faithfulness and the certainty of covenant renewal. God is still faithful, although the people have forgotten their covenant obligations. See Micah 7:15–20. The prophet Ezekiel twice speaks of "a covenant of peace" (34:25; 37:26), which God will make with the people. Note that in Ezekiel 37:24–25, the divine promise includes the restoration of the royal line of David.

No covenant passage in the prophets is more important than **Jeremiah 31:31–34.** The prophet speaks of a new covenant, a covenant of the heart, which will usher in a universal relationship with God. This passage is quoted in its entirety in the New Testament (Heb 8:8–12) and will be considered in Session 2. In Jeremiah 33:14–16, Jeremiah associates the fulfillment of

God's promise with a reestablishment of David's line (a passage Christians have connected with the messianic destiny of Jesus). Another well-known, important passage is **Isaiah 55:1–5.** The prophet speaks of a new covenant between God and the people, based on God's love for David.

Suggestions for Further Study

Research

1. Review the covenants between God and the Hebrew people through Abraham, Isaac, and Jacob. Who made the covenant with whom? What was promised and expected by each of the parties?

2. Review the material on the prophets. How did they interpret God's promises in relation to the covenant traditions?

Reflection

1. Through the covenants, God made a commitment to the people. Do you see yourself as one who inherited this commitment made by God? What is your response to God who has so wholeheartedly made these promises to you? In what ways have you responded to the saving grace you have received?

2. Here is a summary list of references that you should be able to locate from this session. Several are starred for special attention:

   Genesis 9:13 (the rainbow promise)
   Genesis 15:6 (Abraham's faithfulness)
   Genesis 28:10–22 (the promise to Jacob at Bethel)
   Exodus 6:2–8 (covenant with Israel through Moses)
   *Deuteronomy 26:5–9 (Israel's "little creed")
   Joshua 24 (covenant renewal at Shechem)
   *Hosea 11 (God's covenant love)
   Amos 2 (surprise denunciation of Israel's sin)
   Micah 4 (vision of peace)
   *Jeremiah 31:31–34 (a new covenant of the heart)
   *Isaiah 55 (an everlasting covenant for all)

Notes

1. See Alice L. Laffey, *An Introduction to the Old Testament: A Feminist Perspective*, 38–41.

2. 1 Sm 16:1, 4, 13, 17–19. Christians related the prophecy to Jesus (Mt 2:1–6; Jn 7:42).

SESSION 2

Promise and Covenant: The New Testament

Session Overview

The Church saw Jesus as a special fulfillment of the Old Testament promises. The epistle to the Hebrews especially focuses on this theme. Paul also refers to it specifically in several epistles, and there are important references in other books.

Key Bible Readings

Mark 14:24
1 Corinthians 11:23–26
Hebrews 1:1–2; 8;
   10:11–18
Hebrews 13:20–21
Galatians 3:15–29
2 Timothy 2:11–13

Key Words

mediator
Pentecost
testament
will

A Bridge from Old to New

The Jewish people returned from the Babylonian Exile full of hope that they could return to the glory of the days of David and Solomon. These expectations were never fulfilled. The Temple was rebuilt and Jerusalem partially restored, but the political prestige won by Solomon never returned. The Hellenistic conquerors of Palestine treated the Jews with either uneasy tolerance or with outright persecution. Hellenistic oppression was ended by the Maccabean revolution, yet the respite lasted scarcely a century (166–63 BC). The Romans came with their garrisons and taxes (63 BC). In this time of political and social oppression, John the Baptist and then Jesus stirred up expectations that fulfillment of God's promise was at hand.

Theme 1, Session 3, discussed the events following the resurrection of Jesus when the Church was called dramatically into being. Peter's Pentecost sermon is recorded as the first public challenge from the new faith. Review Acts 2:14–42. Peter concluded the message by calling the people to repentance and baptism as realization of God's promises (Acts 2:38–39).

Jesus and Fulfillment

The gospels record only one explicit reference to God's promise made by Jesus. At the meeting in Jerusalem where the two disciples report how the risen Jesus revealed himself to them at Emmaus, Jesus appears and declares that "the promise of my Father" will shortly be fulfilled (Lk 24:44–49). This refers partly to the effective presence of the Holy Spirit among the people, and this promise begins to be realized precisely at the event of Pentecost.

There is evidence, however, that in a broader sense Jesus considers his total mission to be the fulfillment of God's covenant promise. This is implicit in his invitation to faith, which is a frequent feature of his preaching. Sometimes it is also very explicit. Recall the sermon at Nazareth in Luke 4:16–30, where he says, "Today this scripture passage is fulfilled in your hearing" (4:21), referring to Isaiah 61:1–2 with its announcement of "glad tidings." The Gospel of John emphasizes this concept in quoting Jesus many times as saying, "I have come" or "I came" and as referring to "the one who sent me" (for example, Jn 5:43; 7:28; 10:10; 17:4, 8, 18, 21).

The claim of covenant connection is also explicit in Jesus' words at the Last Supper. Read Matthew 26:28; **Mark 14:24;** Luke 22:20; **1 Corinthians 11:23–26.** Paul writes to a community split into factions. He sees the eucharistic memorial as a way to unify all who recognize Jesus as Lord.

> Whenever believers share this bread and this cup, they recall the Lord's command to do this in memory of him. In so doing, they recall his death as they await his coming in glory. Three stages of time, the past (the original Last Supper and Jesus' death), the present (the community's celebration), and the future (the parousia) are brought together in this action. Anyone who performs this act unworthily, that is, separating one of these aspects from the other, sins in not fulfilling the Lord's command.[1]

In the eucharistic memorial, then, Christians remember the sacrifice of Jesus and recognize the call to enter into the new covenant sealed by Jesus' life, death, and resurrection.

The Epistle to the Hebrews

So central was the concept of the covenant being fulfilled in Jesus Christ that the Church has called its scriptures the New Testament, which is another way of saying new covenant. The Hebrew scriptures, also held sacred by Christians, are called the Old Testament or old covenant. The writer of the letter to the Hebrews reflects this double meaning of "covenant/testament" in Hebrews 9:1 and 15–22, where the word is translated to the more common term "will" in the NAB. (Lawyers speak of one's "last will and testament.") This passage is difficult. We shall understand it better as we learn more about this letter, but for the present just observe this word shift.

In **Hebrews 1:1–2,** the author states the old/new contrast at the outset: Whereas God's past communication to the people was varied and partial, now God has spoken fully "through a son," that is, Jesus Christ. The writer then spells out how the son is better than the former channels of God's revelation. This highlights the transition from old to new covenant and a continued demonstration of God's faithfulness in process.

In **Hebrews 8,** Christ is a heavenly high priest; and therefore he functions with a new and better covenant, which "is enacted on better promises." In Session 1, Jeremiah 31:31–34 was emphasized. That passage is quoted in full in Hebrews 8:8–12 and provides the thematic text for the whole letter. The new covenant is effective; "he declares the first one obsolete." The

Jeremiah quotation is offered as evidence that the transition is not by chance. Jeremiah 31:33–34 is quoted again in **Hebrews 10:11–18** in relation to Christ's sacrifice for sin. This theme is also reflected in Jesus' words at the Last Supper.

Hebrews 13:20–21 is sometimes used as a benediction in worship services. Notice that it begins with the resurrection and then speaks of "the blood of the eternal covenant."

Paul and God's Covenant Faithfulness

Hebrews 12:24 refers to Jesus as "the mediator of a new covenant." This association of mediator and covenant occurs also in Paul's writings, although his lines of thought proceed quite differently. Read **Galatians 3:15–29.** Paul is arguing that God's people find the basis for their life not in the old law but in God's promises. Here again, the multiple usage of the words covenant, testament, and will is employed. Since the covenant-promises were given through Abraham before the covenant-law was given through Moses, the earlier form of God's will is not annulled by the latter. In Galatians 3:19–20, Paul also argues that because the law came by an intermediary (mediator), it is less final than the promises God gave directly to Abraham. "The law does not, however, oppose God's purposes, for it carries out its function (22) so that *righteousness* comes by *faith* and *promise* not by human works of the law."[2]

One of Paul's most curious arguments is in Galatians 4:21–31. He constructs an allegory from events in Abraham's life. Abraham had a son by a slave woman (a common practice in the social structure and not a moral problem). Later Isaac was born to his wife, Sarah, in fulfillment of a promise made by God. Try to follow the thought in which mountains are meant to represent the offspring of the two women

and the corresponding covenants. In Ephesians 2:11–16, the author relates Gentiles in the Church to the Abraham covenant with its symbol of circumcision. Gentiles were "strangers to the covenants of promise," but now the saving act of Jesus Christ has brought them into the covenant people of God.

In Romans 9–11, Paul theologizes about the relationship of Jews and Gentiles. In 9:4, Paul associates the "Israelites" with the covenants and promises; but he goes on to show that the Jewish people have generally rejected God's plan and that God has accepted the Gentiles. Paul, however, denies that God rejected Israel (11:1). Proof of God's fidelity is the existence of Jewish Christians like Paul himself. Then, in Romans 11:26, Paul asserts that "all Israel will be saved," and part of his supporting scripture recalls Jeremiah 31:33. The gifts of God are irrevocable. Another of his involved arguments occurs in 2 Corinthians 3, where there seems to be another recollection of Jeremiah's words, and the Moses-law covenant seen more clearly. Note also 2 Corinthians 1:18–20, where God's faithfulness to his promise is related to Jesus Christ.

Other New Testament Resources

Stephen's speech in his own defense in Acts 7 stresses God's covenant and promise. In 7:5, there is the promise of land and progeny. In 7:8, this is ratified by the "covenant of circumcision."[3] In 7:17, the deliverance from Egypt is referred to as the time "for the fulfillment of the promise."

2 Timothy 2:11–13 contains a saying that must have been current in the Church after the middle of the first century. It is a remarkable statement about Jesus Christ. How does this sum up our theme?

In Theme 1, Session 4, the message of the Book of Revelation was shown to focus on the victory of salvation. While the word "promise" does not occur in this book, the future of God's people is assured by God's affirmation (see, for example, Rv 3:20–21 and 22:16). God's faithfulness becomes actualized in the victorious Christ (Rv 5:12–13; 19:11–13; 22:6). Old and new are all one in God through Jesus Christ (Rv 1:4–6, 8; 21:5–7; 22:13).

Suggestions for Further Study

Research

1. Review Acts 2. How did the author see Jesus and the experience of Pentecost as a fulfillment of Old Testament promises?

2. Review Luke 4:16–30. How did Jesus see himself in relationship to the Old Testament in this passage?

3. Review Galatians 3:15–29. How does Paul relate faith in Christ to the covenants God made with Abraham and Moses?

4. Review 1 Corinthians 11:23–26; Acts 2:37–39. How do these sacraments of initiation express the ways we join and are supported by the Church?

Reflection

1. What are the ways you believe God has been faithful to you in your life of faith?

2. Pay special attention to the following verses. You may wish to memorize the starred passages.

   *1 Corinthians 11:23–26 (The Last Supper)
   *Acts 2:39 (promise to God's people)
   Acts 7 (Stephen's defense)
   Romans 9–11 (Jews, covenants, Gentiles)
   Galatians 3, 4 (Paul on the new covenant)
   Hebrews 8, 9 (the new covenant)
   *Hebrews 13:20–21 (a benediction)
   2 Timothy 2:11–13 (God's surprising faithfulness)

Notes

1. *Collegeville Bible Commentary*, 1123.

2. See HBD, note for Galatians 3:19–22.

3. The sons of Jacob are referred to as "the twelve patriarchs" (Acts 7:8).

THEME 3

God's People Reflect on God

SESSION 1

Thinking about Who God Is

Session Overview

Reflecting on the experience of a saving and faithful God raised questions about who God is and how God is related to people and all creation. The Bible deals with such questions by stories such as the narratives of Genesis 1–11, rather than by abstract reasoning. These and other early traditions show the difficulty of understanding God through only human descriptions, particularly in regard to "where" God is and the uniqueness of God, the nature or reality of other gods, and the several names by which God is known in the Old Testament.

Key Bible Readings

Genesis 1–3; 8:20–22;
  9:11–17
Psalm 139:1–18
Isaiah 40:27–31
Exodus 25:10–22;
  20:1–6

Key Words

anthropomorphism
El Elyon, El Shaddai,
  Yahweh Sabaoth
prehistory
The Fall
theology

The Transition to This Theme

This theme presupposes that the people of God came to be what they were because of their experience of the saving actions of God in the Exodus (Theme 1), and the extension of those experiences was an awareness of the faithfulness of God in covenant relationship (Theme 2). These experiences and this awareness made some people think deeply about God, but the Old Testament does not specify how that thinking developed. Questions about God did arise. We find these questions scattered through the scriptures, and some answers to them are proposed. These questions will occupy the three sessions of Theme 3.

The corporate consciousness of the Hebrew people began with the experience of God's liberation in the Exodus event. The Hebrews thought and wrote in concrete terms. They did not develop a theoretical concept of God. The Hebrews were at home in history, not in philosophy. If we were to ask them what they thought about God, the Hebrews would likely have replied in terms of what God had done and how they had been involved in these actions. Even when the Hebrews declared the

Lord's faithfulness or recalled God's promises, it was by remembering their experiences of God rather than by drawing logical deductions (recall Dt 6:20–23). This means that a "doctrine" of God or a question like "Does God exist?" is really foreign to most of the Old Testament.

Throughout the literature of the Old Testament, the Hebrew people arrived at new perceptions of God based on their ongoing experience of God's revelation. Christians believe that thinking about God reaches its definitive experience in the New Testament (new covenant). For Christians, questions about God receive their unique and, in a sense, final answer in Jesus Christ.

This theme is organized in three sessions, but the division is really artificial. Session 1 explores what is implied about God when one probes the background of God's saving faithfulness. Session 2 considers the relationship between God's love and justice. Session 3 asks how it could be that the unknowable God has become known.

This program covers the Bible in broad, comprehensive themes, but at the same time tries to master key aspects of the component books. Some of the materials would be appropriate in several sessions. The three subjects of this theme are not neatly confined to the passages studied, but are woven here and there throughout the material. Thus, when we consider the relationship between God's love and justice (Session 2), we presume that something of the unknowable God can be known (Session 3), and that both these matters are part of understanding who God is behind and beyond salvation and covenant-faithfulness.

Back to Beginnings

Moses told the Hebrew people in Egypt that the God of their ancestors was acting for them (Ex 3:16; 6:3, 8). The revelation of the Lord to Moses is part of the history of relationships between God and the people. The traditions about God went very, very far back, before the time of any written records. The questions about God, such as: "Where did God come from?" and "What did God have to do with the beginning of the world and human life?" were addressed and answered in stories and narratives in all ancient civilizations as well as by the Hebrew people. This takes us to Genesis 1–11.

If you read Genesis at one sitting, you will realize that the principal storyline of the book begins with Abraham in chapter 12. In a sense, what comes before that is a kind of prehistory, that is, a collection derived from ancient, tribal traditions handed down in stories told around campfires from times long before the Hebrew people used a written language. All people are curious about their origins, and various Near Eastern peoples have left records and narratives telling their stories of creation. The Hebrews were not unique in having such traditions. Their stories of creation, God's part in primeval events, and the earliest life of human beings, however, are for them a new chapter in the history of recounting a true relationship with God and the awareness of human dignity.

These traditions were collected and edited in the years of exile (597–538 BC). The creation stories were special sources of revealed truth about God's relationship to humanity, in contrast to the myths of the predominant Babylonian culture.

Genesis 1–2 contains two accounts of God's creation of the good world and of humanity as the blessed resident and regent. The second creation account begins at 2:4b.[1] The most important point is that the earliest traditions of the Hebrew people associate the origin of the world and the beginning of humankind with the creative power of God.

Genesis 3 tells the story of how humankind first rebelled against the creator. Verses 14–19 tell of the consequences of sin in a poem telling about basic human woes. Chapter 4 shows the expanding consequences of sin, telling the story of the first murder. There are also references to the primitive beginnings of certain skills and arts (Gn 4:21–22).

In much of this material, God is depicted in human terms. These are usually called anthropomorphisms (see Gn 3:8, 21; 4:9). Anthropomorphisms are descriptions of God in terms that are more appropriate for human beings. "References to God's hands or ears, or to his evening walk in a garden (Gn 3:8), or to his being moved by passion, irritation, or regret are typical examples."[2] What do such references suggest as to how those who handed down the stories thought about God? Among a people who mostly thought in concrete terms would you not expect anthropomorphic language? How would you describe God to a child who asked you what God is like?

In order to provide a traditional continuity with the earliest ancestors, genealogical links were constructed, as in Genesis 5. Such lists appear in the writings of other ancient Near Eastern peoples. They were especially valued among the Hebrews in later periods, and even the gospels employ them (see Neh 7:5–65; Mt 1:1–17; Lk 3:23–38). In the Old Testament, the use of genealogies served

> as a continual reminder of the intent of Genesis to set its sights firmly on a human *history* and, contrary to the disposition of ancient myth to drift toward never-never lands peopled with unearthly beings, to play upon the stage both earth- and time-bound with a cast of real characters.[3]

Genesis 5:21–24 implies that Enoch escaped the ordinary experience of death. Remember him for later reference. His son Methuselah has become a byword as the all-time record-holder for birthdays!

Chapters 6 through 9 contain the story of Noah.[4] Here the Lord is so revolted by human wickedness that God is determined to start over again by destroying all but one human family. Other Near Eastern peoples also had ancient memories of a great flood. These stories tell of gods who wish to destroy humanity out of spite. Contrast that with the reasons in Genesis for the flood. The covenant theme is prominent: **Genesis 8:20–22** relates it to the first recorded altar-offering, and **Genesis 9:11–17** connects the rainbow and God's faithfulness. The remainder of this section through chapter 10 bridges the time from Noah's family to the rise of nations.

Genesis 11 continues the genealogical transitions to Abraham. It begins with a tale about the origins of world languages. Note the Lord's part in verses 5–8. In verse 7, God speaks using a first-person plural: "Let us then go down." There is a similar usage in 1:26. This expression is a rhetorical phrase used by the writer, much like a person who has made a personal decision will say "Let's do it!"[5] As has been said before, the book of Genesis was written in very concrete, poetic language. In all of these examples the writers were using this language, which reflects their background, and the vivid imagery that helped them to remember the stories.

God's Self-communication

In Genesis 35:1, there is the simple statement, "God said to Jacob," one of many instances where such communication is indicated (in Gn 12:1, the Lord speaks to Abram). This address to Jacob is the sequel of the ladder-to-heaven dream at Bethel (an important incident: see Gn 28:10–22 and 35:6–15). It is not known exactly how God spoke in such instances, nor can we recover precisely how the earliest readers of the text understood the way such messages were given. It was probably not a simple auditory experience with a voice from an invisible source, but there is certainly some anthropomorphism involved.

There are also instances where a messenger of God is treated as the presence of God. In Genesis 18, "three men" visit Abraham; but without warning, in verse 13, their words become God's words. Then in 19:1, presumably the same three men are described as "two angels." Later they are again "men," and then God again in verses 21–23. In the story of Jacob at the Jabbok ford in Genesis 32, a messenger of God is considered to be the presence of God: note verse 31. In Exodus 19:7–25, the Lord is revealed at Sinai in spectacular, natural phenomena. There seems to be a kind of primitive awe connected with the mountain, and God is not directly accessible to all the people but reaches them through mediators such as Moses.

In Exodus 33:7–23, Moses meets the Lord directly, but not face to face. Other Old Testament persons are also said to have had an immediate experience of God's presence: Elijah (1 Kgs 19:13) and Isaiah (6:1–2). It is difficult to be at all precise about the understanding of God in these early periods, partly because of the nature of the literary records. In Exodus 24:9–18, for example, the stories about the Lord's appearance are difficult to relate to Exodus 33:7–23. The editors who gathered these early traditions did not attempt to synthesize them into one homogeneous story (see also Dt 5:22–27).

Eventually, the Hebrews became convinced that God really could not be seen. In the New Testament, the Gospel of John insists, "No one has ever seen God" (1:18). This will be discussed in Session 3.

Interceding with God

Several stories in the Pentateuch show us examples of intercession offered on behalf of the people. Abraham's three visitors at Mamre (Gn 18) tell him that the Lord intends to destroy Sodom. Abraham intercedes with God, apparently because his nephew Lot lives in Sodom. He succeeds in getting the conditions of destruction modified and Lot and his family removed from the city.

Exodus 32 tells us of Moses' intercession on behalf of the people who had sinned by making a golden calf to worship. The story is sketchy, but God's stated intention of starting over again with Moses (Ex 32:10) is modified, for in chapter 33 Moses is commanded to get on with the invasion of the promised land.

These stories show the intensely personal relationship that existed between the Hebrew people and God. As was noted above, the Hebrews did not have an abstract, theoretical concept of God, but a relationship in which God is involved with the intimate details of their lives. They therefore had no problem speaking directly and forcefully to God when they felt the need (see Jer 16:10–21).

The distinction between God's holiness and the human condition is often marked in the Bible (for example, see Nm 23:19; Jb 9:32–33; 10:2–9; Ps 8:4–5; Hos 11:9). This distancing, however, never obscures the trust that persons are the unique part of creation who are in everlasting relationship with the creator, as seen in **Psalm 139:1–18** and **Isaiah 40:27–31** (see also Ps 8:5).

Can God Be Localized?

In much of the Old Testament, there is a particular place where God meets the people. Early localities include special shrines like Bethel. Eventually, the locus of God's activity would be the Ark of the Covenant. Read the relevant details of its construction in **Exodus 25:10–22.** The Ark becomes in effect the Lord's throne.[6] During Israel's nomadic period, the Ark is kept in the "tabernacle," a kind of portable temple.

Once they are settled in Canaan, the city of Jerusalem becomes by extension the place where God dwells (as in Ps 122:1–2; Zec 8:3). An extended story in 1 Samuel 4–6 shows how the Ark was regarded both in Israel and in neighboring kingdoms.

A corollary of such localization is the recognition that other places may be under the dominion of other gods. The first two of the Ten Commandments are instructive in this regard: **Exodus 20:1–6;** Deuteronomy 5:7–10. The first commandment seems to imply the existence of other gods; it is not yet clear that there really is no other god worthy to be considered a god in the same sense as the Lord. In Genesis 35:1–4, Jacob disposes of "the foreign gods" that his family group possesses. Read 1 Kings 20:23–25 for insight into the sort of belief that lies behind the first commandment.

In order to make clear the absolute difference between God and all other gods, the second commandment forbids all physical representation of the Lord God; that is, Israel must have no idols. The golden calf story focuses on the practical problem of following an invisible god. The aberration recurs repeatedly in Israel's experience. Recall Elijah's confrontation with the prophets of Baal (1 Kgs 18) (see also Ps 115:1–8; Is 40:18–26; 44:6–20). Try to understand what sort of thinking about God is involved. The commandment is all the more remarkable in view of the idolatry prevalent among Israel's neighbors.

Names of God

God is called by names other than Yahweh in the Old Testament (translated "the Lord" in the NAB), but this name occurs well over twice as often as any other (about 6,800 times). Exodus 6:2–3 gives another name that is said to have been used before the name Yahweh was revealed. This is *El Shaddai* in Hebrew, variously translated "God my Breast" or "God of the Mountain." The NAB translates this as "God the Almighty." (Check other modern versions, especially the New Jerusalem Bible.) The name *El* occurs alone in several forms in Hebrew (such as, Beth*el*). The name is perhaps as close to a generic term for "god" as the Old Testament provides.[7] Conversely, *El* occurs in the plural form *elohim,* which may be considered a "plural of majesty" (as a king used to officially say "we" when he meant only "I the king"). *Shaddai* occurs alone, particularly in Job (5:17, and so on). In Genesis 14, Abraham meets Melchizedek, "priest of God Most High." This divine name is a rendering of *El Elyon,* which occurs later in the Old Testament (Dn 4:29, 34, and so on), and in a Greek form in the New Testament (Lk 1:32, 35, and so on).

God is also sometimes called "Lord of Armies," or "Lord of Hosts," *Yahweh Sabaoth.* This name occurs rather frequently in familiar passages: Psalms 24:10; 46:8, 12; Isaiah 6:3, 5; 9:6; and in other places from 1 Samuel 1:11 to Malachi 1:14. (Paul in Rom 9:29 quotes Is 1:9, where the name also occurs.) The name may derive from the Lord leading the hosts of Israel from Egypt (Ex 12:41) or from the Lord ruling over the hosts of heaven (Ps 148:2).

Occasionally, God is called "Lord," where the Hebrew is not YHWH but *Adonai* (Jb 28:28). Out of reverential awe for the divine name, the Jews pronounced *Adonai* ("my Lord") whenever they read YHWH in the text. The Greek word is *kyrios,* which then became the term rendered "Lord" in the New Testament.

Suggestions for Further Study

Research

1. Review the stories in Genesis 3–11. Choose one of the stories and tell it in your own words to your family or a friend.

2. Review Genesis 1 and 2. What do these stories say about the value of creation? What do they say about the value of human life?

3. Review the names of God found in the Old Testament. List them and write a short explanation of each.

4. Review Exodus 20:2–6. How would you describe the image of God found in these verses?

Reflection

1. How do Old Testament portrayals of God clarify or complicate your own understanding of God? What kinds of idol worship do you think are prevalent in the world today?

2. The Old Testament stories show that the Hebrew people had a very intense personal relationship with God. How does this compare with your own relationship with God? Can you speak as directly to God as the people in the Old Testament?

3. You may want to be able to retell the following stories:

   creation
   the flood
   the tower of Babel
   salvation of Lot from the destruction of Sodom
       and Gomorrah
   Jacob wrestling at the Jabbok
   the golden calf

4. It would be helpful for you to be able to identify the following people:

Cain	Methuselah
Abel	Noah
Enoch	Lot

Notes

1. Scholars generally note that the name *Yahweh* does not occur until Genesis 2:4 and following.
2. See Anthropomorphism, HBD 32.
3. Bruce Vawter, *On Genesis,* 26. This book is the classic Catholic resource for reliable, detailed information about the ancient traditions of Genesis 1–11.
4. See also Theme 2, Session 1.
5. See Vawter, *On Genesis,* 54.
6. Yahweh as king is studied in Theme 6.
7. See El, HBD 252–53.

SESSION 2

Exploring the Relationship Between God's Love and Justice

Session Overview

Serious reflection about God raises a dilemma: Experience shows God's constant covenant-love; confrontation with God raises the question of God's justice. A number of Old Testament stories explore the relationship between God's love and justice. Turned outward, the question expands to why evil exists in the world. Two classic considerations are found in Jonah and Job. Christians find the ultimate response to the problem of evil in the cross of Jesus Christ.

Key Bible Readings

Exodus 34:6–7
Psalm 73
Jonah
Job 1; 2; 3; 38:1–13;
   40:1–9; 42:1–6
Revelation 12:7–10
Philippians 2:5–11

Key Words

dualism
theodicy

Raising the Question

After the golden calf incident at Sinai, the Lord showed compassion for the people by calling Moses to receive new tablets containing the divine commandments. Moses had destroyed the first set in frustrated anger. Review Exodus 32:15–19. The Lord continues to be gracious and compassionate toward the people (Ex 33:12–19), and in the revelation to Moses at the giving of the new tablets the Lord makes a remarkable pronouncement that stipulates God's nature: **Exodus 34:6–7.** This is an important record of how the Hebrew people thought about God. They have experienced God's saving faithfulness. They received the promise of God's continuing presence; this was coupled with God's concern for justice.

> The people could be confident of God's presence with them only if their life together was a reflection of God's nature and God's concern for justice. In Israel's attempts to express this notion of community the dominant pattern was that of *imitatio dei* [acting like God]: to assure Yahweh's continued presence with the people meant acting toward other humans as Yahweh had first acted towards them.[1]

The treatment of the Lord's justice, then, recognizes that God's justice is God's saving power. It is God's fidelity to the promises made in the covenant. The Hebrew people had been saved from slavery in an act of grace on the part of God. Their continued freedom rests on their faithfulness to the covenant with God, based on true worship (Ex 20:2–6) and compassion toward one another.

There are several instances when the relationship between God's love and justice is seen. When the Lord sends Samuel to select David as future king, one guideline is, "Not as man sees does God see, because man sees the appearance but the LORD looks into the heart" (1 Sm 16:7).

Two stories in 2 Samuel 12 illustrate the duality of David's relationship with God. First, David's sin is condemned through the prophet Nathan, and David accepts God's judgment. Then David finally accepts the death of his infant son with quiet resignation. The text makes plain the mixture of love and justice. God's justice is not revenge, but a calling of David back to repentance for his sins, as well as a calling to David back into a proper relationship with God and the people.

Other parts of the Old Testament show deeper questioning of this issue by some of God's people. If God does indeed love the people and keep the covenant promises in spite of their unfaithfulness and rebellion, why do they persist in such wicked ways? If God is indeed the Almighty One, how can such opposition be tolerated at all? Where, how, and why, in fact, did opposition to God first arise? In philosophical terms, this is the problem of evil; but the Old Testament is not a philosophical book. In the Old Testament, these questions were approached in unphilosophical ways. Poetry, drama, and story occasionally touch matters that the West, with its Greek heritage, would handle by reason.

Adam and Others

Genesis 3 and 4 contain stories that are related to the questions posed here. When considering these passages, it is fundamentally important to distinguish between what they signify in their context and what Jewish and Christian theologians have made of them. For example, there is a real difference between the story of the disobedience in Eden as it stands in the Book of Genesis and the doctrine of "original sin" that Christian theologians derived from that story.

Consider the question, "Why didn't the Lord God simply destroy Adam and Eve when they went astray?" Instead, they were punished severely, it appears, but in one sense they got away with the rebellion. The apparent success of such rebellion against God is faced frankly in other parts of the Old Testament. For example, see 1 Kings 19:9–18; **Psalm 73:1–14;** Jeremiah 12:1–4. Usually, as in **Psalm 73:15–28,** the person posing the problem arrives at a conviction that God's way is best as an affirmation of faith rather than a reasoned solution.

Another particular form of such questioning is raised repeatedly when God's people are oppressed by their enemies. Often there is a simple complaint that the Lord ought to do something about their plight (Ps 137:7–9). Sometimes this is supported by the suggestion that the predicament is a reflection on the Lord's power (Ps 74:1–11; 79). One answer to the implied dilemma is the response of faith. Psalm 73 can be interpreted this way. This is also the counsel of Isaiah to Hezekiah in 2 Kings 19:10. When God's people are in Babylonian Exile, the poet-prophet is confident that the Lord will respond to their plight (see Is 40:25–31; 43:1–21).

The Problem of the Prophet Jonah

Two Old Testament books deal at length with our present question. Neither finds a simple answer. First consider the story of **Jonah,** some minor details of which are famous. What view of God is embedded in Jonah? How does Jonah expect the Lord to exercise God's justice? What is Jonah's role? Another theme will consider Israel's self-identity in this story; but for now, notice the contrast between what Jonah expects and what the Lord actually does.

Take another look at Jonah 4:2; notice the similarity with Exodus 34:6–7. Are the circumstances of the saying in any way similar? What sort of character does Jonah manifest here? How do you think the reader is expected to react? Notice the abrupt ending of the story. How would you explain why it ended this way?

The Problem of Job

The second book to consider is Job. The book is long and in many ways difficult, but this theme shall be confined to how Job poses the problem of evil.[2] You may have read Archibald MacLeish's play *J.B.,* which was inspired by the Book of Job. The biblical book may likewise be read as a drama. Begin by reading **Job 1–2.** Notice that chapters 3 and following are poetry.

The Book of Job addresses the question of the meaning of undeserved suffering before the silence and inactivity of God. What is one to make of the teaching of the religious tradition, of God's character and purpose in the view of this experience? The author also questions the character of human piety in the face of such suffering. In **Job 3,** Job complains to God, but it is a complaint that is carefully distinguished from accusing confrontation. Keep in mind the testimonial to Job's integrity in 2:10.

In chapters 4 to 28, three friends try to convince Job of God's justice by more or less conventional arguments, which revolve around a naive view of God's justice: innocent persons are spared; only the wicked are punished. Job's suffering must stem from wickedness, they ar-

gue. His only hope is to throw himself on God's mercy. Job responds to each in turn, and he sums up his case in chapters 29–31. Job insists that he is innocent and declares that he does not deserve his present state because of his previous life. He holds his own in dialogue with his friends, but he does not really answer his own questions.

In chapters 32–37, another friend, Elihu, takes up the debate. He acknowledges that the other three have not answered Job. He is angry because he thinks Job has overstated his case. Elihu's solution, however, is neither new nor helpful (36:6–12; compare 5:17). When he has finished, the Lord answers Job; read **Job 38:1–13** and **40:1–9.** Job's final response is in **42:1–6,** where he confesses his ready and complete subjection to the Lord's will and accepts God's justice as a gift and not as something owed to him. In the epilogue (42:7–17), everything turns out right, and Job lives happily ever after!

God's Adversary

Satan appears in the Book of Job as God's adversary (*satan* means "adversary" or "prosecutor" in Hebrew), but satan is also pictured as an "insider." The adversary is a difficult matter to understand in the Bible. The satan of the Book of Job is not the same as the satan or devil known to Christian theology.

The existence of a character of the spirit world is generally assumed in scripture, but there is no theological analysis of its nature nor any detailed consideration of practical implications. It should be noted, however, that biblical tradition, in contrast to many other religions, implicitly rejects dualism: the belief that two great, cosmic powers of good and evil are in an eternal struggle in the world with the outcome in the balance.

The almighty power and sovereign supremacy of God is assumed in the Bible. Indeed, God is somehow the source of everything. (This does not mean that pantheism is an option; that is, everything is not to be *equated* with God.) Any power that a personified evil force may have exists in the light of God's supreme power. Without ever working out the rational problem involved, the texts never portray God as creating evil, nor is the logical ambiguity ever admitted as a valid excuse for human sin (see Jb 2:10; Am 3:6; Is 45:5–7; Ps 33:6–15, 51:3–4; Gn 4:13–15).

In the New Testament, Jesus is portrayed as the antagonist to and victor over the evil one. See the stories of Jesus' temptation (the Greek word is perhaps better rendered "testing") in the wilderness in Matthew 4:1–11 and the Beelzebul controversy in Mark 3:20–27. Theme 1, Session 4, shows that the heart of the Book of Revelation is the liberation God effected by Jesus' victory. The details of the complete and final overthrow of the evil one are described in the apocalyptic language. Note, however, **Revelation 12:7–10,** where several names and labels of the evil one are brought together. The seer implies that all evil opposition to God is one, however diverse or particular it may appear. Chapter 20 has caused much dispute among differing interpreters, but the imagery focuses on the Messiah's victory over evil. In the context of the whole book, surely this is more important than any secondary detail.[3]

The Role of Faith

Job's final answer to his questions is, after all, an answer of faith. Habakkuk 1:2–2:5 contains in brief form that prophet's posing of the problem of evil and the solution of faith. Two other prophets deal with the matter by using the illustration of the potter and his clay. Read Isaiah 64:7 and Jeremiah 18:1–6. In the New Testament, Paul draws an inference from the same image (see Rom 9:19–24).

For the Christian, the ultimate answer to the problem of evil is seen in the cross and resurrection of Jesus. The Son of God suffered and died, willingly and ignominiously, the death of a slave. Then came the resurrection. The Christian response to evil is the cross of Jesus Christ as the time of glory (see John's gospel). The cross as seen in the light of the Easter dawn is the message of **Philippians 2:5–11.**

Suggestions for Further Study

Research

1. The story of Jonah is often popularly associated with the "great fish." How does that creature really relate to the story? How would you tell the story without the fish?

2. The heavenly scene and the earthly speeches seem to constitute two "layers" of tradition in the Book of Job. Which do you think would be the older? (See Job, the Book of, HBC 492–94.) See Ezekiel 14:12–20 for another reference to Job. Also note James 5:11.

3. If you are interested in English literature, investigate the relationship of John Milton's *Paradise Lost* with Genesis 3–4 and Job 1–2, or read Archibald MacLeish's play *J.B.* For philosophical discussions of God's love and justice in a popular style, see C. S. Lewis's *The Problem of Pain* and Harold Kushner's *When Bad Things Happen to Good People.*

Reflection

1. Have you ever asked, "If God loves me, why is this happening to me?" What answer did you work out to your question?

2. The problem of evil is perennial. Think of some examples, then consider the following questions:

How may a biblical answer differ from a secular-philosophical answer?

How might love be conceived as a manifestation of justice?

What about justice as an aspect of love?

How does the biblical notion of justice compare with your sense of what justice is all about?

Notes

1. Paul Hanson, *The People Called*, 43–44.

2. Job will be studied further in Theme 8.

3. The unusual problems of the Book of Revelation will be more fully treated in Theme 10.

SESSION 3

Knowing the Unknowable God

Session Overview

Thinking about God led Israel to sense more and more the absolute mystery of God. Because of their convictions about God's continuing revelation, however, Israel continued to speak of God in human terms. They also recognized angels as divine messengers, but many times the revelation came by God's "Spirit." The Church accepted the Jewish scriptures as the revelation of God. A unique problem arose, however, when the Church became convinced that Jesus revealed God in a new and definitive manner. The gospels treat this in various ways. After Jesus' resurrection, the Holy Spirit is associated with Jesus' revelation. Paul becomes the theological interpreter of this matter, but God's Holy Spirit continues to be the key to revelation.

Key Bible Readings	Key Words
Isaiah 6:1–8	immanence
John 1:1–18	transcendence
John 14:15–26	paraclete
Acts 17:22–34	seraphim
	synoptic gospels
	theophany

Mystery and Revelation

We have seen that the early efforts of God's people to understand the internal nature of God are described in terms drawn from their own life and experience. The more they thought about God, however, the more the mystery of God intrigued them. The better they knew God, the more unknowable God became. Each revelation from God makes evident how much is still unknown.

This is implicit even when God's name is revealed to Moses as Yahweh (represented in translation by "the Lord;" see the article, The Pentateuch, in NAB Study Edition; See also Theme 1, Session 1). The meaning of the name Yahweh is enigmatic, and the relationship that begins with the giving of the name grows with new insights as God is encountered in new historical circumstances. At Sinai, in the covenant code, the Lord gives Israel a new knowledge of God's will. That is, however, the very place where the mystery of God is dramatized by the display of natural phenomena and the mountain taboo, which only Moses is permitted to penetrate (Ex 24:12–18). God becomes at the same time inescapable and imponderable—as Jonah and Job both discover so pointedly.

We, like the Israelites, know that God is revealed in many ways (recall Heb 1:1). Anthropomorphic language is often used in references to God because so much that the people learn about God comes in historical experiences. Sometimes such experiences are perceived to have revealed God directly, although it is usually only a voice or some natural phenomenon that marks God's presence (such as Moses at the burning bush and many of the experiences at Sinai). Another notable occurrence is in the vision recounted in **Isaiah 6:1–8.** Note what Isaiah learns about God in this vision.

God is also often revealed through messengers. Our translations sometimes call these "angels," a word directly derived from the Greek word for "messenger." "Angel" may suggest misleading associations that arise through medieval and Renaissance art. The story of the strangers who promised a son to Abraham and Sarah and rescued Lot and his family from Sodom illustrates how elusive the terminology may be. Recall also Jacob's vision at Bethel, his wrestling at the stream Jabbok, the messenger who instructed Gideon, and so on.

Sometimes the messenger is referred to as the Spirit of God, and often it is hard to tell exactly what kind of messenger is being described. In Genesis 1:2, that which sweeps over the watery chaos is sometimes translated "Spirit" (RSV), sometimes "wind" (NAB), and sometimes "breath" (Ronald Knox). The same Hebrew word can mean all three, as can the corresponding Greek word. (In English, the words "ghost" and "gust" are related.)

In other instances, God's Spirit is almost the same as God's Word. In Isaiah 61:1–3 (see Lk 4:16–19), the prophet declares that "the Spirit of the LORD is upon" him; and Joel 3:1–2 promises that God's Spirit will be "poured out" in the future.[1] God's Spirit comes "mightily" upon persons (as Gideon in Jgs 6:34 and Saul in 1 Sm 10:10), and God's Word regularly accompanies the Spirit. God's Word is powerful as God is powerful (see Is 55:11 and Heb 4:12). It is effective in creation (Gn 1:3, 5, 6, and so on). "The word of the LORD" is the authenticating and moving power of the prophets.[2]

God becomes known in still other ways in Old Testament traditions. The "royal" psalms portray such revelation through the anointed king (see Ps 2:6–7; 21:1–7; 72:1–4). Nature is perceived as a source of divine revelation (see Ps 19:1–6; Jb 38:1–11). "Wisdom" becomes a special way in which God communicates (see Jb 28:20–28; Pr 2:6; 8:12–22; and Theme 7).

Old Scriptures' New Revelation

The early Church understood that God was revealed in the Jewish scriptures. In the New Testament, scripture refers, of course, to parts of the Old Testament, particularly the Torah, the Prophets, and the Psalms (as in Lk 24:44). Jesus refers to Psalm 118 as scripture (Mt 21:42 and Mk 12:10). Paul declares twice in 1 Corinthians 15:3–4 that the saving events of the gospel came about "in accordance with the scriptures," even though it is uncertain what specific texts he has in mind.

The writer to the Hebrews, after summing up the varieties of God's communication "in times past," asserts that God's final and definitive communication is a son (Heb 1:1–2), who is clearly Jesus (2:9). This is representative of the conviction of the first-century Christian Church that Jesus Christ is the epitome of God's self-revelation and that in Jesus the God who has always been beyond human description is now known in human form. Jesus Christ now defines how God is to be understood. Jesus becomes the unique way by which people are to relate to God.

Jesus as the Revelation of God

The old problem of describing the indescribable God now surfaces in a new form. Although other gods are often portrayed as appearing in human guise, the ineffable God of the Hebrew people is different. This God is so holy that by the time of Jesus even the divine name has become too sacred to utter. God's appearance as a human being presses the earliest Christians almost at once to find ways to explain and describe how this could be.

Jesus' early career is dealt with in the gospels. His teaching, as remembered by his followers, is striking and, in some important respects, highly original. People address Jesus as teacher, and he is considered to be a healer, a wonder-worker, even a prophet. The gospels tell us very little about Jesus before the public ministry. It seems clear that his life is relatively simple and unpretentious for nearly thirty years. Thus, if it had not been for the momentous resurrection victory, Jesus might scarcely have been remembered.

Another aspect of the problem appears in the fact that in the gospels Jesus most often refers to himself as "the son of man" (for example, Mt 8:20; 11:19; 16:13; Mk 14:21; Lk 22:48; Jn 8:28; 9:35–37). There has been a great amount of scholarly debate about this title (Dn 7:13), but we may at least conclude that it is meant to emphasize the unique mission of Jesus. It is also part of a pattern of avoiding the term "messiah," which includes ideas Jesus did not accept. We know that the early Church does not continue to use the title for Jesus, probably because other titles seemed more appropriate after the resurrection.

Old Testament stories familiar to us are used by Jesus concerning his role as one who reveals God (see Mt 12:38–42 and Lk 11:29–32). Theme 6 considers how Jesus is thought about as a king. In Hebrews 12:18–24, another familiar theme appears as Jesus is said to be the mediator of a new covenant.

The event known as the transfiguration, Matthew 17:1–8, parallels Old Testament material. We have noted the Exodus theme in Luke's record of the occasion (Lk 9:31). Moses and Elijah probably represented the Law and the Prophets, that is, the substance of the old covenant scriptures. It may also be noted that both Moses and Elijah did not depart this life in an ordinary manner (Dt 34:5–6; 2 Kgs 2:11–12). As happened at Jesus' baptism, there is a divine voice at the transfiguration: The message combines Psalm 2:7 and Isaiah 42:1.

The Gospel of John is often quite different from the synoptics. In **John 1:1–18,** an early Christian hymn adapted to be the "prologue" for John's gospel, there is an unparalleled interpretation of Jesus Christ's role in making God known. These are the often-read verses about "the Word." It becomes clear that John, the evangelist, has in mind Jesus as the embodiment of the Word (verse 14). Whatever more this phrase may also mean, note how appropriately John recaptures the spirit and force of God's word in the Old Testament and how subtly he affirms that this has been actualized in the new word-become-flesh. Another symbol of revelation, namely light, is also woven into this passage. John 1:1 consciously imitates Genesis 1:1, and John 1:4–9 picks up the association of God's word and light in Genesis 1:3.

Jesus and the Holy Spirit

The Spirit of God is associated with Jesus. The story of Jesus' baptism makes this clear (see the four records in Mt 3:11–17; Mk 1:9–11; Lk 3:21–22; and Jn 1:31–34). In the upper-room discourse, according to John, Jesus asserts that the Spirit will take his place and continue what he set out to do. Read **John 14:15–26** and 16:7–15. The Book of Acts shows that the first Christians believe this had happened. Remember how Peter associates the coming of the Holy Spirit in power on Pentecost with the career and victory of Jesus.

Other passages illustrate how the Church relates the Holy Spirit and the message about

Jesus. Acts 10 and 11 recounts the story of how Peter receives divine instruction regarding his attitude toward Gentiles. Notice particularly Acts 10:19, 36–48; 11:12, 15–17. In one of the mission travelogs, there is a unique juxtaposition of the Holy Spirit and the Spirit of Jesus (see Acts 16:6–8).

Paul and Jesus

Study the story of Paul's conversion in Acts 9:1–22. Notice that an encounter with Jesus is instrumental in changing Paul's views about Christ (verse 17). One of the strong, early influences on Paul, which leads to his radical antagonism to the Christian Church, is the stoning of Stephen (see Acts 6:8–8:1). Paul realized that the Christian movement contained the seeds of doctrinal divergence from Judaism. The sermon of Stephen clearly turns his witness to Jesus. Note Acts 6:14; 7:52. Stephen's witness comes to fruition when Paul meets the living Jesus on the road to Damascus. Immediately after his conversion, Paul begins proclaiming that Jesus is the new way by which God is to be known (see Acts 9:20, 22, 27–29).

In **Acts 17:22–34,** there is the digest of a sermon Paul preached to a curious audience in Athens. This is the only time we hear him using what might loosely be called philosophical argument; he even quotes two Greek poets (verse 28). This approach appears to be unusual, but Paul employs it to tell about Jesus, and the effort is reasonably successful.

Paul's letters repeatedly emphasize how God is made known through Jesus Christ. Romans stresses how Jesus has accomplished what earlier revelation did not (see Rom 8:3–4, 11; 10:17). Paul associates God's revealing wisdom with Jesus Christ in 1 Corinthians 1:30; 2:1–2, 7–8, 16. Paul wrestles with the problem of knowing the unknowable in Philippians 2:5–11.

Colossians 2:2–3 states that "all the treasures of wisdom and knowledge" are hidden in Christ.

Revelation Beyond Jesus

Jesus is the summit and culmination of the revelation of God. The Holy Spirit comes to proclaim Jesus from age to age. In each age, the Church, under the guidance of the Holy Spirit, seeks a deeper understanding of the life and mission of Jesus. This revelation about Jesus will go beyond what Jesus was able to say in his earthly ministry. The Gospel of John attributes to Jesus a declaration of the work of the Spirit in deepening our understanding of Jesus (see Jn 16:12–15; see also 20:30 and 21:25). A similar statement from the Pauline tradition is in Ephesians 1:15–23. The mystic-pastor of the apocalypse also claims to be setting forth such revelation (see Rv 1:1–2; 3:20–22).

Suggestions for Further Study

Research

1. What does "theophany" mean? (see definition in HBD 1062–63). Define it in relation to this theme.

2. Review John 1:1–18. List every title, word, or phrase that refers to Jesus.

3. Review John 14:15–26; John 16:7–15; Acts 16:6–10. What is the relationship of the Holy Spirit to Jesus according to this text? What is the task of the Holy Spirit according to this passage?

Reflection

1. How can you find Jesus in your life today?

2. Consider the following questions:

   - How is revelation in scripture related to God's Spirit?
   - How can you think of Jesus as a truly human being and yet the unique revelation of God?
   - How is Jesus "present" today? How do you relate this to the presence of God's Holy Spirit?

3. You may wish to be able to identify the following passages:

Psalm 2:7	Acts 9:1–22
Isaiah 6:1–8	Acts 17:22–31
John 1:1–18	Philippians 2:5–11
John 14:15–26	Hebrews 1:1–2

Notes

1. Quoted by Peter in his Pentecost sermon (Acts 2:17, 18). See also Genesis 2:7; Job 27:3; Nehemiah 9:20; Zechariah 7:12.

2. For some examples among many, see Isaiah 2:1; 38:4; Jeremiah 25:3; Hosea 1:2; Zechariah 4:1–6; and the long story of 1 Kings 13.

THEME 4

People Live in God's World

SESSION 1

Views of the World in the Old Testament

Session Overview

Our study has its setting in the eastern Mediterranean world. God's concern for the whole world, however, is evident throughout the Bible from Genesis on. Prophets urged a wide worldview, and poets celebrated God's universal power. Nature was sometimes viewed as harsh, sometimes as benign. Attention to geography and archeology aids our understanding and appreciation of the environment in which God's Word was revealed.

Key Bible Readings

Genesis 9:8–17;
    11:1–9
Amos 9:7
Isaiah 45:1–13,
    22–23; 65:17–25
Job 38:1–18
Psalm 24:1–2

Key Words

Anatolia
The Day of the Lord
servant
tells

Why Palestine?

It is now time for us to focus on the setting of the world where God's Word was revealed to the people. The life of God's people centers in a tiny land at the eastern end of the Mediterranean Sea, an area about the size of the state of Vermont. How could such a small territory become so important? What connection is there between the religious history of the people and their geographical setting? What was their view of the rest of the world? These and related questions must now claim our attention.

Palestine was precisely at the crossroads of the ancient world. It is at the point where three continents join. Important nations arose in the Mesopotamian valleys to the east, in Asia. The old civilizations of the Nile Valley in Africa lay to the southwest. The Asian lands of Anatolia and the European nations of Greece, Macedonia, and Rome were in the north and west. The routes all of these empires and peoples traveled crossed through Palestine, where the Hebrew people settled. When Alexander the Great (356–323 BC) set out to conquer the Persian empire, he passed this way; and the history of the Middle East was permanently changed.

Living in such a strategically important area had a great impact on the life of the people who lived there. As we study more about the people of God who called this their "promised land," we must keep in mind the relationship of the geography to their life and faith. In Ezekiel 5:5, the Lord declares that Jerusalem is "in the midst of the nations." Do you think these people would have become so important if they had lived somewhere else? Of course, we can't answer that question; but considering it will help us get a broader understanding of the history of God's people.

Israel's Relationship to the World

The nomadic narratives of the Israelites, tracing their journeys after the Exodus, reflect views about the world in which those movements occur. Sometimes they reflect the historical situation of the time that is being described, and sometimes they reflect the theological concerns of the writers and final editors of the text. Very early, the Lord apparently was thought of as a nature-god whom the people could persuade to manipulate the forces of nature for their well-being. According to 1 Kings 20:23–28, some people considered Yahweh to be a mountain god. In Theme 3, we discussed later views of God. We must now see how such views about God relate to the world.

A superficial reading of the Old Testament may lead one to think that the people of God were not concerned about the surrounding world except when invasions forced their attention. The development of a national, monotheistic faith might suggest that other peoples and lands were relatively unimportant. From texts that declare God created the world and then chose one people for the central role in sacred history, one could get the impression that everything that is not Hebrew must somehow be of secondary importance. Several portions of the Old Testament imply just that.

Nevertheless, there runs through the Bible an inescapable and increasingly serious belief that the whole world is God's concern. Consequently, God's people dare not ignore their relationship to this world. There are two aspects to this: the theological, which involves thinking and believing; and the practical, which demands social, political, and religious action. God's people often find the practical aspects very difficult to implement.

Genesis Again

This problem of the relationship of God, the people, and the world is presented at the very beginning of our Old Testament canon: review Genesis 1 and 2 carefully. Notice what the creation stories imply about God and the world. Adam and Eve are given stewardship over certain parts of nature (see also Gn 9:1–3). The idyllic existence in Eden soon ends, however; and toil becomes necessary for human survival (3:17–19, 23). There is no indication here that nature has become evil. The curse against the *ground* is the result of human failure. Although the world is pictured in some later contexts as the arena for the forces of evil, this is not God's intention. God maintains sovereignty over all creation in spite of the consequences of wrong human choices. Review the details of the curse against Cain in Genesis 4:11–14. Note that Cain is given a sign of God's protection in spite of his sin.

The story of the great flood (6–8) indicates that the Lord's displeasure is directed against evil humankind, not against the whole creation. Compare 5:29 with 8:20–22. The rainbow covenant, **Genesis 9:8–17,** glorifies a natural phenomenon and relates to all earth's creatures. In the story of the tower of Babel, **11:1–9,** the Lord's action is again directed against humanity.

The dividing of the world's population through language differences is God's response to human presumption.

The story of Abraham deals with God's choice of one family to be the channel of divine blessing upon humankind, and this is a revelation of God's faithfulness.[1] This narrative is developed against a backdrop of the whole Near Eastern world. Abraham emigrates from Mesopotamia and lives for a time in Egypt (Gn 12). He encamps at a number of places in what we call Palestine, which was then settled largely by Canaanites.[2] In Genesis 14, he becomes involved with the political fortunes of certain kingdoms (no longer identifiable); this story is somewhat aside from the rest of the traditions about him. The story about the blessing by Melchizedek (Gn 14:18–20), a mysterious figure from Salem (pre-Israelite Jerusalem), is a window on how God was understood to relate to the gods of the people around Israel. In Hebrew, "God Most High" is *El Elyon,* the name for the supreme Canaanite god. In the biblical story, Abraham uses this name together with "the Lord" in conversation with Melchizedek (14:22). Here is early evidence of a developing awareness that the God of Israel is indeed sovereign over the world. Thus God's people are related to the world by their place in creation and through the traditions of their ancestry.

Israel and the Promised Land

When the Lord defeated the power of Egypt and the Exodus initiated the long trek to a promised land, the people saw immediate proof that God is sovereign over the world. The Egyptian magicians could duplicate Moses' manipulation of nature, but only the Lord was supreme over life and death. At Sinai, the Lord was revealed in natural phenomena. When Israel confronted hostile tribes and kingdoms during the desert wanderings, deliverance by the power of God gave the people further evidence that they were inextricably bound to the world they lived in. It was indeed God's world.

The promise of a land in which to settle implied that God can dispose of the world in any way that suits the divine purpose. Thus, it was possible to believe that Israel might be involved in the destiny of the whole world. God's promise to Abraham implied just that. However, it must be noted that Abraham owned permanently only a burial plot, which he purchased (see Gn 23). This gave Abraham's descendants their first, however small, property rights in the land that God promised would be their own. Israel repeatedly forgot that the relationship with God required that Israel be the agency for divine blessing in the world.

Israel's national expansion and God's will did not always coincide. Solomon appears to have introduced international sophistication to the Israelite scene along with territorial expansion. Elijah and Elisha both had varied and exciting encounters with foreign peoples. Omri, king of Israel, was a very successful ruler from a political viewpoint; but the record in 1 Kings 16:25 says that he "did evil in the Lord's sight beyond any of his predecessors." Ultimately, it was failure to come to terms with their proper place in the political and religious scheme of things that brought about the downfall of Israel and then Judah.[3]

Prophets and the Worldview

The message of the divine destiny of God's people was prominent in the proclamation of the latter prophets (see Is 19:23–25).[4] Amos pronounced God's judgment upon Israel along with the fate of the neighboring kingdoms (Am 3:1–2). In **Amos 9:7,** the prophet goes a step further and declares that the migrations and relocations of Gentile nations are under God's will and control. Many of the prophets spoke of a time when the powers of the world come to a final reckoning with God's sovereignty. This was usually referred to as "the day of the Lord" or simply "that day" (see Is 13:9–11; Ez 30:3; Jl 3:1–3, 11–14).

The Jews were not proselytizers, and it is a wonder that the prophets were not more perplexed about how Israel was to be a blessing to the nations. Amos, who was so pessimistic about the political future of his nation, offers a note about restoration at the very end of the book; but the focus is on the land of Israel, not the world. In a passage that is later applied to Jesus (in Mt 2:6), Micah looks to a future ruler in Israel, whose greatness "shall reach to the ends of the earth" (5:2–4); and the point is developed in detail (see 7:16, 17).

The relationship of Israel and the nations is treated in Second Isaiah (Is 40–55). This part of Isaiah was written during the period of the Exile in Babylon (587–538 BC). Cyrus, the Persian ruler who allows the Jews to return to Palestine, is referred to as the Lord's "anointed" in 45:1. The key figure is called the "servant" (as in 42:1). Sometimes it seems this is an individual (53); but elsewhere it indicates God's people, an elect remnant, are designated to be the agents of hope in the world (41:8, 9; 49:6; 55:5). The prophet repeatedly emphasizes the universal sovereignty of the Lord (Is 40:15–17, 28; **45:1–13, 22–23;** 48:12–14).

In the Exile, many Jews must have been tempted to conclude that a Babylonian god had proven stronger than the Lord. They would have found it hard to understand how God could allow them to suffer this terrible indignity. The theological reflections found in **Isaiah 65:17–25** are therefore remarkable. The prophet has not given up on this world. He casts his hope in terms of "a new earth" and "new heavens," but it is not otherworldly.[5]

God's power over the created world is fully affirmed in the final chapters of **Job 38:1–18.** The poet-dramatist declares that any aspect of nature that Job may behold is under the power of God. Even Leviathan, a creature representing ugly, evil nature, is subject to the divine will (40:25). Job is finally impressed and acknowledges God's sovereignty in a brief confession (42:1–6).

The Psalms repeatedly and beautifully express the conviction that God made the world, continues to rule it, and so is its complete possessor. Perhaps the most familiar lines are **Psalm 24:1–2** (see also Ps 19:2–7; 95:3–5; 103:19; 139:7–12).

Facing a Dilemma

The world power of God is a mysteriously difficult subject in the Hebrew scriptures. The Hebrew people certainly found it troublesome. The problem was persistent: How can the world be the creation and possession of God and yet at the same time be alienated from and even opposed to God? How can God's people be the Lord's agents in the world without becoming ungodly from their contact with the world? Indeed, how can God's universal sovereignty be reconciled with the choice of one people for a special, exclusive relationship? There is no final resolution of these questions in the Old Testament.

We may review the Book of Jonah as an example of this dilemma. It is clear from Jonah 4:1–2 that the reluctance of the prophet to go on a mission to Nineveh arises precisely because he fears he may be successful! He is unwilling to face the possibility of the Ninevites becoming his religious associates. See also Jonah 4:11, where God expresses the divine concern for the pagan city and all its life. Jonah speaks for a narrowly exclusive view among his fellow Jews, who are unwilling to undertake the role that God has set for them in the world. The book is a dramatic call for God's people to become what they must be if they are to fulfill the divine will.

The problem carries over into the intertestamental period. The Maccabean rebellion, which gained Jewish independence, did not clarify the theological dilemma. The separation of the Jewish nation from the world was reasserted, but it became evident that their future demanded a workable understanding of the relation between God's people and the rest of the world. When the Romans took over, they at first allowed the Jews some religious privileges; but finally Caesar could no longer tolerate their primary loyalty to God.

Nature and Worldview

We have been focusing on the relationship between God's world and Israel's national life and religion. There is a great deal more to be said about nature. For the writers of scripture, nature is intimately related to faith and history. Creation is prime evidence of this. God created nature and had judged it to be very good (Gn 1:31). All human activity takes place in relation to nature, and the destiny of all creation is under God's sovereign sway and purpose. Unlike the fearsome nature gods of the surrounding cultures, nature is seen as revealing the presence of God's activity in the world.

The grim side of nature is sometimes indicated to be a sign of God's displeasure. Sometimes (but not always), disasters in nature are declared to have been sent as punishment from God. This is how the death of Egypt's firstborn is interpreted at the Exodus. A gruesome story about Dathan and Abiram bears the same interpretation (see Nm 16:12–35. For other examples, see 2 Sm 21:1; 1 Kgs 8:35–36). The experience of Job, however, is evidence that natural hardships are not always an indicator of spiritual failure. We should note how important the interpreters of natural events become.

Usually nature is benign. The promised land was "flowing with milk and honey." Several of Israel's annual festivals are connected with the cycle of nature's productivity.[6] The Psalms are full of praise of nature and nature's God (see 65:5–14; 104:1–24; and so on). Prophets often associate the future happiness of God's people with a wonderful increase of nature's bounty (see Is 35; Am 9:13–15).

We might expect that such concern with nature would function as sure proof of God's sovereignty and would lead inescapably to recognition of God's rule. "The heavens declare the glory of God" (Ps 19:2). "His is the sea, for he made it: and the dry land which his hands have formed. Come, let us bow down in worship . . ." (95:5–6). There is no indication, however, that contemplation of natural phenomena produces sufficient revelation to lead people to become devoted to the Lord God. The glory of nature needs the complementary revelation of God's Word to interpret the signs of God's presence.

Geography and Archeology

It should be clear from this discussion that a general grasp of the geography of the lands of the Middle East is indispensable in the study of the scriptures. All study Bibles have some maps. See the maps in Appendix 8 of this *Resource Book*. Church and public libraries usually have Bible atlases in which you can make more detailed study.[7] You should begin by fixing in mind the relationship of Palestine and the neighboring areas that were mentioned at the beginning of this session.

It is helpful to become familiar with the broad topographical areas of Palestine. Mountains are prominent in biblical narratives; locate Sinai and Zion. The Jordan River figures in many stories. In Genesis 13:11, Abraham's nephew Lot chooses to live in its valley. The Jordan appears again and again, until in the gospels it is the locale for John the Baptist's ministry and hence is a springboard for Jesus' public ministry. It empties into the Dead Sea (called by several names in scripture), which is the lowest point on earth (1,294 feet below sea level). The Jordan Valley is nearly 700 feet below sea level when it leaves the Sea of Galilee; and this fact of topography often is reflected in biblical narratives even when the river is not mentioned. For example, Luke 10:30 speaks of a man who *went* down *from Jerusalem to Jericho* (which is not far from the Dead Sea). Texts usually speak of going *up* to Jerusalem because of its location on a mountain (even though the Mount of Olives is higher).

Geographical features like this are more or less constant and have changed little since biblical times. The features that were constructed by human work, on the other hand, are not so changeless; and few of these are as they were in biblical times. Hence, we must to turn to archeology to help us understand these parts of the past.

Cities in Palestine were rebuilt repeatedly on the ruins of earlier habitation. There has been a settlement at Jericho since about 8000 BC. Towns and cities persisted in the same locations usually because the area was readily defensible and had a water supply. Sometimes elaborate tunnels were dug to provide access to water in case of siege. Read 2 Kings 20:20, where King Hezekiah's water tunnel is mentioned. It was rediscovered in modern times, and an inscription on the wall verified the history.

The mounds produced by the succession of leveling and rebuilding are called "tells" by archeologists. *Tell* is an Arabic word for a hill, natural or artificial. Techniques for excavating these tells have been refined so that the ages of the succeeding layers can be determined and much about their history may be recovered. Archeology has become a complicated and independent research and study discipline that is very valuable to biblical scholarship.

Suggestions for Further Study

Research

1. Using a topographical map from a Bible atlas, study the major geographical features of the holy land and locate the following cities:

Beer-sheba	Jericho
Bethel	Megiddo
Damascus	Rabbah
Dan	Samaria
Gaza	Shechem
Hebron	Tyre

2. Examine the chronology of the history of Israel found in Appendix 7. What major nations interacted with Israel? During what periods of time did this interaction occur?

3. Review Genesis 1:1–2:4 and the psalms referred to in the text. What do they tell us about God's relationship with nature?

4. Reread Isaiah 40–55 and the Book of Jonah. What do these readings tell us about Israel's responsibility to other nations?

Reflection

1. If you should travel to the Middle East today, what would you want to see? Why?

2. What particular relevance does this theme have for God's people today with regard to:

   • our care of the earth?

   • our relationship to the world's peoples?

3. What places in your life and memory are especially significant reminders to you of your relationship with God?

Notes

1. See Theme 2, Session 1.

2. Perhaps his "business" was caravans, as Professor W. F. Albright has suggested.

3. Details of this history will be provided in Themes 5 and 6.

4. Review Introduction, Session 1, for the term "latter prophets."

5. This hope is considered at length in Theme 10.

6. These are discussed in Theme 9, Session 1.

7. The *Harper Atlas of the Bible* is an especially comprehensive resource.

SESSION 2

Good News in All the World

Session Overview

The Christian faith arose in the world of the Jewish scriptures, but it soon spread through the wider, first-century world. The initial stage of Jesus' mission was carried out in Palestine, but his outlook embraced the whole inhabited world. He was intensely aware of the world of nature. His followers moved out of the Jewish milieu, at first hesitantly, then boldly under Paul's leadership and influence. Paul, a Roman citizen, took his mission to the West, confident that the whole world was God's. Although some New Testament texts treat the world as evil, God's sovereignty is affirmed throughout. A good future for the world is guaranteed through Christ's victory.

Key Bible Readings

Matthew 6:26–30; 28:16–20
Luke 12:54–56
John 3:16–17
Acts 11:1–18; 13:44–48
Romans 8:18–23; 13:1–7
1 Peter 2:13–17
2 Corinthians 5:17–20
Revelation 21:22–26; 22:1–2

Key Words

Syrophoenician
Gentiles
deacons
Hellenistic
dualism

Jesus, Nature, and the World

Jesus was born into a religious and social environment deeply influenced by the Jewish scriptures. The impact of this fact can hardly be overemphasized. From infancy through youth, Jesus was introduced into Jewish religious life (Lk 2:22–24, 39–47). He adjusted very well, according to Luke 2:52. As we consider the setting of Jesus' public ministry, two political facts are important: First, two hundred years before Jesus' time, the Jews had gained independence under the Maccabees, who were highly honored. Second, one hundred years before his time, the Romans had conquered Judea. The Roman presence was deeply felt and resented by most of Jesus' hearers. For a pointed reminder of how this affected his followers, read Acts 1:6–7.

Jesus' public ministry was primarily in Galilee and its environs. His instructions to the twelve disciples when they were sent on a mission include a charge to restrict their travel to Jewish territory (Mt 10:6). The story of an encounter with a Syrophoenician woman (15:21–28) implies a similar limitation, but Jesus softens its sharp edge by his kind (and possibly humorous) conversation. His unpopular interpretation of Elijah's cure of Naaman the Syrian (Lk 4:25–26), however, indicates that his outlook was broader. The story of Jesus' visit to Samaria in John 4:1–42 is another indication of a wider horizon for his ultimate mission.

Jesus recognizes the power of evil in the world, and he speaks freely about it, though in terms and concepts current in his day. In John he refers three times to "the ruler of the world," and it is clear he has an evil power in mind (12:31; 14:30; 16:11). In each instance, Jesus' mission is bringing the power of that ruler to defeat (see also Jn 16:33). In his farewell discourses, Jesus also speaks of the "world" much as we should refer to secular circles; this is in contrast to the company of his chosen followers (15:19; 16:20; 17:6, 14–16). Jesus understands his ministry to be a challenge to and the defeat of the power of evil in the world. Jesus signifies that the authority of evil is being broken by his message and mission (see also Lk 10:17–20).

The gospels tell that Jesus spoke much about nature. His sayings and stories are full of references to the countryside. One of the best-known passages is **Matthew 6:26–30** from the Sermon on the Mount. The familiar parable at 7:24–27 also has a nature setting. Much of his ministry is conducted outdoors. Recall how many incidents take place on or around the Sea of Galilee. In **Luke 12:54–56,** he makes weather observations. His illustrations and lessons show him to be in the closest rapport with the natural world around him.

In Luke 13:4, Jesus refers to an otherwise unknown accident and declares that it was not an act of divine retribution: The people killed by the falling tower in Siloam were not more guilty than everyone else who lived in Jerusalem. Thus, natural events are not used as punishment by God; but they should cause people to *repent,* that is, to redirect their lives to God's will.

The Gospel of Mark tells of the occurrence of an unusual darkness during the early after-

noon hours when Jesus hung on the cross—as if to portray nature as feeling the horror of the occasion (Mk 15:33). Matthew relates that there were other strange phenomena including an earthquake, which led the attending centurion to declare that Jesus was God's son (Mt 27:54).[1]

Several details in Luke expand the horizon of Jesus' teaching; see the remarks about a centurion (7:4–5), the parable of the good Samaritan (10:29–37), and the healing of the ten lepers (17:11–19). The Gospel of Mark shows concern for non-Jewish readers (see 7:3–4, 34). In spite of some deference to Jewish readers, **Matthew** ends with "the great commission," **28:16–20,** which includes a command to "make disciples of all nations." (The Greek word translated "nations" may be also rendered Gentiles.) In Luke 24:47, the risen Christ tells the assembled disciples that "repentance, for the forgiveness of sins would be preached in his name to all nations." **John 3:16–17** is probably the best-known passage in the gospels; note carefully what it says about God and the world.

The Early Christian Mission

It was inevitable that the first Christian communities should face with a new intensity a challenge from the world around them. It is helpful to consider how the critical experiences of Judaism in the Hellenistic world helped to prepare the way for the new movement. Translation of the Hebrew scriptures into Greek was a major sign that Jewish faith could survive outside Palestine. The Septuagint version became the Bible of the Christian missionary Church and is frequently the source of scriptural quotations in the New Testament. Paul often used the Septuagint, although it is not always possible to identify his source. Many times he is probably quoting from memory. In other instances, it is not always possible to decide whether the author is using the Septuagint, another of several versions, or making a fresh translation from the

Hebrew. Other Jewish literature from this period reflects Judaism's struggle to accommodate to the contemporary world. Many historical examples of the presence of "God-fearers" like Cornelius related to the synagogue show the positive impact of Jewish ethical standards on the Roman world. It remained for Christianity to move deliberately into that world as a field for mission.

The early Church claimed the authority of Jesus for its mission (as in Mt 28:18–20). At Pentecost, following Jesus' resurrection, people from other lands were in Jerusalem, evidently because of their relationship to Judaism; and they were immediately drawn to the Christian faith (Acts 2:5–11). Peter connects this with Jesus' intention and promise (2:38–39). The early Christian evangelism caused friction among some of the first Christians, who came from diverse backgrounds. When the momentum of this faith led some Christian leaders to accept Gentiles, difficult tensions arose in the Church.[2]

Conflict in one such situation led to the appointment of the first deacons (see Acts 6:1–6). Note that the names of these men were Greek rather than Jewish. Two of these deacons soon attracted attention and caused problems. Stephen's powerful preaching was opposed by Jews of non-Palestinian background (6:9–11). His defense, which is told at length in Acts 7, infuriated his enemies; and they instigated his violent death. Philip engaged in a successful mission to Samaria (8:4–25), which caused the Jerusalem leaders to check the situation. He also preached effectively to an Ethiopian official in a chariot (8:26–40). The key moment is when Peter, head of the Church, visited and—prompted by the Holy Spirit—baptized Cornelius and his household. Read **Acts 11:1–18.**

Paul's Mission

Paul accepted the implications of God's universal sovereignty and moved boldly into the Gentile world. His letters provide the beginning of a theological basis for a world Christian mission. In **Acts 13:44–48,** read about one of Paul's radical moves. During this same journey, Paul and Barnabas had a remarkable brush with Greek religion at Lystra in Asia Minor (14:8–18). During Paul's next journey, he visited Athens and there encountered Greek religion and secular philosophy (17:22–34). This latter occasion marked a critical step for the Christian movement into the Gentile world.

Paul's letters reflect this movement out of the confines of Palestine. In Galatians 2:6–10, he recounts how the Jerusalem church approved his Gentile mission. In his correspondence with the Corinthian Church, he counters the pagan influence of their city (see 1 Cor 5:1; 6:9–11; 10:23–29; 2 Cor 6:14–16). The list of personal greetings in Romans 16 contains Greek and Roman names. Slavery was widely practiced and accepted in that time; and Paul makes many references to the subject, sometimes very delicately. The letter to Philemon concerns a slave Onesimus; see also Ephesians 6:5–9; Colossians 3:11, 22–24; 4:1; 1 Timothy 6:1–2; Titus 2:9–10.

Paul's travels expand the geographical horizons of the first-century Church. Study his movements on a map. When he writes to the Church at Rome, which had already thrived for some years, he expresses his hope to visit them, intending to go on to Spain (Rom 15:22–25). Those plans did not work out, but he eventually did reach Rome (Acts 28:11–16). This was after a hazardous voyage on the Mediterranean Sea in the first century. In Theme 5, Session 4, we will explore Paul's travels from a biographical perspective.

Rome and the Pagan World

Much historical and archeological information about the first-century Greco-Roman world is available, and it is helpful to relate such data to New Testament study. Roman imperial power was part of the pervasive backdrop. New Testament writers do not view this uniformly. Roman authorities crucified Jesus, yet he prayed for those who carried out the sentence (Lk 23:34). Paul implies in 1 Corinthians 2:8 that Rome acted in ignorance. Stories in Acts indicate that Paul was somewhat proud of his Roman citizenship; at any rate, he took advantage of it (see Acts 16:37–39; 22:25–29; 23:26–27). The existence of Roman might, however, posed a problem in a world where God is believed to be sovereign. Paul deals with this in **Romans 13:1–7.** Prayer for civil authorities is enjoined in 1 Timothy 2:1–2.

But human governments are not permanent fixtures in God's world. Paul's positive relationship to Roman authority is finally reversed. Although he exercised his right to appeal to Caesar, tradition is unanimous that he was eventually put to death by Caesar's might.

Colossians 1:23 states that "the gospel . . . has been preached to every creature under heaven," but this is surely a rhetorical exaggeration. Paul here wants to emphasize the universality of Christ's message. In Romans 1:18–25, Paul intimates that all people should be able to perceive God in the created world and therefore to acknowledge God's power. In 2:15, he says that there is law "written in their hearts," which renders all people liable to God's judgment. In 10:8, he quotes Deuteronomy 30:14 to make a similar point. Acts 14:16–17 quotes Paul at Lystra to the same effect.

The World and Evil Powers

In the New Testament, "world" has a variety of shades of meaning; but it never means "orderly universe" as we might understand today. Sometimes "world" is used to mean heaven-and-earth; sometimes it indicates the inhabitants of creation (see Mt 25:34; Acts 17:6; Rom 1:20; Heb 1:6). It may mean the "age" in which people live (see Jn 12:25; 1 Cor 1:20; 1 Jn 3:17; 4:1). "World" may signify a negative contrast to God's way (see Jn 16:20; Gal 6:14; 2 Tm 4:10).

Occasionally, there are echoes of an older idea that the power of evil temporarily rules in the world (see Eph 2:2; 6:12; 2 Thes 2:3–4). While the power of evil is potent, it is ultimately subject to God's sovereignty. Paul rejects the ancient belief in dualism: the idea that two somewhat equal forces, one good and one evil, are struggling for the control of the world. Evil has been doomed by the victory of Christ (see Rom 8:38–39; Col 2:15). This will be further considered in Theme 10, Session 3.

The epistle of James uses "world" to mean all that is in opposition to God (1:27; 4:4), and the sovereignty of God is emphasized in a unique and practical way (see 4:13–15). The legitimacy of human governments is recognized in **1 Peter 2:13–17;** but in 4:12–17 there is a warning that this relationship is likely to change for the worse. In 1 John "love for the world" is opposed to love for God (see 2:15–17; 3:1; 4:4–5; 5:4–5).

The Future of the World

What will become of the world is directly related to what Christ has already done (see Eph 2:11–15). Paul often ties this to a theme of creation. In **Romans 8:18–23,** he writes that "all creation" yearns for the fulfillment anticipated through Christ and "the children of God." God purposes to form "a new creation" out of persons who will be "ambassadors for Christ" (see **2 Cor 5:17–20**; Gal 6:15).

Theme 10 will go into detail about the future of the world. God will finally suppress all opposition. God may be all in all (1 Cor 15:28). The Old Testament expectation of a renewed world will be accomplished (see Gal 4:26; Heb 11:10). This is particularly set forth in **Revela-**

tion 21:22–26; 22:1–2, where the renewal of nature is a special part of the picture.

Suggestions for Further Study

Research

1. Using the *Resource Book* and a Bible dictionary, summarize the different meanings of the word "world" in the New Testament.

2. Make a list of references to nature in the sayings of Jesus. How do the references to nature made by Jesus compare to the views of Paul?

3. Review Acts 2; 8:4–40; 11:1–18; 13:1–3, 44–48. Summarize the way each of the incidents described helped the Church spread its mission to the Gentiles.

Reflection

1. The text refers to the question of whether God can be understood from nature. What difference does the answer make with reference to the Church's mission of evangelization?

2. In what ways does Christian faith lead to concern for the needs of the world?

3. You may want to memorize the following verses:

   - Matthew 28:18–20
   - John 4:24
   - Romans 8:28
   - 2 Corinthians 5:17

Notes

1. Mark 15:39 and Luke 23:47 do not connect the centurion's testimony with an earthquake.

2. Further dimensions of this movement are examined in Theme 7, Session 4.

THEME 5

God's People Have Leaders

SESSION 1

Patriarchs, Judges, and Kings

Session Overview

As the early history of God's people unfolds, human leaders are always prominent. The patriarchs, particularly Abraham and Joseph, are the chief actors in the Genesis drama. The midwives who resist the oppression of Pharaoh make the career of Moses possible. Moses is both a religious and political leader. Joshua is the first national hero. A succession of judges function as local chiefs. Samuel is the transitional leader into the monarchy period, where the first kings serve more to rally the people into a nation than to rule them. Ruth shows how women were able to take initiative in a male-dominated society.

Key Bible Readings

Genesis 45:1–15
Exodus 18:13–26
Deuteronomy 1:1–8
Joshua 24:14–28
Judges 4; 21:25
1 Samuel 3:1–18; 17
Ruth 1:16–17

Key Words

Deuteronomy
Shibboleth
khesed

Another Start in the Pentateuch

In Theme 3, we saw how God communicated with the Hebrew people and directed their destiny through leaders appointed for such critical tasks. The Bible story, indeed, can be told in large part by surveying the lives of the leaders involved. How these leaders carried out their vocation to show God's way and bring God's message is the subject of this theme.

Abraham could be considered the first of the great, God-appointed leaders who exercised his role in a limited clan setting. He is the model of fidelity to God, leaving his home to follow wherever God would lead him. Because of his obedience he became a source of blessing for the people (Gn 12:1–3). The story of Joseph's rise to a position of power in the Egyptian nation is one of the great stories from the ancient world. Review briefly Genesis 37, 39–41. The part Joseph played in relation to God's people becomes evident in the rest of Genesis. Notice especially **Genesis 45:1–15** and the interpretation of Joseph's role in 50:20.

The Role of the Midwives

Interspersed between the story of Joseph and Moses is the story of the midwives who refused to bow to the oppression of Pharaoh and obeyed God. The midwives Shiphrah and Puah risk the displeasure of Pharaoh and refuse to kill the male children of the Israelites because they "feared God" (Ex 1:21).

Moses' life is saved by his mother, who hid him for three months; his sister, who watched after him when he was placed in the river; and finally by Pharaoh's daughter, who took him into her home (Ex 2:1–10). Through the co-operative efforts of these women to resist the oppression of Pharaoh, God raises up the rescuer of the Hebrew people.[1]

The Career of Moses

Moses was clearly a leader of God's people. The focus on Moses in the previous themes was on events and ideas rather than on his character. Here we turn again to Moses' career and give particular attention to the man himself and how he responded to God's appointment. The story of his early life is recounted in Exodus 1:15 to 2:10. In what ways would these remarkable circumstances affect his later career? His call at the burning bush climaxes an important chain of events (see Ex 2:11 to 4:23).

Moses' power struggle with Pharaoh is related in Exodus 5–11. From the many details, pick out a general outline of the story. The Lord is the chief actor in the events associated with the Exodus; Moses and Aaron are the mediators for the Lord (12:50–51). Note how close the relationship is between the Lord and Moses in Exodus 14:10–31. The last sentence of this passage is remarkable, for it marks the exalted esteem in which the Israelites held the memory of Moses.

Exodus 17 contains several items of peculiar interest. The story about water from the rock has already been referred to in Theme 2, and there is a parallel in Numbers 20. The battle with the Amalek is notable for the story about Moses' hands being raised in blessing during the battle. A sequel to this latter incident is found in **Exodus 18:13–26.** Moses is counseled by his father-in-law, Jethro, to share the role of mediation between God and the people.

Recall Moses' part in the events at Mount Sinai. Exodus 19; 24; 32; 33:7–23; 34:1–13, 27–35 are pertinent passages. Moses continues to lead the wilderness journey away from Sinai. These stories are found in the Book of Numbers. Chapters 11 and 12 are connected with Exodus material (see Theme 2, Session 1).

Next we read about twelve spies who go into Canaan (Nm 13). The people are dismayed when most of the spies give a negative report. The Lord is angered by this lack of trust, and Moses again mediates on behalf of the people (Nm 14:13–25). The incredible difficulty of Moses' task is evident from the rebellion against him and Aaron, which is recounted in chapter 16. Numbers 20:1–13 parallels the incident about water from the rock in Exodus 17 with the significant difference that the story in Numbers shows how Moses succumbs to the sin of disobedience against God. Verse 12 shows the consequences of Moses' lack of faith. The story of the serpents in Numbers 21:4–9 was noted in Theme 2.

A short look at the Book of Deuteronomy rounds out the picture of Moses and the Pentateuch. Read **Deuteronomy 1:1–8.** This whole book is written as a second recounting of God's law set in the form of farewell discourse by Moses. (The name Deuteronomy means "the second law" in Greek.) There are significant differences between Deuteronomy and comparable parts of the other Pentateuchal books. Note the reason for keeping the Sabbath commandment in 5:15; compare Exodus 20:11.[2] Deuteronomy includes the end of Moses' career and his death. Read Deuteronomy 32:44–52 and chapter 34.

The place of Moses in biblical tradition can hardly be overestimated. Moses is the model prophet and mediator between God and the Hebrew people. In Deuteronomy 18:15–22, there is a promise of a later "prophet like" Moses. Peter's sermon in Acts 3:17–26 applies the prophecy to Jesus. Indeed, several passages in the gospels that refer to "the prophet" are probably to be associated with the image of Moses (for example, Jn 1:25; 7:40). The importance attached to the Passover and wilderness events in the gospels further emphasizes the significance of Moses. He may be regarded, indeed, as the Old Testament model of God-appointed leadership. He is also the model of those who mediate between God and the people.[3] As the law-giver, Moses sometimes stands in the New Testament as the virtual equivalent of "Torah." See, for example, John 1:17, 45; Mark 1:44; Luke 16:29. Moses exercises some priestly functions in Exodus 17:15; 24:2; 32:1; and at times he acts as a ruler (Ex 18:13–26; Nm 11:10–17; 12:7).

Joshua and the Conquest of Canaan

At the beginning of the book that bears his name, Joshua assumes the awesome role as Moses' successor (Nm 27:18–23). Joshua is a successful leader because he lives in obedience to God. As long as the Hebrews follow the leadership of Joshua, they receive the blessings of God. His first task is to lead the people across the Jordan River into the promised land. Having circled the Dead Sea, the Hebrews were now approaching from the east at a point approximately across from Jericho. Joshua 2 tells an intriguing story of how two spies whom Joshua sent ahead are saved from capture in Jericho due to the help of Rahab. After crossing the Jor-

dan, twelve memorial stones are set up in Gilgal, the rite of circumcision is performed, and the Passover is kept. Then the celebrated battle of Jericho occurs in Chapter 6. The main purpose of the story is to show that when the Hebrews obey God, they will be successful and receive the land as God's gift. "Because Joshua has such undaunted faith in his divine guidance in the war, he was not only successful, but his reputation became great throughout the land."[4]

It is not possible to cover all details of Joshua's conquest of the land. Many of the stories are not essential for general understanding of the period. Close reading of some passages, however, suggests that the conquest was not simple nor complete in this period (compare Jos 13:1 with 11:16–23). Available archeological evidence leaves many questions unanswered. Pass on to Joshua's final charge to the people in chapters 23–24. Note especially **Joshua 24:14–28,** where Joshua calls for continued obedience to the covenant made with God.

The Period of the Judges

After the death of Joshua and his generation, there is a sharp decline in devotion to the Lord. This brings on political disaster. Read Judges 2:6–15. The leadership in this period seems to have been sporadic and mostly limited to one tribe or another. These leaders are the judges, who are portrayed as leaders sent by God to call Israel to obedience (Judges 2:17). One example of what we have already seen in Theme 1, Session 2, is Gideon. Because Israel did not listen to the judges, its successes are neither national nor permanent (2:16–23). The stories are interesting, but we shall note only three.

Deborah is one of the famous women of the Old Testament. Her story and some poetry attributed to her are in **Judges 4** and 5. Another woman, Jael, plays a somewhat gruesome part in the same story. Read the story of Jephthah in chapter 11. The disastrous consequences of a vow he makes pose an ethical dilemma. A less important incident in 12:1–6 has put the word "shibboleth," which means a test word, or a secret password, in our vocabulary. Stories about Samson are more extensive. See chapters 14–16. Read all the material about this tragicomic character, for he is well known in literature.

The last chapters of Judges (19–21) show that the Hebrews have degenerated into warring factions, massacring and destroying each other. Their disintegration and inability to defend themselves from external enemies shows vividly the consequences of their disobedience to God. Note the last verse of Judges, **21:25.** It is an apt summary of the political and moral situation in those transitional times.

The Leadership of Samuel

The life of Samuel dominates the first twenty-four chapters of the books known by his name. In Theme 1, Session 2, he is designated "the last of the judges and the first of the prophets" (1 Sm 3:20 and 7:15). The stories of Samuel's birth and childhood show that from the beginning he was a man dedicated to the service of God. Note that there are some general parallels to the stories about Isaac and Moses. Read 1 Samuel 1 and 2:18–20. Samuel's call from the Lord in **1 Samuel 3:1—18.** is of special interest, demonstrating how he was ready to hear and obey God.

Read 1 Samuel 7:3–13 and analyze Samuel's role in Israel. In verses 9–10, he functions as a priest mediating between God and the people. He also plays a major part in establishing the monarchy; the stories are in chapters 8–10. Note his warning to the people of the consequences of preferring the obedience to kings rather than obedience to the Lord. The kings are considered in Theme 6.

Saul and David

Saul's role as leader connects directly to his becoming king. 1 Samuel 11 tells how a deed of military prowess brings him to prominence in Israel. Saul is made king in an assembly held at Gilgal, the site of the first encampment after the Hebrews crossed the Jordan. There Samuel addresses the people and recounts "the saving deeds of the Lord." (Many of these deeds are already familiar to you.) Shortly after this, Saul disobeys God by wrongly performing a priestly function that is outside his prerogative. Samuel then tells him that his royal line will not continue (1 Sm 13:8–15).

Samuel anoints David to be Saul's successor (1 Sm 16:1–13). There are two stories of how David came to Saul's attention. In 16:14–23, the musical ability that is evident later in David's psalms plays a part; **1 Samuel 17** is probably better known. David wins the battle with Goliath because of his devotion to the Lord. David continues to be connected with the family of Saul (1 Sm 18:1–4; 20). References to David's rise to the throne are scattered through to 2 Samuel 21. The deterioration of Saul's character and his removal from kingship are related to his failure to obey God. The details are scattered through the rest of 1 Samuel.

Three stories in these chapters may be highlighted. 1 Samuel 25 tells a romantic tale of David and Abigail. Although it was a man's world, Abigail, through personal initiative and courage, helps David avoid the descent into the blood feuds that plagued the Hebrews in the time of the judges. Thus, she makes a significant contribution to David's growing awareness of how to act as a just king.

1 Samuel 28 is a bizarre tale of how Saul consults a witch or medium at Endor. Not only does this give insight into the breakdown of Saul's character, but it also offers commentary on folk religion of that time. In chapter 30,

David makes an expedition to avenge the capture of Ziklag, where he made his home while in exile. Note his generous treatment of the rear guard of his company.

David is certainly one of the most important figures in the Old Testament, and his name appears more than fifty times in the New Testament. Only Moses and Abraham are mentioned more often (see, for example, Mk 2:25–26). In the next theme, we shall consider David's role as the ideal king. In Theme 9, we shall mark his fame as a sacred, liturgical poet. (Seventy-five of the psalms are attributed to him.) In summary, note the divine tribute to David in 1 Samuel 13:14, which is repeated in Acts 13:22.

The Story of Ruth

The main theme of the Book of Ruth is *khesed,* which means loyalty or faithfulness born of sense of caring and commitment. "*Khesed* is a Hebrew term used to describe God's relationship to Israel as well as the relationship among members of a family or community."[5] Ruth shows how God is manifested in the loyalty which the family members show to one another. The story also depicts Ruth and Naomi courageously taking the initiative in establishing a relationship with Boaz. Because of their actions, the family that would give birth to David was maintained.[6]

This romantic tale is set during the period of the judges (1:1), but the end of the book makes it clear that the tradition was recorded no earlier than the time of David. The admirable traits of Ruth, her noble, loving womanhood, are often cited in the biblical tradition of Jews and Christians. Note **Ruth 1:16–17,** where Ruth binds herself in a covenant relationship with the Lord by pledging herself to Naomi. Ruth, David's great-grandmother, was a "foreigner," and because of her faithfulness she was included in Jesus' family tree (see Mt 1:5).

Suggestions for Further Study

Research

1. Using a Bible dictionary, locate and read the articles on Joseph, Moses, Joshua, Deborah, Jephthah, Samson, Samuel, Saul, David, Abigail.

2. Read the article Women in the Bible in Appendix 2. What does the article tell you about the general position of women in the Bible?

3. Read the Book of Ruth and the relevant material in a Bible commentary. What does the story tell you about how God acts in the lives of ordinary people?

Reflection

1. What are the characteristics you would look for in a leader appointed by God?

2. Consider how biblical leaders discussed in the session may serve as role models for religious leadership today.

3. Think of some modern leaders who seem right for their time. How do you think Old Testament writers would have reported their leadership?

4. If you were called to be a leader in your parish, how would you try to assure that your leadership would be blessed by God?

5. You may want to summarize these stories:

   • Joseph's relation to his brothers
   • Joshua's last charge to Israel
   • Deborah's victory
   • the choice of David to be king
   • David and Jonathan

6. You may want to memorize Ruth 1:16–17.

Notes

1. See Rita J. Burns, *Exodus, Leviticus, Numbers* (Wilmington, DE: Michael Glazier, 1983), 32–36.

2. See also the law of release for slaves: Deuteronomy 15:12–18 and Exodus 21:2–6.

3. See Mediation, Mediator, HBD 618–19.

4. HBC 239.

5. HBC 262.

6. See Alice Laffey, *An Introduction to the Old Testament: A Feminist Perspective* (Philadelphia: Fortress, 1988), 205–10; and John Craghan, *Esther, Judith, Tobit, Johan, Ruth* (Wilmington, DE: Michael Glazier, 1982), 198.

SESSION 2

Prophets and Later Leadership

Session Overview

Elijah, the prototype prophet, and Elisha, his successor, struggle against a corrupting, alien religion. Later, Isaiah, Jeremiah, and Ezekiel play key roles at critical times in the life of Judah, extending through the Exile. The return from Exile brings to the fore Ezra, the scribe, and Nehemiah, the governor, who help the struggling Jewish community meet the demands of their new national life. Five important groups of leaders emerge later in Judea: Scribes, Pharisees, Sadducees, Essenes, and Zealots.

Key Bible Readings

1 Kings 17:8–16;
  22:5–28
2 Kings 5; 19
Amos 7:10–15
Jeremiah 1
Ezra 1:1–7
Nehemiah 6

Key Words

hasidim
scribes
Pharisees
Essenes
Sadducees
Zealots
Mishnah
Talmud
rabbi

A New Focus

In Theme 6 we will take a careful look at the kings of the Hebrew people. Other persons in the times of the kings exercised special leadership under a driving sense of God's special guidance, and we shall study these "prophets." You may find it helpful at this point to refer to the chronology chart in Appendix 7. After Solomon's reign, the Hebrew nation was divided into two kingdoms, Israel and Judah. Descendants of David were kings of Judah in the south; a succession of dynasties ruled Israel in the north. First and Second Kings (denoting the necessity of using two scrolls to contain the material) deal with affairs in Israel where Elijah and Elisha are prominent prophets.

Elijah, Prototype of Prophets

The duel between Elijah and the priests of Baal on Mount Carmel is probably the most noteworthy story of prophetic leadership in the early period of the kings.[1] Read the story in 1 Kings 17 and 18 and continue on through chapters 19 and 20 with the following notes:

94

- **17:8–16** Can you identify Jesus' use of this story?[2]

- 17:17–24 Many miraculous events are associated with Elijah. They are intended to show God's power at work.

- 18:3 This Obadiah is not the same person as the author of the book of that name; there are several other Obadiahs mentioned in the Old Testament.

- 18:26 Baal was a Canaanite sky god. The "hop" of the priests was a ritual dance.

- Chapter 19 The Lord is revealed to Elijah at Horeb ("the mountain of God," in place of Sinai in the tradition of the northern kingdom). The voice (Word) of the Lord brings reassurance to the prophet and gives him a new appointment. Here Elisha is introduced as the successor to Elijah.

- Chapter 20 Other prophetic leaders are mentioned, though not by name.

Micaiah and Elisha

1 Kings 22:5–28 describes the activity of court prophets, like Micaiah, who are a kind of professional guild. It becomes apparent here that all prophets are not God-appointed leaders. Isaiah proves to be the true interpreter of the Lord's will. The story gives important insights into prophetic roles and functions.

2 Kings 1 begins with a grim story that sets forth the austere reputation of Elijah's power. 2 Kings 2 tells how Elijah left the earthly scene. Elisha's cry in verse 12 indicates the astonishing awe in which Elijah was held. Elisha immediately assumes the role that his mentor had filled. The material in 2 Kings 2:23–24 presents an unattractive, even fearsome, picture of Elisha.

2 Kings 3:9–20 is a miracle story about Elisha. Verse 15 suggests how the prophetic gift may sometimes have been exercised. Chapter 4

clearly parallels the Elijah stories in 1 Kings 17. The story in **2 Kings 5** was mentioned in Theme 1, Session 2. Where is this story of Naaman referred to in the New Testament?[3]

In 2 Kings 6:8–23, Elisha is directly involved in the leadership of Israel. In 9:1–3, he takes a hand in a change of dynasty, just as it was predicted he would (10:17; compare 1 Kgs 19:16, 17; 21:20–22).

Amos

Elijah and Elisha lived in the ninth century BC. Their leadership style seems to be direct involvement, whereas the prophets after them are better known for their powerful messages. Here we shall survey the careers of several of these prophets. The prophetic messages will be examined in several later themes.

Amos lived in the southern kingdom of Judah, but prophesied in the northern kingdom of Israel. See 1:1 and **Amos 7:10–15** for a description of the context of his activity. Amos denounced the injustices present in his society. The wealthy grew rich on international trade while using dishonest business practices to exploit the poor. Small farm holdings were consolidated into large estates, with dishonest judges making decisions for the rich at the expense of the poor. The wealth amassed by the rich was used for their own pleasure rather than for building up the community (Am 6:3–7). Little is known about Amos. Although the text of his message survives, the results of his efforts can only be guessed. But his critique of social injustices still calls Christians to responsibly protest social injustices in society and to assume responsibility for the needs of the poor today.

Isaiah's Career

The Book of Isaiah in the Bible was written in three parts. The first part, Isaiah 1–39, discussed below, was written between 740–701 BC. The second part, Isaiah 40–55, was written during the Babylonian Exile, c. 587–539 BC. The third part, Isaiah 56–66, was written by a third prophet in the fifth century BC, after the repatriation to Jerusalem.

Isaiah ben-Amos, whose teaching is presented in the present Book of Isaiah, chapters 1–39, was active in the southern kingdom of Judah in the latter half of the eighth century. We have some information about his life and public career. His call (already noted in Theme 3) is dated "in the year that King Uzziah died," which is 742 BC, according to modern calculation (see Is 6:1–8). During this period, the kingdoms of Judah and Israel are unhappy buffers between Assyria, where power is rising, and Egypt, whose power is on the wane. Early in Isaiah's public life, Israel falls (721 BC), but Judah believes that the dynasty of David will never end (see 2 Sm 7:16, 17). Nevertheless, the political situation of the southern kingdom becomes extremely precarious. The role Isaiah plays at this time may be surmised from parts of Isaiah 1–39 and a few other references. Read chapter 20 to see how the radical prophet acted. Theme 1, Session 2, refers to the invasion of the Assyrian king, Sennacherib. 2 Kings 18 tells of the ensuing siege of Jerusalem. **2 Kings 19** relates Isaiah's activity in the deliverance of the city, and chapter 20 recounts King Hezekiah's deathbed encounter with the prophet.

2 Chronicles, a somewhat idealized review of the history of the southern kingdom, credits Isaiah with having written records of the monarchy in his time (2 Chr 26:22; 32:32), but such books have not survived. Isaiah is married, the "prophetess" is his wife, and has two sons to whom he gives names intended to convey messages to his contemporaries. The first son is named Shear-jashub, meaning "a remnant will return"; and the second, Maher-shalal-hash-baz, means "the spoil speeds, the prey hastes." Read Isaiah 8:1–4; an older son is also mentioned in 7:3 without further comment. Parts of Isaiah's message are directed toward the future, especially chapters 9 and 11, but these are more appropriately taken up in later themes.

Jeremiah's Career

Jeremiah's activities are substantially better known than those of Isaiah's career. Note the similarities between the two prophets' calls.

Jeremiah plays an important role all during the last years of Judah. His career extends through the downfall of the southern kingdom in 587 BC. The Babylonians have conquered Assyria, and a power struggle has developed between Babylon and Egypt. Judah, of course, is caught in the middle. Babylon wins a famous battle at Carchemish (605 BC) and becomes the ruler of the Middle East. Not long afterward Judah revolts, but Nebuchadnezzar subdues Judah and sets up a puppet state. Judah revolts against Babylon again, is defeated, and Jerusalem is leveled (587/6 BC).

Jeremiah urges the people to hold fast to the covenant with God and to follow wiser courses in their political dilemmas. More than once the prophet is in trouble with the political and religious leaders of Judah. As a dramatized witness against the grim future, he does not marry (Jer 16:1–9). Read what happens to him in 19:14–20:6. In chapter 26, he is brought to trial but acquitted because of his prophet status. In Jeremiah 36:1–19, Jeremiah is instructed to dictate God's message onto a scroll. This is read in the Temple, and later before the council of princes, by Baruch, Jeremiah's scribe. See what finally happens to the scroll (Jer 36:20–26) and how Jeremiah replaces it (verses 27–32). Later (37:11–21), Jeremiah is arrested; but because of the king's friendship, or fear, he is given some freedom. Chapter 38 tells how the prophet is put into a cistern for his outspoken appraisal of the national situation. He is saved through the help of one of the king's servants.

When Jerusalem falls, Jeremiah is treated well by the conquerors (Jer 39:11–14). His message is really misunderstood both by his own people and by their enemies. Allowed the choice of good treatment with the Exile in Babylon or continued residence in Judah, he chooses the latter. The people who remain in Judah are restive, and after the appointed governor is murdered, they determine to go into voluntary exile in Egypt. (The term "Chaldean," which occurs in Jeremiah 41–43, is another name for Babylonians.) Jeremiah vetoes this decision, but they force him to go along. There he continues to be spokesperson for the Lord and vigorously opposes the rise of idolatry among the exiles.

Lamentations, Nahum, and Others

The Book of Lamentations, traditionally ascribed to Jeremiah, contains a series of "acrostic" poems lamenting the situation after the destruction of Jerusalem. An acrostic poem distributes the entire Hebrew alphabet of twenty-two letters in each of the first four chapters and then, in the final chapter, uses the same device through the use of twenty-two short verses. Linguistic experts and biblical theologians think it is unlikely that the book was written by Jeremiah himself, but this need not hinder our appreciation of the beauty and appropriateness of the poetry.

Other material that comes from this period includes some of the minor prophets, for example, Joel, Obadiah, Nahum, and Malachi. Limitations of time and space preclude particular study of these books. You may note them here

in passing. Brief summaries of their contents may be found in a Bible dictionary.

Ezekiel's Career

Another "major" prophet is Ezekiel. Theme 1 looks at one of his famous visions (Ez 27); later themes will consider other passages. Here the focus is on his relationship to events of his time. While the exact chronology of his prophecies is not entirely certain, we may tentatively divide the book into approximately equal halves. In 24:1–2, Ezekiel hears that Jerusalem is under siege. It appears that the prophet is among an early group who were exiled to Babylon about 597 BC. The first half of his prophecies, then, consists mainly of warnings about what is still to come. After Jerusalem falls, his emphasis shifts to woes against Judah's enemies and hopes for the exiles. The book culminates in a vision of the restoration of the temple.

Ezekiel's character is unusual, to say the least, and his prophetic practice differed considerably from that of his contemporaries (see, for example, 4; 12:1–16). His book, however, deserves more careful study than it usually receives, and it shall be studied in other themes.

Post-exilic Leaders

Jeremiah foretold that the Babylonian Exile would last seventy years (Jer 25.11–12; 29:10). The chronicler who produced both Chronicles and the books of Ezra and Nehemiah specifically mentions this when he tells how that period came to an end (2 Chr 36:21–23). The following is a brief study of the principal leaders of the return from exile.

The chain of events in Ezra and Nehemiah is difficult to untangle, but we can get a general overview of what is recorded. Begin with **Ezra 1:1–7.** The rest of chapters 1–6 deals with the return of the exiles. Much of the detail here need not concern us directly at this time. Our focus is on the leaders. Note the mention of the prophets Haggai and Zechariah in 5:1.

Nehemiah's leadership is both political and religious. Ezra's mission is concentrated primarily in religious affairs. Nehemiah's first task is to rebuild the walls of Jerusalem. Walls begun by the first defenders are in place. Nehemiah is opposed by Sanballat, who seems to be the official from whose territory the Jewish restoration state is being carved out. The story is sketchy in Nehemiah 1–7; read **chapter 6.** We can roughly identify the time, for Nehemiah appears to have been governor of Judah during two periods under Artaxerxes I, king of Persia (464–424 BC).

In Nehemiah 9:6–38, Ezra rehearses a broad outline of Israel's history. This is in the form of a national confession to the Lord. Note the affirmations in verses Nehemiah 9:17, 31–32. The rest of the Book of Nehemiah contains more about religious reforms than about political events. You can get some feeling for the temper of the times. The rest of Ezra is of similar import.

The Maccabean Period

The principal source of information for the period between Ezra and Nehemiah and Jesus is found in first and second Maccabees. Theme 1, Session 2, mentioned the brief period of Hebrew national glory in the mid-third century BC under the leadership of the Hasmonaean clan, especially Judas Maccabaeus.

After the period of the return from Babylonian Exile, Jewish leaders are no longer "prophets." The words of Psalm 74:9 characterize the times: "Deeds on our behalf we do not see; there is no prophet now." After the death of Judas Maccabaeus, the writer of 1 Maccabees

notes, "There had not been such great distress in Israel since the time prophets ceased to appear among the people" (9:27). During the Exile, of course, the lack of a temple brings the priesthood into obscurity, but during the centuries immediately following the Exile, priests attain considerable influence. When the temple is rebuilt and its services and staff extended, the office of high priest becomes very powerful. Priestly writers served to edit important religious documents. When the temple is given a new grandeur under Herod the Great, late in the first century BC, the priests have prestige but are not popular leaders among the people.

Leadership at the End of the Old Testament

At about this same time, experts in the study of Torah come into prominence. Already in the Maccabaean era persons devoted to Torah are known as *hasidim*, "pious ones." The natural leaders of these "Hasideans" are the scribes, who since the Exile are responsible for copying the sacred books and are also the experts at interpreting them as the law of God for the people.

In the middle of the second century BC, two groups known as Pharisees and Essenes emerge from the Hasideans. Both groups are marked by intense dedication to doing the will of God as they believe it to be revealed in the Law, but they differ in their interpretations of it. Along with the Sadducees and Zealots, these are commonly named as the major parties or factions in Judaism at the beginning of the Christian era.

None of these groups exercised leadership among God's people in the style of the great figures studied in this theme. The Pharisees come closest to being recognized leaders. The common people looked to them to set standards in religious matters. The Pharisees were concerned to make God's will clear for every area of life, so they developed an elaborate system of rules. The intention was to put a "fence" about the law to keep people from coming to ruin by transgression. This came to be regarded as "oral law." It was considered to have divine authority, and by Jesus' day those who accepted Pharisaic doctrine gave it a place alongside the written Torah. In the second century of our era, this material was written down and became known as the Mishnah. The elaborations of Mishnaic law were extensive and are called Talmud. The scribes were natural allies of the Pharisees, and these two groups are often mentioned together in the gospels. Lay teachers of the law came to be addressed as *rabbi,* a Hebrew word meaning "my master." In Jesus' day, these were well-known leader-figures. This is apparently why Jesus is occasionally so addressed.

Like the Pharisees, the Essenes developed from the Hasideans. The Essenes, however, withdrew from the common life of the people and became, at least in part, monastic. They are generally regarded as the people who produced and preserved the Dead Sea Scrolls.[4] It is disappointing that there are no clear interrelationships between the Essenes and the infant Christian Church.

The Sadducees were mostly from priestly, aristocratic families. Jerusalem was their center, for the temple was their official responsibility. Their religious stance was conservative. Politically, they fostered the status quo, which meant they superficially supported Roman rule. They had little influence among most of the people.

The Zealots did not really form one party. The name was apparently applied to any organized resistance to Rome, or more generally to any individual who resisted an enemy of Judaism. Mention of them dates from early in the first century of the Christian era. Many Zealots acted from deeply religious motivation, and they produced some prophet-like leaders.

Suggestions for Further Study

Research

1. Using a Bible dictionary, look up the meaning of the word "prophet." Who are some people in the world today who might fit the description?

2. How were the prophets Micaiah, Elijah, Elisha, Amos, Isaiah, Jeremiah, and Ezekiel involved in influencing the political life of Israel and Judah?

3. Using a Bible dictionary, read the articles on Ezra and Nehemiah. What leadership roles did they play during the restoration?

4. Review the entries about the major parties of first-century Judaism (Scribes, Pharisees, Essenes, Sadducees, Zealots) in a Bible dictionary.

Reflection

1. Who do you think is a prophetic voice in the Church and society today? How do you see that person challenging you to examine the priorities in your own life?

2. Religious groups influence political decisions in one way or another. What historical examples can you think of outside the Bible? In contemporary society? How should religious leadership be exercised?

Notes

1. See Theme 1, Part 2.
2. See Matthew 14:13–21; 15:32–38; Mark 6:30–44; Luke 9:10–17; John 6:1–14.
3. See John 9:7; Luke 4:27.
4. See Scrolls, the Dead Sea, HBD 915–17.

SESSION 3

The Baptist, Jesus, Mary, and the Apostles

Session Overview

The appearance of John the Baptist as a prophet of "the kingdom of God" creates a sensation. The end of John's career marked the beginning of Jesus' public ministry, which brings Jesus to prominence as a distinctive, unique leader. After his death and resurrection, Jesus' ministry continues and is extended, initially by Peter and John. In Acts, Peter is the spokesman for the early Church. Paul also emerges as an outstanding leader.

Key Bible Readings

Luke 1:26–38
Luke 3:1–20
Mark 11:1–19, 27–33
John 18:33–38
Acts 1:15–26; 10; 9:1–22
Galatians 1:13–2:14
2 Corinthians 11:22–33
Acts 15; 25:1–12
2 Timothy 4:6–18

Key Words

apostle
disciple

John the Baptist

The gospels agree that Jesus is preceded by a popular, prophet-like figure, known as "the Baptist" because of a distinct feature of his ministry. In the story of John's birth, Luke 1:5–25, 57–80, note similarities to Old Testament stories we have read. Continue with **Luke 3:1–20.** The time of John's ministry is probably AD 26–27. Herod Antipas is ruling at this time. He and Philip are sons of Herod the Great, whose kingdom was divided by the Romans following his death in 4 B.C.

Imagine the excitement when people begin to believe that a genuine prophet has appeared after so long a silence! Matthew 14:5 and Mark 1:5 reflect the popular estimate of John. Matthew 11:9–11 gives Jesus' appraisal. Luke 3:15 suggests that many people are raising the question whether John may be the messiah. He denies this and insists that another is coming who will better merit that title.

The end of Malachi (3:23–24) promises that Elijah will appear before "the day of the Lord" (a term for the end-time). The gospels tell of popular discussion as to whether John the Baptist could be the returned prophet. According to Matthew 11:10–15 and Mark 9:1–13, Jesus identifies John with Elijah; but in John 1:21 the Baptist categorically denies that he is Elijah. These texts are not implying reincarnation but are dealing with the interpretation of prophetic roles; both Jesus and John could be correct.

John exercises a prophet's function by denouncing Herod Antipas's private life. As a result, the Baptist is imprisoned and eventually put to death. Read the basic story in Mark 6:14–29. Later interpreters have embellished the story extensively.

Mary as One Obedient to God

Read **Luke 1:26–38.** Just as Moses was saved by the intervention of courageous women who refused to carry out the orders of their oppressors, Mary plays a significant role in the salvation of humanity. Like the God-appointed leaders of the Old Testament, Mary accepts in humble obedience the word from God. Luke portrays Mary as "the handmaid of the Lord" (Lk 1:38). "Here Mary's enthusiastic response to the angel depicts her from the very beginning of the account as one who cooperates in God's plan of salvation."[1]

As a result of her positive response to God's Word, Luke sees Mary as the model believer (Lk 1:45). "Pronounced blessed; and because she is favored, she will be declared blessed by all generations."[2] John portrays the mother of Jesus as one involved in the fulfillment of Jesus' hour and as the mother of the beloved disciple (Jn 19:25–27).

Beginning of Jesus' Career

This theme treats some details of Jesus' life from the perspective of God-appointed leadership. Although his followers come to believe that he is more than a leader, most contemporaries of Jesus' public ministry seem to recognize him as a teacher, a charismatic healer, and probably a prophet.

Jesus' career is related to that of John at several points. Read Luke 1:5–25 and compare it with the story anticipating Jesus' birth. Perhaps Jesus' and John's mothers were kin, although they appear to have belonged to different ancestral tribes. The hymnlike poem attributed to Mary is very much like the song of Hanna (1 Sm 2:1–10). Read Luke 2:41–52, noting again a similarity to the Old Testament materials.

According to Mark 1:14, Jesus begins his active public life when John is arrested. Some time before that, Jesus comes to John and receives baptism. Matthew, from his later perspective, recognizes a theological problem in this act. Read Matthew 3:13–17. Why was Jesus baptized by John? Did this mean that John was the greater one? The accounts in Mark 1:9–11 and Luke 3:21–22 are somewhat simpler. Whatever else Jesus' baptism has come to signify, it surely marks Jesus' acceptance of his special role in the destiny of God's people.

Mark 8:27–30 seems to describe a turning point in Jesus' career. In a discussion about his "public image," his disciples say that some people think he is John the Baptist or Elijah reincarnated. Herod seems to have entertained a similar idea, identifying Jesus as John "raised from the dead." See also Mark 6:14–16 and Luke 9:7–9. In Jesus' first recorded preaching at Nazareth (Lk 4:16–27), the references to Elijah and Elisha suggest that Jesus may have been partly responsible for such ideas. In Mark 8:29, Peter announces that he considers Jesus to be the Messiah (note the more elaborate parallels in Lk 9:20 and Mt 16:16).

Jesus as a Public Leader

Early in his ministry, Jesus gathers an intimate group of followers. These are sometimes called "disciples," sometimes "apostles." Learn the meanings of these two terms.[3] Suggest why Jesus would choose twelve followers. For this band, his leadership was both physical and spiritual (see, for example, Mk 10:32–34; Mt 10:24–25; Jn 13:13–17). Upon occasion, Jesus states boldly the claims of his leadership (Mk 1:16–20; Mt 10:37–39; Mk 10:17–22, 35–45; Jn 10:7–11, 14–16). The gospels make it clear that Jesus chose and trained the apostles so that they would proclaim his gospel to the other disciples and to the entire world (Mt 28:16–20).

Jesus exerts influence among widening public circles by the force of his actions and the intriguing power of his words. The twelve are chosen from a larger group (Lk 6:13). Women also helped Jesus and the apostles (Lk 8:1–3). When Jesus' popularity fluctuates, so does the number of his followers (Jn 6:66–67). He was renowned as a healer, a function exercised by some of the early prophets. He rejects efforts, however, to make this the focus of his ministry. In a story of the healing of a paralytic, Mark 2:1–12, he tries to redirect the meaning of the event (see also Jn 5:13–14; 11:23–24).

Other passages portray Jesus as reluctant to be thrust into public prominence. This is particularly true in Mark (see Mk 1:43–45; 3:11–12; 5:43; Mt 9:30; Lk 9:21). He expends himself for the crowds that follow him (Mk 8:1–3), but he frequently retires for personal refreshment of spirit (Mt 14:23) or for a private opportunity to teach the Twelve (Mk 3:7–9, 13). The transfiguration is a special instance (Mk 9:2–8); an inner circle of three is singled out to participate with Jesus.

On one occasion, Jesus does take the spotlight; we refer to it as the triumphal entry into Jerusalem. He does not, however, capitalize upon the strategic momentum of this event. Try to discover what the texts tell about Jesus' intention (Mt 21:1–17; Lk 19:28–48). If Jesus had aspirations to be a political leader, this was the opportunity for him to make his move. In **Mark 11:1–19,** these events are spread over several days. The apparent deliberateness of his movements hardly suggests a political coup in progress.

The Gospel of John places the triumphal entry in the same general sequences as the synoptics; but the clearing of the temple is a part of Jesus' early Judean ministry, which is given only in John 2:13–25. This difference and the synoptic variations show that the editor of John probably moved the story in order to emphasize the raising of Lazarus as the final dramatic confrontation between Jesus and his enemies (Jn 11). The sharp, calculatedly clever exchange between Jesus and some of his religious opponents in **Mark 11:27–33** seems clearly to place Jesus' goals beyond the immediate, mundane setting. Consider also the conversation with Pilate in **John 18:33–38.**

The Twelve

It would be a mistake to conclude that Jesus' aim was directed only toward otherworldly goals and that he exerted no immediately effective leadership. His life and teachings directly affected the lives of his followers. Recall the meanings of the terms "disciples" and "apostles." A circle of twelve receives Jesus' special attention and instruction. Three of these form a more intimate circle: Peter, James, and John (for example, see Mk 9:2). When one of the original twelve is lost as a traitor, the infant Church deems it important to select a successor (**Acts 1:15–26**). Note the qualifications specified for Judas's replacement. The symbolic value of twelve as leaders as the successors of the twelve tribes of Israel is clear.

There are other persons whose leadership in the early Church is important enough to merit the title "apostle." Make a list from Acts 14:14; Romans 16:7; 1 Corinthians 15:7; Galatians 1:19. Traditions and legend record very meager details about the later lives of the twelve; the concern here is only with New Testament data. There is some significant information about Andrew, James, Philip, and Thomas; you may consult a Bible dictionary for this. Their leadership qualities are more implied than demonstrated. Judas Iscariot is a special case. John 12:6 and 13:29 name him as the treasurer for the twelve, so he must have had recognizable ability. Indeed, we may assume Jesus saw significant potential in each of those he chose. We know next to nothing about the other apostles.

Peter

While the twelve are banded about Jesus, Peter is the leader and spokesperson. For example, when Jesus begins to anticipate the end of his earthly career, Peter speaks for the group in protest against this unwelcome declaration. This marked a turning point in Jesus' ministry, and it immediately follows Peter's "confession" that he—and perhaps the others—thinks Jesus is the Messiah. In the transfiguration experience, it is again Peter who speaks out. See also his role in the garden of Gethsemane (Mt 26:36–56; Jn 18:10–11).

According to Mark 1:16–18, Jesus calls Peter directly from his fishing business. John 1:40–42 indicates that Peter's brother Andrew has already been attracted to John the Baptist as one who will fulfill Old Testament expectations. Peter's real name is Simon, a common name borne by several other New Testament persons. Jesus promptly gives him a nickname—in Aramaic, *cephas*, a word meaning "rock"; in Greek *petra*, whence "Peter"—and promised to build his Church upon this Rock. This nickname appears to be somewhat ambiguous, for Peter is not always like a rock. Sometimes he speaks

more quickly than he thinks, as in Mark 9:5–6. His actions are often impetuous (for example, Mt 14:26–32; Jn 18:10; 21:7). The bitter story about his denial of Jesus (Mk 14:53–72) is a telling indictment against Peter, but Luke 22:31–34 has a word of hope about his future.

Church tradition says that the Gospel of Mark contains Peter's memoirs. If this is true, the wording of Mark 16:7 is particularly poignant. Matthew's version of Peter's confession at Caesarea Philippi (16:13–20) adds the giving of the keys to the kingdom of heaven to Peter. John 21:15–23 contains a conversation between the risen Jesus and Peter, which reflects further traditions about Peter in the early Church.

Beginning at Acts 1:15, Peter's leadership in the early Church is specific. The prominent part he played at Pentecost is given in Acts 2:14–42. In chapters 3 and 4 he and John are the particular representatives of the new movement. In the story of Ananias and Sapphira (Acts 5:1–11), Peter appears as a fearsome, charismatic leader; and in verses 14–15 he is treated with almost superstitious regard. This is further developed in Acts 9:32–43.

Peter's experience with the Roman centurion, Cornelius, is recounted twice in **Acts 10** and 11.[4] This story shows Peter taking the initiative to evangelize the Gentiles. Here an experience like Pentecost happens to Gentiles, and Peter is a central figure in the event. The last story on Acts concerning Peter is in 12:1–19. His relationship with Paul is noted later, and in Theme 10 we look at the two letters that bear Peter's name.

Catholic tradition, as shown by St. Peter's Basilica in Rome, holds that Peter later became bishop of Rome. The Pope, as bishop of Rome, is considered to be Peter's successor as shepherd of the flock of Christ (see Mt 16:18; Jn 21:15–17).

John, James, and Others

The apostle John's leadership in the early Church, according to Acts, is exercised in association with Peter. Tradition has assumed that "the disciple whom Jesus loved" mentioned in the fourth gospel (for example, 13:23–24; 19:26; 20:2; 21:7) is the apostle John,[5] although the name is not used. The three letters attributed to John were perhaps not written by the apostle himself, for in the second and third letters the author calls himself "the elder," an unlikely alternative for "apostle." Probably the elder is associated with a tradition that stemmed from the apostle's preaching. The seer of Revelation gives his name as John, but it is uncertain whether or not he is the apostle.

John's brother James (Jacob in some modern translations) is one of the inner circle of Jesus' disciples. We know little more about him except that he appears to have been the first martyr from among the apostles (Acts 12:1–2). Several other men are named James in the New Testament. One of these becomes an important leader and is referred to as Jesus' brother during the public ministry (Mk 6:3; Jn 7:5). Paul implies (1 Cor 15:7) that a special appearance of the resurrected Jesus brought James into active prominence in the Church. In Acts 12:17, he is singled out as a special person in the Jerusalem congregation. In Acts 15, he served as moderator of a Church council. See also 21:18. In Galatians 2:9, Paul refers to James, Cephas, and John as "reputed pillars" of the Church.

Paul

An outstanding leader in the first-century Church is Paul. His original Jewish name was Saul, but he became known by the Latin sound-alike "Paul" (see Acts 13:9). We usually follow the course of his career from the relevant chapters of Acts, but we should check and adjust de-tails by reference to his letters wherever possible. Certainly, his letters are the primary source for studying his thoughts. There is a chart listing the events in Paul's life in HBD 759.

For Paul's personal background, read Acts 21:39; 22:3–5; Romans 11:1; 2 Corinthians 11:22; Philippians 3:4–6. He has no doubt about his leadership status: He affirms and defends his call as an apostle in Romans 1:1; 1 Corinthians 1:1; 2 Corinthians 1:1; and especially Galatians 1:1, 11–17. The story of his special call is told three times in Acts: **9:1–22;** 22:6–21; and 26:4–20. An early mission in the Church is mentioned in 11:25–26.

The longest biographical passage in Paul's letters is **Galatians 1:13–2:14.** There is scattered information in **2 Corinthians 11:22–33;** 12:7–10 (see also 10:10); and Galatians 4:13–15. Some of the details in these references are hard to correlate with the materials in Acts, but the general outline is clear enough. Note Paul's declaration of independence from the Jerusalem leaders and his clash with Peter. All the epistles reflect the strength of Paul's leadership in the churches.[6]

Paul's "missionary journeys" remain a most notable achievement. Retracing his steps even today is a very difficult undertaking. Maps charting these trips appear in Appendix 8 of this book and in HAB 172–73. There is some value in remembering at least the general features of each of the journeys, but many of the details can be passed over quickly in this survey. The background of the original journeys is sketched in Acts 13:1–3. Barnabas was already an important leader in the churches, and at the beginning of the first trip he is presumably the leader of the evangelization team, a fact which helps to explain references to "Barnabas and Saul" in Acts 11:30; 12:25; and 13:2.

The record of the first journey is in Acts 13:4–14:26. The group travels through Cyprus, north to the southern coast of Asia Minor (modern Turkey), makes a circuit north and then eastward, retraces the route to the sea, and returns to Antioch in Syria. Among the details, note Paul's sermon at Antioch in Pisidia with its familiar scripture, and the strange encounter with pagan religion at Lystra.

Acts 15 marks an important break in the travel stories. Here is what is often called the first Church council. Note the intervention of Peter (Acts 15:6–12). The council's decisions do not seem to have changed Paul's mission. See also Acts 21:17–26.

The second journey runs from 15:36 through 18:22. The dispute about Mark is patched up later, as we may infer from Colossians 4:10 and 2 Timothy 4:11. Paul's new associate is Silas, also referred to as Silvanus. They travel overland to some of the places visited on the first expedition. Then they head northward to the area near ancient Troy, and there Paul has a dream that is interpreted as a call to go to Macedonia—thus taking the gospel to Europe. The Macedonian man is not identified, but has been conjectured that it is Luke. Luke is usually considered to be the author or compiler of Acts. It is interesting that at this point in the narrative the pronouns shift from "they" to "we."

At Philippi, Paul and his companions are imprisoned.[7] Paul's sermon at Athens is noteworthy, for its mode of presenting the gospel is unique in the New Testament. Paul stays a year and a half in Corinth. Though we have few details, he maintains himself by working at his trade as a tentmaker or leather worker. His usual strategy in a new community is to begin with the local Jewish people, but rejection by the Corinthian Jews leads to a radical turn to the Gentiles. Paul senses anew his special commission to evangelize the Gentiles (Acts 19:8–10). Mention of Gallio in Acts 18:12 is important because it provides an approximate date for the incident: Outside sources for the time of Gallio's proconsulate establish the time as late 51 or early 52.

The transition to the third journey is quite abrupt in Acts 18:22–23. The story continues through Acts 21:15. The principal ministry during this trip is a two-year stay at Ephesus. Apollos appears to be a remarkable leader; we should like to know more about him. The story of the riot in that city provides details about the area and its life. The great theater seating at least 24,000 may be visited today. The story of the young man who falls asleep while Paul is preaching at Troas is often retold.

Paul seems to have attracted opposition almost from the beginning of his Christian ministry. The hostility comes to a head when he returns to Jerusalem after the third journey. The story runs from Acts 21:27 through 26:32. You need not remember details now, but **Acts 25:1–12** with Paul's appeal to Caesar is the turning point in the action. The Roman administrative capital was at Caesarea on the Mediterranean coast. Travel between there and Jerusalem was relatively easy, so the shifts in the scene are no problem.

Paul's journey to Rome, sometimes referred to as the fourth missionary journey, is famous for its story of the shipwreck; read Acts 27 and 28. In Rome, Paul is placed under house arrest, but apparently he conducts an effective ministry.

The New Testament does not tell about the end of Paul's life. **2 Timothy 4:6–18** probably contains some of his last recorded words, but we are uncertain how that passage relates to the Acts narrative. Since our information is so sketchy, we find it difficult to fit the pastoral epistles (1 and 2 Timothy, Titus) into what we know of Paul's life from the rest of the New Testament. Some of the Church traditions in these letters seem to reflect a time later than Paul's ministry.

Suggestions for Further Study

Research

1. Read an article on John the Baptist in a Bible dictionary. What was his basic message? How did he lead the way to Jesus?

2. From your reading of the gospels, list the times when you think Jesus showed special qualities of leadership. Make a list of the passages in which you found these examples.

3. Read the summaries of the disciples found in a Bible dictionary. Which of them impressed you the most? What apostolic qualities do you think are important for the Church today?

4. Reread Acts 15. What was the role of James and Peter in guiding the Church through the conflict over accepting new members? What were the issues involved? List some issues in today's Church that you think might lead to similar difficulties.

5. Outline Paul's career by using a chronology of his letters found in a Bible dictionary.

6. Lists of the disciples are found in Matthew 10:2–4; Mark 3:16–19; Luke 6:14–16; and Acts 1:13. John mentions possibly eight of them here and there. Compare the listings found in these references.

Reflection

1. List the kinds of leadership demonstrated in the New Testament references of this session. What is the relative effectiveness of each type?

2. Which Christian leaders of the last two centuries have exerted significant influence in the modern world? Can you identify leaders who are affecting the world today?

3. In what ways is Mary's obedience a model for modern Christian leadership?

Notes

1. Joseph Fitzmeyer, *The Gospel According to Luke,* Vols. I–IX, (Garden City, NY: Doubleday, 1981), 341.

2. *Ibid.,* 341.

3. See Apostle and Disciple in HBD.

4. See also Theme 1, Session 1.

5. Known as "the son of Zebedee," as in Mark 1:19.

6. For example, 1 Corinthians 4:14–21; 11:1; 1 Thessalonians 4:1–2; Philemon 8–9, 21; and Acts 8:4–25 demonstrate that the Jerusalem leaders carry a great deal of authority. Philip is a "second team" leader (see also Acts 6:1–6; 8:26–40; 21:8–9).

7. See Theme 1, Session 4.

THEME 6

God's People Have
Kings and a King

SESSION 1

The Lord, Kings, and a United Kingdom

Session Overview

From the very early times, God's people thought of the Lord as king. When they eventually acquired a human king, he was, in a sense, a vice-regent for God. Samuel anoints Saul and later David. David consolidates the kingdom, and his dynasty lasts for over four centuries. Solomon's reign is the peak of Israel's prosperity, but under his son the kingdom splits.

Key Bible Readings

Judges 9
1 Samuel 8:4–9; 10:1,
    9–13; 10:20–25;
    11:14–15; 12:1–2,
    13–15; 15:22–23
2 Samuel 2:1–11; 5:1–
    5; 7:12–16
1 Kings 3:1–15; 11:9–
    13; 10:23–29; 12

Key Words

apostasy
royal theology

The Lord and the Kings of Earth

We cannot be certain when God's people first thought of the Lord as king. In Egypt, they were under the rule of pharaohs, who assumed the role of gods. When the power of the Lord was pitted against the pharaoh, it would have been natural for the Israelites to make the reasonable association that the Lord was their ruler as the pharaoh ruled the Egyptians.

Early legends of Mesopotamian peoples treat their rulers as having the particular, special favor of their gods. In Canaan, moreover, Israel was surrounded by peoples who thought of their gods as monarchs. It would have been surprising if Israel had not come to associate royal terminology and practices with its God (see Ex 15:18; Dt 33:5). Thus, as we consider the development and course of Israelite monarchy, we must not lose sight of the place of the Lord as the ultimate king.

The period of settlement in the promised land (as introduced in Theme 5, Session 1) was one of uneven leadership. After the strength of Joshua, there follows the age of the judges, with relative chaos mitigated by times of hope. The judges are more or less tribal leaders, often with some military prowess. In Judges 11:27, the Lord is called Judge. One of the more successful judges is Gideon, whose leadership against Midianite oppression has already been noted in Theme 1. One of his sons, Abimelech, makes an abortive attempt to set himself up as king (**Jgs 9**; the entire story is in Jgs 8:33–9:57). The time of the judges finally ends with the tribes of Israel destroying each other (Jgs 19:1–21:25). Is it any wonder the people looked for a single ruler who would unite the people and lead them out of anarchy?

The Establishment of Monarchy: Saul

The Israelites finally get a king, in circumstances like those that brought several of the judges to the fore. The Philistines pose a general threat, and the crisis leads to the crowning of Saul as king. The record in 1 Samuel 8–11 indicates that this comes about in four steps: (1) **8:4–9;** (2) **10:1, 9–13;** (3) **10:20–25;** (4) **11:14–15.** How do you see them fitting together? Summarize in your own words what happened.

We have met Saul as a national leader in Theme 5, Session 1. It is important now to reconsider his career in light of his appointment as king. Remember that the record is edited in the knowledge of what happened later. From the outset, the rule of an Israelite king is specifically evaluated according to the king's obedience to the Lord. Read **1 Samuel 12:1–2, 13–15** and note the attitude toward the monarchy. Further remarkably detailed commentary is given in 8:10–18. Chapter 13 tells how Saul disobeys the Lord and is told that his kingdom would not endure (1 Sm 13:10–14). Details of the stories seem almost primitive, as the next step (15:16–31) makes startlingly clear. Note, however, the striking oracle in **15:22–23,** which stresses the importance of obedience.

The narrative treats the shift of power from Saul to David in a series of stories that reveal a deep sense of the interplay of personalities and the course of Saul's psychological breakdown. Saul goes into a jealous rage against David as the aftermath of a parade celebrating a military victory (1 Sm 18:6–12). Saul continues to try to kill David. Saul's son, Jonathan, becomes David's fast friend and tries to protect him. Twice David spares Saul's life when opportunities for revenge arise. As an aspirant for the throne himself, David did not want to set the precedent of assassinating God's anointed. Saul's final failure in his consultation with the medium (or "witch") at Endor, and his death by his own hand in battle at Mount Gilboa by the plain of Jezreel, follow (details may be found in 1 Sm 19–31).

David

As previously noted, David's rise to prominence is interwoven with the stories about Saul. During the last years of Saul's reign, David led an almost Robin Hood–like existence. The country was divided between the northern and southern tribes, a rift that later becomes permanent. David's centralization of political and religious authority in Jerusalem when he becomes king reflects his attempts to overcome these divisions. The first stage is told in **2 Samuel 2:1–11,** when David is anointed king in the south at Hebron; the dynasty of Saul survives in the north. The rivalries and machinations of David's military leaders, especially Joab, and the northern forces under Abner tell a grim tale (2 Sm 2:8–3:39).

David becomes king of the united country, **2 Samuel 5:1–5,** and establishes his capital at Jerusalem, which is strategically near the border between Judah and Israel. (From this point forward the term "Israel" will refer to the ten northern tribes and "Judah" will refer to the remaining two in the south.) Subsequently, the Ark is brought to Jerusalem, so the religious and political consolidation is complete in about the year 1000 BC. David proposes to build a "house" for God, but is told instead that God will build a house for him (2 Sm 7:1–17). His son, Solomon, will build the Temple. God promises that David's house and kingdom "shall be made sure forever," that is, the Dynasty will be perpetual (see **2 Sm 7:12–16**). The text tells more about how David organizes his rule and neutralizes his enemies.

The stories are not limited to glory and praise of the king. Up to the point of his kingship, David is praised and finds success because of his devotion to God. Once he is in office, however, he begins to act not for God but for himself. The sordid episode of how he marries Bathsheba in chapter 11 reveals a serious weakness in David's character. In 2 Samuel 12:1–14, the prophet Nathan brings him to devastating self-condemnation. David's willingness to accept God's judgment is told in 2 Samuel 12:15–23. This set of stories ends with the birth of Solomon.

A lengthy section, 13:1–19:15, deals with the internal dissension in David's family as the result of his sin. It describes the rape of Tamar by her half brother Amnon and the revenge of another of David's sons, Absalom. Absalom appears to have been strong-willed, ambitious, unscrupulous, and spoiled. He leads a rebellion against his father and is temporarily successful. David's disobedience to God has led to tragedy for the whole country. David experiences deep personal anguish after the execution of Absalom by Joab (see 2 Sm 19:1). The remaining material may be passed over for now.

Solomon

Solomon succeeds David as king and establishes his throne (1 Kgs 1–2). Under his rule, the king-dom is quite different. David acquired territory by warfare and welded the north and the south into a union, however shaky. Solomon consolidates the kingdom by political shrewdness and military organization. He takes full advantage of the period of peace without interference from outside civilizations.

His reign has an auspicious religious beginning. Read **1 Kings 3:1–15**. Solomon's prosperity is seen as the result of his willingness to obey God. The building of the temple is a far-reaching achievement (1 Kgs 5–7), and the dedicatory prayer attributed to Solomon is impressive (1 Kgs 8:22–61). This temple and its successors become a focus for Jewish religion. Solomon's reputation for wisdom is marked at this point, but we shall consider it in detail in Theme 8.

The writer of 1 Kings hints at misgivings about Solomon's religious "pluralism" from the outset of his reign (note 3:3b). This is associated with his prolific marriages to foreign wives (which probably have political significance). In chapter 11, the negativism becomes specific; **1 Kings 11:9–13** may be compared with Deuteronomy 7:1–5, where the religious peril associated with foreign wives who bring the worship of their foreign gods with them is specified. Solomon's disobedience is seen as laying a foundation for future disaster. Try to distinguish in your mind the nature of the monarchy under Saul, David, and Solomon. Read **1 Kings 10:23–29** for some indication of how far national development has come.

What a change has taken place in Israel-Judah! Now they are a nation with international relations. The king's court is elaborately pretentious and grand. Solomon's political and military establishment is extensive. He adopts "modern" ways (for example, the use of chariots). But the cost of all of this for the people is the importation of foreign gods and the oppression of forced labor (1 Kgs 5:27).

Beginning about this time, a kind of "royal theology" develops. The king is portrayed as the adoptive vice-regent or "son" of the Lord. It may be seen in what are often called "royal" psalms (see Psalms 2, 21, 45, 72, and 110). These may be used in celebrations where the king plays a central role. They are balanced by other psalms, where the ultimate rule of the Lord is affirmed (see particularly Ps 93; 95; 96:10; 97:1; 99:1–5).

All this magnificence appears to be more than the nation can bear. Only two generations back it was still a rather loose confederation of tribes. Disintegration threatens the nation in 1 Kings 11:26–40, and the death of Solomon (11:41–43) bodes ill for the future.

Division of the Kingdom

The intertribal rivalries, which seem never to have ceased, flare up violently at this juncture. Solomon's son Rehoboam is unable to maintain the centralized power of his father. The subsequent division of the kingdom dominates the political picture and affects the religious situation from this time on; read **1 Kings 12,** which tells the critical story. Though Rehoboam is not a good king, the dynasty of David continues and indeed survives as long as Judah remains a kingdom. Jeroboam, who led the rebellion of the northern tribes, does not have a long–lived dynasty. His son Nadab rules three years and is assassinated. Israel, without a capital and cultic center, has frequently changing dynasties.

Jeroboam's success as a revolutionary is short-lived. The narrative plainly associates this with his religious apostasy (note 1 Kgs 13:1–5). The breakup of Israelite national life focuses upon the isolation of the northern tribes from the central worship in the Jerusalem temple and their failure to follow David's successors, who rule in consequence of the Lord's promise. Jeroboam's sin becomes a byword, and the later narrative stigmatizes him for it (see 15:26, 34; 2

Kgs 23:15). The measure of royal success is henceforth measured to the degree of conformity to the Lord's "way."

Beginning with the story of David, we have the parallel records of the "chronicler." Bibles that have any notes at all indicate in margins or footnotes the parallels between Kings and Chronicles. Sometimes the materials are identical; in other instances, there is substantial difference. Chronicles treats only the kings of Judah, reflecting the story from a southern viewpoint. The parallels make the amount of material to be read prohibitive in the compass of this study, so we shall move back and forth between the two narratives to maintain continuity but keep the references manageable.

Suggestions for Further Study

Research

1. Look up the references to Saul, David, and Solomon in a Bible dictionary. What contribution did each make to the building of the kingdom? To what does the Bible attribute their successes? To what does it attribute their failures?

2. Look up the articles on Rehoboam and Jeroboam I in a Bible dictionary. What do they tell you about the conditions which led to the revolt of the northern tribes against Judah?

Reflection

1. Few kings rule today in our world, and the role of monarchy has changed dramatically in modern times. How does this affect our idea(s) of God as "king"? How else could we picture the role of God in the universe as we

perceive it now? How do these images help or hinder your study of the Bible?

2. Solomon built on David's work of uniting the kingdom, building important national symbols such as his palace and the Temple to match the values of the surrounding cultures. He did so through the use of heavy taxation, forced labor, and the introduction of many pagan Gods. In what ways do we put the values of this world before God? In what ways have we allowed the values of our society to eat away at our faith in God?

3. You may want to memorize the following verses:

- 1 Samuel 15:22
- 2 Samuel 1:19–20; 2:26
- Psalm 2:7

SESSION 2

Kings and the Divided Kingdom

Session Overview

The northern kingdom, Israel, undergoes many changes in dynasty, and most of the kings are not obedient to God. Israel is overthrown by Assyria. Judah continues the Davidic dynasty and, despite dark days, has some notable rulers. The fall of Jerusalem and Exile in Babylon mark the end of the kingdom. Much later, a brief period of national freedom is achieved by the Maccabees.

Key Bible Readings

1 Kings 14:22–31;
21:1–26
2 Chronicles 22:10–
23:21
2 Kings 17:1–24;
22:3–13
Jeremiah 52:1–16
Psalms 89:2–5, 36–41,
47, 50

Key Words

Hasmonean
Megiddo
Exile

The First Years of Division

Jeroboam's son reigns after him in Israel, but he is assassinated and succeeded by a new dynasty, which lasts only two generations. You will find the biblical text somewhat difficult to follow, especially when parallel rulers in Israel and Judah are described. Many times their names are similar, adding to the confusion. Refer to the chronology chart in Appendix 7 which provides a list of the kings of Judah and Israel. It is more important to understand the intent of the text than to memorize its detailed content.

It is fairly obvious that the writer is adapting sources that have not otherwise survived (see 1 Kgs 11:41; 14:19; 15:31; 16:5). Several references, such as 14:29, refer to "Chronicles," but it is very doubtful that these are the books we call by that name since our Chronicles were produced after the books of Kings.

The moral and religious situation in Judah appears to be scarcely any better than in Israel; read **1 Kings 14:22–31.** The inroads by foreign powers ultimately bring to ruin the fortunes of both south and north. Although Rehoboam's grandson Asa is generally credited with faithfulness to God, he bribes the king of Syria to attack Israel, a policy that eventually leads to destruction (2 Chr 16:1–8). Omri founds a strong dynasty in Israel (c. 876–842 BC). He comes to the throne in a chaotic time and establishes a new capital at Samaria. Years later Assyrian records refer to Israel as "the house of Omri." This "international" mention contrasts with the terse record in 1 Kings. Again this is probably because of Omri's religious shortcomings. His son Ahab (c. 869–850 BC) marries a pagan, the Phoenician princess Jezebel.

Kings in the Times of Elijah and Elisha

Ahab receives rather extensive attention because of the activity of Elijah at this time. Judah has a strong king, Jehoshaphat, during the same period (details of his reign are given in 2 Chr 17–20). The careers of the two kings intersect when they become allies against Syria (1 Kgs 22 and 2 Chr 18). This proves to be a misadventure for Judah and a fatal move for Ahab. The story is fascinating, particularly because of the activities of the prophets involved. The single, memorable appearance of Micaiah is noted in Theme 5, Session 2.

Ahab and Jezebel are infamous, the epitome of opposition to the way of the Lord in Israel (see 1 Kgs 16:33). Their crucial confrontation with Elijah is treated in Theme 1, Session 2. Another story about the evil royal couple is in **1 Kings 21:1–26.**

The contents of 2 Kings is a formidable challenge in our study. The details summarized here are important to remember, because they contribute to understanding the sweep of the biblical story and because they are important for "biblical literacy." The names of the kings are hard to keep straight; in several instances, kings of Israel and Judah even have the same name; in other instances, there are inconsistencies in spelling. Furthermore, it is impossible to arrive at a chronology that will satisfy all biblical experts, but the variations are relatively small.

Elisha succeeds Elijah and plays the role of king-maker, not only in Israel but in Syria. He anoints Jehu, who puts an end to Omri's dynasty. Jehu also deals a severe blow to Baal worship, but the writer of Kings insists that Jehu did not abandon the sins of Jeroboam I.

Evil family relations seem to survive and spread at this period. Jehoshaphat's son marries Athaliah, Omri's granddaughter (daughter of Ahab and Jezebel). When her son dies after a short reign, she assumes rule in Judah. She is the only woman to become sole ruler in Judah or Israel, and her reign is a break in the succession of David's line. She tries to purge completely the male heirs of David. But her grandson, the infant Joash, is saved. Read how the boy Joash becomes king in **2 Chronicles 22:10–23:21**.

The reign of Joash is important because of the restoration made in the temple. The requisite funds are collected in an interesting way (see 2 Kgs 12:9–15). On the negative side, Joash buys off the king of Syria to keep him from attacking Jerusalem, thus signaling again the declining fortunes of the monarchy. In 2 Kings 13:10 and 14:23, we observe the coincidence of kings of Judah and Israel (Joash and Jehoash) with variations of the same name.

Read 2 Kings 13:14–20 and note how important the prophet's role is in relation to the king's power (recall Nathan and David). This indicates a sort of indirect recognition that the Lord is ultimately the true king. Observe also the striking example of how the prophets use symbolic actions to convey the divine message.

The End of Israel

The shifting circumstances of Israel and Judah are reflected in the catalog of kings. The two kingdoms go to war with each other, and at one point the wall of Jerusalem is actually breached. The territorial expansion of Israel reaches its zenith under Jeroboam II (786–746 BC). He receives brief mention in 2 Kings 14:23–29, for "he did evil in the sight of the Lord," as did Jeroboam I. The reign of Jeroboam II, however, lasts forty years, and he recovers lost territory. These expansionist activities brought wealth to a new class of landowners, but at the expense of creating a class of servants and slaves who were exploited by the rich. It is these social and economic abuses which provoked the sharp oracles from the prophet Amos (for example, Am 2:6–8). Jeroboam II's son, Zechariah, in contrast to his father, reigns only six months (2 Kgs 15:8–12), foreshadowing the end of the northern kingdom.

The demise of Israel is swift. There is a rapid succession of kings, and for a while they pay tribute to the Assyrian king, known in secular history as Tiglath-Pileser III (745–727 BC). Attempts to join alliances against Assyria prove disastrous and Samaria soon falls to the Assyrians (722 BC). Since it is extremely difficult to arrive at exact chronology of this early time, the year of the fall of Samaria is sometimes given as 721 BC. The writer of 2 Kings is sure that Israel's end comes for religious reasons; read **2 Kings 17:1–24** for the details. This territory has a population of mixed nationality from this time on, which lays the foundation for later antipathy between Jews and Samaritans as reflected in the New Testament.

The End of Judah

Two more kings of Judah are to be noted. During the reign of Hezekiah, the land was delivered for Sennacherib of Assyria—a story already treated in Theme 1, Session 2, and in Theme 5, Session 2. Lengthy attention is given to Hezekiah in 2 Chronicles 29–32. His great-grandson Josiah comes to the throne as a boy.

The chronicler gives good marks for Josiah's early years (2 Chr 34:1–7). The most notable series of events in his time begins with the repair of the Temple and the discovery there of a "book of the law," **2 Kings 22:3–13.** Josiah institutes sweeping reforms based on this book. The year is usually reckoned to be 621 BC, just a century after the fall of Samaria. A special Passover is kept, and the covenant relation with the Lord is celebrated anew. Because of these reforms, Jerusalem becomes the cultic center for God's people. Any worship of the Lord from any other center such as Shechem, Bethel, or Dan is considered evil. Because of the details of the reforms, it is generally agreed that the book that was found was an early edition of our Book of Deuteronomy. The books of the Bible from Joshua through 2 Kings are written from the point of view of the deuteronomist reform, thus the continual criticism of the kings of Israel for worshiping outside of Jerusalem.

Josiah dies in a battle with the king of Egypt near Megiddo (see Chr 35:20–27). He is the last notable king of Judah and perhaps one of its best. The downfall of the kingdom is swift after his time; the end comes a little over twenty years later.

The last four kings live with almost constant foreign interference, first by Egypt, then by Babylon. Zedekiah, the last of Judah, is a puppet under Babylon. His two predecessors have been deported to Babylon, and his reign is insignificant. When he engages in a rebellion, Nebuchadnezzar besieges and overthrows Jerusalem, leveling the city and destroying the Temple. We have already noted Jeremiah's relation to these events (Theme 5, Session 2). Read the details in **Jeremiah 52:1–16.** The year is 587 or 586 BC.

When There Is No King

This is the end of kingship in Judah and Israel in the sense of national monarchy. Now God's people are under other rulers, not their own kings. The Exile is a time of reflection and evaluation of the people's relationship with God. The belief that God fought for Israel as a warrior, defeating all enemies and promising all blessing, has to be reevaluated in terms of their experience of defeat. They saw the tragedy of the loss of their national existence as the just punishment for their disobedience to the Lord. They also began to arrive at a deeper and more spiritual view of God's action in the world. As a consequence of their reflection, the people began to think about their relationship with God in two ways:

(1) Their belief in the sovereign power of their God and the related sense of their own divine destiny lead them to attribute some acts of foreign rulers to the direction of God's will. In Isaiah 45:1, the Persian king Cyrus is called God's "anointed," thus giving him what we should call a "messianic" role (see also 2 Chr 36:22–23). This is not a new theological development, but it plays a new part in the consideration of the kingship of God.

(2) The Israelite people expected a restoration of the human line of kings. God's covenant-promise to David was the principal basis for this hope (see 2 Sm 7:16 for the specific statement; see also Ps 132:11–18). The tension produced by the collapse of the Davidic monarchy is boldly stated in **Psalms 89:2–5, 36–41, 47, 50.** At the end of the Exile there appears among those who return to Jerusalem a leader named Zerubbabel, who is listed as a grandson of one of the last kings of Judah. As such, he is a descendant of David, and we might expect to find an effort to restore the kingly line.

The prophet Haggai gives some ground for this (Hg 2:20–23), but Zechariah indicates that the power passed into priestly hands (Zec 6:9–14), and we hear no more of Zerubbabel until Luke mentions him as an ancestor of Jesus (Lk 3:27).

The Maccabaean revolution (introduced in Theme 1, Session 2) brings God's people a brief time of national glory. It is in this period that the cycle of legendary stories in Daniel 1–6 was written about 167–164 BC to comfort the persecuted Jews during the reign of the Seleucid Greek king Antiochus IV Epiphanes. The stories tell about a young Jew and his friends in the Babylonian court during the Exile. The purpose of the stories is to glorify the triumph of their devotion to God and thus provide reassurance for others of God's people who are facing the critical challenge of paganism. The lesson is clearly stated in Daniel 6:25–28; the kingship of the God of the Jews is absolutely superior to the rulers of Babylonia, Media, and Persia— names that symbolized the Seleucid Greek rulers who persecuted the Jews at the time Daniel was written.

The succession of Hasmonean rulers achieves a semblance of royal posture and power which lasts about a century, but there is no move to reestablish the throne of David. When imperial Rome subdues and occupies the land (63 BC), the people turn to the desperate hope that somehow God will intervene and establish a king from the house of David. Recall that the king is anointed for office and that the Hebrew word for "anoint" gives us the term "messiah," so we refer to the expectation of a restored kingship as "messianic." In the Roman period the hopes of the Jews were not uniform in detail, but they were widely held. They underlie the New Testament, and we shall return to the subject in the next session.

Suggestions for Further Study

Research

1. Read the article on First and Second Kings in a Bible dictionary. What information does

it contain that shows how the rulers of Israel and Judah were evaluated?

2. Examine the chronology of the kings of Israel and Judah in Appendix 7. Choose six of the kings and read the articles about them in a Bible dictionary. Learn at least one important detail from the life of each of the following rulers:

Jehoshaphat	Joash of Judah
Rehoboam	Jeroboam II
Jeroboam I	Hezekiah
Omri	Josiah
Ahab	Athaliah

3. Read the articles on messiah and the Book of Daniel in a Bible dictionary. What do they tell you about how Israel kept faith in God's sovereignty in the exilic and post-exilic periods?

Reflection

1. What modern examples can you think of where people faced national or racial despair? How did they handle it?

2. The stories about Daniel raise two questions: How do individuals cope with an absolute confrontation by a pagan government? How do people respond to a government demand that is counter to personal religious belief?

SESSION 3

Jesus and the Kingdom of God

Session Overview

For many Jews, dreams of a restoration of their kingdom surfaced in the message of John the Baptist and became a key in the proclamation of Jesus. God's rule is embodied in a special, new way in Jesus' mission and destiny. Paul develops the faith that Jesus is uniquely the anointed one so long hoped for. Revelation focuses the future of God's kingship on the victory of Jesus Christ.

Key Bible Readings

Mark 4:26–29
Matthew 13:44–52
Mark 12:35–37
Matthew 22:1–14
1 Corinthians 15:24–28
Revelation 11:15–18
1 Timothy 1:17

Key Words

kingdom of God/heaven
repent

The Message of John the Baptist

When John the Baptist comes on the scene, the Jews have been under Roman rule for about a century. It has been twice that long since they have heard the voice of a prophet. John is conscious of standing on the brink of a new age, so it is no wonder he creates a stir. Our gospels mark this (Mt 3:5–6; Mk 1:5), and he is mentioned by the Jewish historian, Josephus.

Matthew says that the keynote of John's preaching is "Repent, for the kingdom of heaven is at hand" (3:2). All the gospels present John and his ministry as an immediate anticipation of a "mightier" one, who is to usher in a new time. The gospels say in various ways that John claims to have divine confirmation that this new time will be marked by Jesus' new revelation of God.

Jesus' Key Proclamation

In the Gospel of Mark when Jesus begins his public preaching in Galilee, his message picks up John's theme: " 'This is the time of fulfillment. The kingdom of God is at hand. Repent, and believe in the gospel' " (Mk 1:15). The gospels agree that Jesus intimates that somehow, in his person and mission, the divine demands of God's sovereign power are confronting the people and requiring a radical reordering of their lives ("repentance"). This immediacy is clearly indicated by "at hand."

Here we must examine the phrase "kingdom of God" more closely. Bible scholars agree that "kingdom" in both Old and New Testaments refers first to sovereignty, reign, or rule and only after that to the place where the rule is exercised. Recall Omri and Jeroboam II, whose reigns are found wanting by the writer of Kings because of their religious deficiencies even though the political extension of their nation is at maximum development (1 Kgs 16:23–26; 2 Kgs 14:23–29). Now Jesus proclaims, not the end of Roman provincial domination and the reestablishment of the Hebrew nation, but the mighty presence of God as the King so long eclipsed by earthly rulers.

In Mark 4:11 (and the parallels already cited in the last paragraph), Jesus speaks about the "secret" of the kingdom—the Greek word gives us the term "mystery." This is illustrated by a parable in **Mark 4:26–29.** Read also **Matthew 13:44–52.** Jesus' message is so surprising that he regularly couches it in stories so that it may stay with the hearers and move them to ponder its meaning until they are able to internalize its fundamental import. Our long familiarity with Jesus' words may become a barrier to grasping their challenging message for ourselves. We should be alert to a new openness to Jesus' proclamation of the kingdom of God.

A similar approach may provide a key to understanding Jesus' attitude toward the messiah-role. In Jesus' time there was no fixed technical meaning for the term messiah. "In some circles, it denoted a political or priestly agent sent from God as part of the triumphant establishment of God's power."[1] During the first century AD, the Jews became increasingly restive under the Ro-

mans. There were various protests and revolts and various messiahs. These were seen simply as political leaders to throw off the Roman yoke and set up a Jewish kingdom. Jesus makes it clear that this is inconsistent with his understanding of the kingship of God and the consequent purpose of his mission. On one occasion, Jesus enters a discussion about the title and bases his enigmatic teaching on Psalm 110:1; read **Mark 12:35–37.** Perhaps his reticence about such history-laden titles explains in part his seeming preference for the less loaded designation "son of man."

Kingdom, Present and Future

Jesus speaks of the coming of the kingdom sometimes as though it is present, sometimes as though future. The most familiar words are in the first part of Matthew 6:10, the Lord's Prayer: "your kingdom come." The second part of Matthew 6:10 (not in the parallel Lk 11:2) is usually considered to be a further interpretation: "your will be done, on earth as in heaven." Since Jesus certainly thought that God's will is to be realized as fully as possible here and now, we probably ought to categorize the kingdom of God as both present and future. Some gospel passages are notoriously difficult in this respect. Compare Matthew 16:28; Mark 9:1; Luke 9:27. What do you make of the different nuances in these parallel passages? It seems we must analyze carefully each statement of Jesus and interpret it in the light of all we know about his whole proclamation.

Jesus speaks about entering the kingdom, and it is clear that he means a relationship, not a place (see Mt 5:20; 7:21; Mk 10:15, 23–25; Jn 3:5). He also speaks of receiving and of inheriting the kingdom. These sayings could refer to either the present or the future.

Several of Jesus' sayings in Matthew refer to a king, where the implication is evident that

God is the king (see 18:23–25; **Mt 22:1–14**). When Jesus mentions the king's son, we quite readily jump to the identification of Jesus as God's son, but this is in light of generations of Christian theologizing. Jesus' hearers would perhaps understand the reference to God and the marriage celebration, but the identification of the son would almost surely elude them.

After all, as far as we can tell, Jesus avoided assuming any kingly titles or prerogatives. It is ironic (though probably clear to the gospel writers) that at his trial Jesus is charged with pretensions of kingship (Mk 15:2, 9, 12, 18) and Pilate's final mockery is the title-board on the cross, "the King of the Jews" (Jn 19:19–22).

The Gospel of John mentions the kingdom of God only in Jesus' discussion with Nicodemus (3:3, 5). The idea, however, is presented in other ways. Statements about "life" and "eternal life" imply a kind of equivalent—particularly references to "having" life (see Jn 3:16, 5:24; 6:40; 10:28; 20:31). The "I am" affirmations of Jesus are in many instances indirect references to prerogatives of God (see Jn 6:30–35; 8:12; 10:11; 11:25; Ps 23:1; Ez 34:15).

Paul, the Kingdom, and the Christ

The theme of Paul's preaching while a prisoner in Rome is, according to Acts, "the kingdom of God" (28:30–31). Paul mentions the phrase only rarely in his letters (Rom 14:17; 1 Cor 6:9–10; 15:50). Perhaps he uses the phrase sparingly because much of his writing is addressed to churches that have little Jewish tradition, or perhaps the socio-political context of his ministry rendered the phrase liable to misunderstanding. Kingdom of God might convey all sorts of nonbiblical conceptions in a pagan environment. But Paul does definitely proclaim that God is sovereign, for example, **1 Corinthians 15:24–28.**

There is another facet to Paul's proclamation that relates to his infrequent use of kingdom of God. The designation of Jesus as "Christ" occurs with unusual frequency in Paul's letters,[2] and often he uses the phrase "in Christ" to characterize relationships that in the synoptic gospels might be referred to the kingdom of God. Examples are Romans 9:1; 12:5; 1 Corinthians 3:1; 2 Corinthians 2:14; Philippians 2:1; 1 Thessalonians 4:16. When we remember that "Christ" is the Greek equivalent to "messiah," it is clear that Paul has made the connection that could not be understood until after Jesus' victory over death. Jesus is indeed the Messiah, although he did not fulfill the expected role nor has he re-established a national, Davidic monarchy. With Paul, this affirmation about Jesus' identity in the historical expectation of the people of God becomes so pervasive that "Christ" appears as a name for the ascended Jesus, even when the messianic overtone is quite sublimated. This substitution of "Christ" for "Jesus" however, does not occur as often as we assume; consider Romans 8:17; Galatians 6:14, 17; 1 Thessalonians 2:6–7.

In Mark, the first gospel to be written, Jesus is finally identified by Peter as the Messiah. But then Jesus goes on to explain three times that he is not a political messiah, but a suffering messiah.

The Kingdom and the Church

In this interim period between the proclamation of the kingdom of God in the preaching and saving activity of Jesus Christ and the fulfillment of the kingdom in the last days, Jesus established the redeemed community of the Church. The Church takes the place of Israel (see Mt 16:18).

The Church is a sign and anticipation of the kingdom where those who are called by God are to reflect what it means to live in hope of the final redemption for all in Jesus Christ. This understanding of the role of the Church is found in the documents of Vatican II:

> Henceforth the Church, endowed with the gifts of her founder and faithfully observing her precepts of charity, humility, and self-denial, receives the mission of proclaiming and establishing among all peoples the kingdom of Christ and God, and she is, on earth, the seed and beginning of that kingdom. While she slowly grows to maturity, the Church longs for the completed kingdom and, with all her strength, hopes and desires to be united in glory with her king.[3]

The Kingdom Forever

We can look at this last element of the final return of Christ only briefly here, but we shall reserve detailed study of future-hope until Theme 10. Paul writes very briefly, almost cryptically, about the future reign of Christ in 1 Corinthians 15:20–28. In verses 24 and 25, Paul seems to treat the reign of Christ as a perfecting preparation for the end. The finale will find "God all in all." God's rule will be complete and absolute. This fulfills the phrases in Jesus' prayer: "on earth as in heaven." The Church celebrates the kingship of Christ in the liturgical observance of the Feast of Christ the King on the last Sunday of the liturgical year.

The Book of Revelation uses king and kingdom imagery often. In 1:6, Jesus Christ makes God's people "a kingdom"; see also 1:9; 5:10. In **Revelation 11:15–18,** God is praised in a heavenly hymn for inaugurating a kingdom where he will reign forever. In 17:14, "the lamb" is the conqueror, called "king of kings"; and the same title is applied in 19:16 to the Christ-figure in another guise.

The same appellation appears in Pauline tradition in 1 Timothy 6:15. In a benediction in the same letter at **1 Timothy 1:17,** the somewhat different phrase "king of the ages" is ascribed

to "the only God." This supreme attribution ties together what we have pursued in this theme. (It is significant that Jewish liturgy to this day often repeats the Hebrew equivalent when addressing God.)

We may note, finally, that the scripture emphasizes the conviction that God will reign in fullness. There are only passing pictures of what conditions will be like in that reign. Speculation about details of the future of the kingdom of God has scant biblical warrant. The certainty of God's reign has been established "in Christ." Vatican II comments "All men are called to this union with Christ, who is the light of the world, from whom we go forth, through whom we live, and towards whom our whole life is directed."[4] In Revelation 20:4–6, God's people and Christ share in the beginning of the final kingship. In 21:24, all the glory of earthly kings comes into the new Jerusalem. In 22:3–5 there is a final glorious summary of the reign "forever and ever."

Suggestions for Further Study

Research

1. Read about the social and political situation of the Jews in the time of Jesus. What does this tell you about the expectations they might have about a messiah? (see IOT, chapter 1, for information).

2. Using a Bible dictionary, research Jesus' teaching about the kingdom. Make a list of what the kingdom of heaven/God is "like" in Jesus' parables.

3. Using a Bible dictionary, explore the terms used by Paul and John describing the kingdom. What term does John use more frequently?

4. Look up "salvation" in a Bible dictionary. What does it say about how the kingdom arrived in Jesus and how it is coming in the future?

Reflection

1. Which parables of the kingdom most influence your understanding of it? In what ways and why?

2. How do you think of the kingdom of God as present? As future? How do you reconcile these two aspects of the kingdom?

3. How has your concept of the kingdom of God been modified by studying this theme?

4. You may wish to memorize the Beatitudes: Matthew 5:1–12. Begin by learning verses 3–5 and 10.

Notes

1. HBD 630.
2. Statistically, 72 percent of the New Testament occurrences of the Greek term *christos* are in Paul's letters.
3. *Constitution on the Church* 5.
4. *Ibid.,* 2.

THEME 7

God's Law Demands a Righteous People

SESSION 1

The Law of God

Session Overview

The material in Genesis through Deuteronomy contains the instruction that regulates the moral and religious life of God's people. The several law codes in these books have requirements that became the basis for standing in right relationship with God. There are many other details that apply to a previous time, for the material is recorded in a historical framework.

Key Bible Readings

Exodus 24:3–8
Genesis 17:1–2; 15:6;
   22:1–18; 31:49
Leviticus 19:2
Exodus 20:1–17
Deuteronomy 5:6–21
Exodus 25:21–22
Leviticus 19:17–18
Deuteronomy 6:4–9,
   20–25; 30:11–20

Key Words

Covenant Code (Book
   of the Covenant)
Decalogue
Deuteronomic Code
Holiness Code
kosher
mediator
righteousness
Shema

Background of the Torah

Jews refer to the first five books of the Bible as the Torah, and it is the most sacred part of the scriptures for them. The word "Torah" in Hebrew means "instruction" or "teaching," and it is understood to be God's instruction(s). The Hebrews believed that God's will is revealed in the Torah. Often in the rest of the Bible, Torah is called "the Law." When we hear the word "law" we are likely to interpret this in terms of oppressive regulation or unwelcome restraint. Jews did not (and do not) so regard Torah.

For the Hebrews, then, the Law epitomizes the forms of response that God's gracious covenant calls forth. Thus, while we have difficulty thinking of law apart from laws, Law in Torah context is more than laws. We must keep these distinctions in mind as we study this material. In terms of our theme title, Law is not an end in itself: its purpose is to produce a condition in God's people that is called "righteousness." Righteousness can be defined as the state of being in the right or of being vindicated.[1] In the biblical context, it means living as a friend in a harmonious relationship with God. The nature of the relationship is that the people recognize that they have been rescued by God. Living in harmony with God means worshiping God in truth and acting toward one another with the same compassion one has received from God.

The context for understanding the Hebrew experience of Law is the Exodus event. The Hebrew people had been slaves in the rigid religious structures of the Egyptian religious/political system. They had been delivered from slavery by God in an act of grace. Brought to Sinai, they were now being called to form a bond of covenant with the gracious God who had brought them to freedom.

The best-known part of Old Testament law is the Ten Commandments or Ten Words. The setting is at Sinai: note the Exodus connection in 20:2. The Ten Words are a self-contained unit. They are also, however, a kind of prologue to the section that follows, Exodus 20:22–23:19, which is often referred to as the Book of the Covenant, or the Covenant Code. The words and the code are considered a "gift" of the Lord to his people.[2]

The order of events in Exodus 19–24 is not intended to provide a historical picture of how things actually happened at Sinai; indeed, we can hardly recover a sequence of details. There are extensive portions of the biblical text cited in this session. The more you read, the better, but it is helpful to read through the *Resource Book* material first. In this study, we will be concentrating on the ideas and religious duties rather than the circumstances of their formulation. In **Exodus 24:3–8,** notice how the people's relationship with God is based on three premises. The first is to be bound to God in a covenant relationship (as was seen in Theme 2); the second is worship of the true God (treated in Theme 9); the third is to follow God's law as a response to the gift of freedom which has been given. The response of God's people is inextricably bound with these three motifs. In Deuteronomy 30, tangible rewards are promised to those who respond rightly to God's commands. The relationship between God and the people is a very personal one (Dt 30:6, 11–14).

Genesis

The interconnection of God's promise, command, and the people's response is written into the Hebrews' earliest history and even their "prehistory." Command and promise are connected in the Eden stories (see Gn 2:15–17). Human accountability to God's requirements is highlighted by Adam and Eve's primeval sin (Gn 3) and by Cain's fratricide (Gn 4:8–16). In the Noah saga, the reason for the destroying flood is the wickedness of humanity (6:5–7, 11, 12); Noah's righteousness is the reason he was saved (6:8, 9; 7:1). God makes a covenant for Noah's descendants that places demands upon them (9:1–17).

Abraham becomes the model of Old Testament righteousness. In **Genesis 17:1–2,** the Lord challenges the patriarch and makes a covenant offer. The succinct testimony in **Genesis 15:6** is taken up by Paul and James in the New Testament as evidence of Abraham's standing with God (see Rom 4:3, 9; Gal 3:6; Jas 2:23). James's reference to Abraham as "the friend of God" is derived from 2 Chronicles 20:7 and Isaiah 41:8. Some of the stories about Abraham do not show his best side (Gn 12:10–20; 16:1–9; 20:1–18; 21:9–16). His reputation rests on other chapters of his life. Abraham's entertainment of three divine strangers is one such (chapter 18), and perhaps most noteworthy is **Genesis 22:1–18.** This latter plot is grim, but Abraham trusts God implicitly, and God shows mercy, graciousness, and steadfast love. The story shows that Abraham's faith in God's promises was seen as an act that brought righteousness to him. Abraham expressed the "right" attitude of humanity seeking to live in relationship with God.[3]

Other narratives about the patriarchs show the inexorable effects of failure to act righteously. In Genesis 27, Jacob usurps the birthright-blessing belonging to his older brother Esau, and Jacob subsequently suffers from the treachery of others and the consequences of his own acts. In one story, his father-in-law, Laban, tricks him, and the two continue to try to outwit each other. Their final agreement is marked by setting up a memorial heap of stones at Mispah. The familiar words given in **Genesis 31:49** are not intended as a "benediction" but as the confirmation of a pact of nonaggression. Later Jacob has to confront Esau, and he is "very much frightened" (32:6–8). The night before their meeting, Jacob wrestles with an unknown adversary, and receives the name "Israel" as a result of the confrontation (32:22–32). Fortunately, the ensuing meeting with Esau is friendly.

In the Joseph story-cycle, personal integrity ("righteousness" in God's view) is prominent. Joseph's moral uprightness is shown in the incident with Potiphar's wife (chapter 39). Joseph's brothers suffer for their cruelty to him when they meet him in Egypt (Gn 42:6–38; 43:18; 44:1–34). In the end, however, Joseph attributes the outcome to God's good will (Gn 45:5–8; 50:20).

The Law Codes

We have noted that the Law promulgated at Sinai is often called the Covenant Code, and it is rightly tied to the narrative events at that point. In the rest of the Pentateuch, most of the storyline is related in one way or another to the further establishment and interpretation of the law and its relationship to the corporate life of the people. In Leviticus, a succinct summary of how God's people are to live stresses "holiness." Read **Leviticus 19:2.** In Deuteronomy, the same purpose is focused on justice. Read Deuteronomy 6:24–25.

Commenting on the law codes, Paul Hanson writes:

> The Hebrew Bible's careful attention to laws and ordinances, therefore, is not a sign of impoverishment, but of its persistent attention to the strictures that affect everyday life. As the author of James insisted, a living faith in God will express itself in acts of compassion toward those in need. And a living community of faith will translate its experiences of divine grace into forms of community that safeguard the liberating dynamic that nurtures healing and reconciliation in all areas of life.[4]

But the people did not always act "holy," nor did they faithfully follow God's commands. Even the leaders were fallible. Moses was disobedient to God at "the waters of Meribah" (Nm 20:10–13). Miriam and Aaron spoke against Moses (chapter 12), and so did others (chapter 16). As a consequence of their disobedience, they did not see the promised land. Some of the actions of the people at this stage may be disturbing to us. Our reaction is the result of sensibilities that have been developed over thousands of years of life as God's people living under God's Law and gaining experience in the covenant relationship. An example of the earlier expectations of righteousness which Christians may find confusing is the jealous zeal for the Lord manifested by Phinehas (Nm 25:1–13).

The giving of God's covenants and Law is usually associated with human mediators. Noah and Abraham played such roles, but Moses is the classic example (see Dt 5:2–5; 18:15–19; and recall Jn 1:17, "through Moses"). We shall see in the next session how the application of the Law becomes the task of the prophets.

In Torah, the giving of the Law has, as it were, two foci. The narrative spreads the first presentation through Exodus and Leviticus (with two concentrated sections); the second is in Deuteronomy—a name which means "the second law" in Greek. We have noted the probable connection of the Deuteronomic material with the reform under Josiah. The final literary form of all of Torah is later than that and was influenced by the theological concerns of the later editors. At this point, we need to make a somewhat extensive survey of the material.

Exodus

Review the Decalogue (Ex 20:1–17), which is the quintessence of the Law. Tradition says these ten "words" were written on stone tablets, which the Lord gave to Moses on Sinai and which were placed in "the Ark of the Covenant" (Nm 10–33). Echoes of the Ten Commandments are scattered throughout the Law. They are restated in **Deuteronomy 5:6–21;** study the difference.

The remaining chapters of Exodus are briefly outlined below. Read as much of the text as you can, and note particularly what is emphasized here.

Chapter 21: Treatment of slaves and other human beings (note 21:23–37). This section is known as the *lex talionis.* The purpose of this section is not merely the enforcement of rigorous justice, but also the prevention of greater penalties than would be just. As such, they are a great social advance over the laws of the surrounding cultures.[5]

Chapters 22 and 23: Continuation of the above plus festival directions and instructions about the promised land and avoidance of its pagan peoples.[6]

Chapter 24: Moses as mediator with the Lord (see also 19:8–9; 20:18–19).

Chapters 25 through 28: Dwelling of God and its furnishings (note particularly **Ex 25:21–22**).

Chapter 29: Ordination of the Aaronic priests (see also Lv 8).

Chapters 30 and 31: Tabernacle matters; summary of Sabbath regulations (see also 35:1–3).

Chapter 32: The golden calf episode.

Chapters 33, 34: Narrative of events.

Chapters 35 through 40: Execution of the orders given through Moses.

Leviticus

All of Leviticus is surveyed in brief below. Again, read as much of the text as you can, noting particularly what is emphasized here.

Chapters 1 through 16: Directions for worship in the Hebrew community and attendant laws.

Chapters 17 through 26: Sometimes called the Holiness Code, a designation derived from the kind of life called for by the regulations in the text. It reflects historical, economic, and social backgrounds somewhat changed from those of the Covenant Code. Scholars think the roots of the Covenant Code are in the period at the beginning of Israel's settlement in the new land, while the Holiness Code is associated with the time near the end of the monarchy.

Chapter 17: Mostly laws about blood (some related to kosher meat).

Chapter 18: Prohibition of incest and other sexual irregularities.

Chapter 19: Miscellaneous (note particularly **Leviticus 19:17–18**).[7]

Chapter 20: False worship; sexual mores.

Chapters 21 through 24: Rules for priests, festivals, and worship.

Chapter 25: Rules regarding sabbatic years and jubilee; also redemption of slaves in other circumstances.

Chapter 26: Laws and promises for "the two ways."[8]

Chapter 27: Various vows.

Numbers

The Book of Numbers ostensibly covers the journey of the Israelites from Sinai to "the plains of Moab by the Jordan at Jericho" (35:1). Included are somewhat tedious details of various censuses of the tribes (whence the name of the book) and some laws and regulations. A few of the stories appear in other sessions of our study.

Deuteronomy

We have not dealt with Deuteronomy in any comprehensive way. This is a good point at which to skim the entire book. Remember that it is a kind of restatement of Hebrew covenant religion from a historical perspective that professes to be somewhat later than Exodus-Leviticus-Numbers. The regulatory portions are often referred to as the Deuteronomic Code.

Chapters 1 through 3: Moses' review of the way from Sinai (here called Horeb) to Moab on the east bank of the Jordan.

Chapter 4: Concluding exhortation of this first address.

Chapter 5: Recap of the Ten Words.

Chapter 6: Exposition of Israel's relationship with the Lord. The passage in **6:4–9** is particularly important. Verse 4 is called the *Shema*, from the first word in the Hebrew text. It is the central prayer of Judaism. Jesus quoted it as the "first of all" commandments

(Mark 12:29–30; see also Leviticus 19:17–18, noted above). Chapter **6:20–25** is a creed-like statement of the interconnection between law and promise.

Chapters 7 through 11: Instruction and warning about Israel's life in the promised land, with historical recollections as examples.

Chapters 12 through 19: Centralization and regulation of worship; conduct of justice.

Chapter 20: Rules for making war.

Chapters 21 through 25: Miscellaneous laws.

Chapter 26: Conclusion of this section. The credal liturgy in verses 5–9 has already been marked in Theme 2, Session 1.

Chapters 27 and 28: Story of a dramatic ceremony to be enacted at Shechem. A series of curses is to be pronounced from Mt. Ebal, and blessings are to be given from Mt. Gerizim (see also 11:26–30). The final section, 28:58–68, threatens a terrible reversal of the promises.

Chapters 29 and 30: Moses' final address; note **30:11–20.**

Chapter 31: Transfer of leadership to Joshua.

Chapters 32 and 33: Moses' "song."

Chapter 34: The end of Moses' life.

Suggestions for Further Study

Research

1. Using a Bible dictionary, research the meaning of Torah. In what way does the description of law differ with popular conceptions of the meaning of law?

2. Review Genesis 3–4:16; 6:5–9:29; 11:1–9; and 22:1–18. What are the consequences of the actions of those who disobey God? What are the blessings promised to those who obey?

3. Review the two versions of the Ten Commandments found in Exodus 20:1–17 and Deuteronomy 5:6–21. Look up the Ten Commandments in a Bible dictionary. Study the purpose of the Ten Commandments in the life of the Hebrew people. What relevance do you see for the Ten Commandments today?

4. Review Exodus 20:18–23:19, Leviticus 17–21, and Deuteronomy 12–26. What do you think is the major purpose of these codes in guiding the life of the people?

Reflection

1. We have seen that the Torah was given to the Hebrews in the context of God's act of salvation. What changes in behavior do you think are the sign of people who claim to live out their commitment in faith to God today?

2. You may wish to master the following texts word for word.

   • Exodus 20:2–17 (Begin by learning the ten "words" without the extended explanatory material given with several of them.)
   • Leviticus 19:18b
   • Deuteronomy 6:4–9

Notes

1. See HBD 871–72.
2. See John 1:17.
3. See note for Genesis 15:6 in NAB.
4. Paul Hanson, *The People Called*, 42.
5. See note for Exodus 21:23 in NAB.
6. On Israel's separateness, see also Exodus 19:5–6. In 23:29–30, there are hints that the invasion of Canaan was not the immediate sweep, as the tribal allotments might lead one to suppose.
7. Compare Matthew 5:21–24 and Mark 12:28–33.
8. Compare Psalm 1.

SESSION 2

Prophetic Call to Righteousness

Session Overview

With Samuel, the ethical emphasis of the Law comes to the fore. The writing prophets (Amos, Isaiah, Jeremiah, and others) apply the demand for right motives and action in a variety of circumstances. This is followed through the post-exilic period and noted in several Psalms.

Key Bible Readings

Joshua 8:30–35
1 Kings 2:1–4
1 Samuel 12:16–25
Isaiah 8:16–20
Micah 4:1–4
Amos 2:6–8; 3:1–2;
  5:24
Isaiah 1:16–20; 52:13–
  53:12; 55:6–9
Jeremiah 7:1–11
Micah 6:6–8
Habakkuk 2:4
Malachi 3:16–18
Daniel 5:27
Psalms 19:8–15;
  119:9–11, 18, 105

Key Words

Hexateuch
the Former Prophets

Torah Before the Prophets

We have studied the basis of Israel's obligation in the codes of Torah. These codes spread over most of the national life of the Israelite people. Recording and editing the laws came relatively late in the history, but some of them certainly date from the very early years. Laws were usually known and in force long before they were codified. According to John McKenzie, "The conception of law as a sacred covenant obligation is unique with Israel, as far as is known, and it is fundamental in the Old Testament conception of society as governed by the will of God, and of history as determined by man's attitude to the law."[1]

Joshua is sometimes treated as an addition to the Pentateuch; hence scholars may refer to the first six books of the Bible as the Hexateuch. Joshua 1:7–8 suggests such a connection. Joshua 8:31 and 23:6 refer, however, to "the book of the law of Moses," and the process of canonization limited the Torah to the first five books of the Bible. The ceremony described in **Joshua 8:30–35,** moreover, pinpoints an event commanded in Deuteronomy 27:4–8, and thus reflects the theology of the Deuteronomic history of which it is part.

130

The period of the judges was somewhat chaotic, and the moral and religious tone was assessed to be low most of the time (see Jgs 2:7–14, 16–22). Each individual decided "what he thought best" (21:25). The law is hardly mentioned, but wrongdoing is specified as "forgetting the Lord" (3:7). God's commandments are assumed. Pursuit of foreign gods, which was a prime fault of the time, breaks the first two of the Ten Words, and the neglect of worship of the true God leads to disastrous social consequences.

Samuel and Sin in the Monarchy

Covenant law has an indirect influence on the books of Samuel and Kings, partly because of the narrative nature of those books. The law is always implicit but seldom cited. David's charge to Solomon does mention "the law of Moses," and there are other words associated with the law. See **1 Kings 2:1–4.** There is also a stir about the law in the reign of Josiah (2 Kgs 22–23:30). The Books of Chronicles make more frequent reference to the law, but this might be expected because of their theological approach to history.

Samuel's prophet role marks the beginning of the prophetic call to righteousness that appears in so much of the rest of the Old Testament. In **1 Samuel 12:16–25,** we find a clear example of how Samuel exercised his great influence in the early days of the monarchy. Other prophets also play important parts. The relationship of the prophet Nathan to David has already been mentioned.[2] Elijah and Elisha become key figures during critical periods of Israelite national life. Later Judaism referred to the Books of Joshua through 2 Kings as "the Former Prophets."

The kings of Israel and Judah are judged in the records according to their religious moral performance: Did they do what was right? The sins of Jeroboam I, "which he made Israel to sin," point to this relationship of law and righteousness. The standards that the people are called to adhere to and the suffering inflicted on those who did not obey (as in the tales of the Elijah-Ahab-Jezebel cycle) often seem harsh to us because we have had the benefit of many more years of communal experience as God's people. The prophets and those they advised acted according to their perception of God's will, and it is important to stress how far the moral standards of Israelite law exceeded those of neighboring peoples.

The Prophetic Message

The prophets were called by God to speak and write forcefully about the situations in which they were involved. The characteristic preface to their proclamations is, "Thus says the Lord." This does not mean that they are preempting the Law-tradition. They exhort the people to remember the covenant with the Lord which calls them to righteousness, and the Law is everywhere a presupposition, expressed or not. The Law is the deposit of God's will for the people. It calls them away from idol worship and to treat one another as they had been treated by their saving Lord.

Again and again, the prophets deal with the reciprocal relations of Law and sin, righteousness and covenant. There is a broad spectrum of application, varying in detail according to the life circumstances of the prophet involved. The prophets emphasize the connection between law and life.

In **Isaiah 8:16–20,** the word translated "instruction" (8:16) is *torah* in Hebrew. In Isaiah 42:18–43:7, the poet-prophet observes that although the people have suffered because of their sin, God will save them, and the Law is essential in this saving action (Is 42:21). Hosea 4:6 and 8:1–12 warn against disregard for the Law.

Jeremiah 31:31–34 plainly associates Law with covenant.[3] God's new covenant is promised thus: "I will place my Law [Torah] within them, and write it upon their hearts." The new is explicitly a sequel to the old.

Micah 4:1–4 contains a well-known prophecy of future peace. The precondition is that "for from Zion shall go forth instruction (Torah)." In one of the last verses in our Old Testament, Malachi 3:22, God speaks of "the Law (Torah) of Moses my servant, . . . the statutes and ordinances." There is no mistaking the intimate connection between the Law and the prophets' demands and promises.

Amos

No book of the Old Testament has a more striking call to the right action than Amos. The Book of Amos begins with oracles denouncing the transgressions of Israel's neighbors, and even Judah is blamed for not keeping God's Law. Then, in **Amos 2:6–8**, a remarkable explosion occurs: Israel is the audience to whom Amos is proclaiming his message. Suddenly and unexpectedly, Israel's sins are enumerated in detail and roundly denounced! Amos was prophesying in a time of prosperity for the northern kingdom of Israel. Tragically, the wealthy were hoarding the goods, the land, and all the benefits of this prosperity without even a pretense that any would trickle down to the poor. Instead, the poor had their land stolen, their taxes raised, and their lives oppressed. Amos witnesses to the judgment of God against the selfish behavior of those who do not remember the gift of freedom given in the Exodus or realize the gift of their prosperity. Chapters 3–6 survey the coming judgment. Read the whole book to get the full impact.

Notice **Amos 3:1–2;** it is precisely because of God's favor that Israel will be punished. They were looking for "the day of the Lord" (5:18), which they anticipated as a time when all wrongs against them would be righted. Amos declares that they should rather dread that day because God's justice will deal impartially and strictly with them. The extent of their wickedness is spelled out (Am 8:4–6); they are exhorted to "seek good, and not evil" (5:14). The epitome of his message is in **Amos 5:24.**

God's ultimate rebuke would seem to be located in the words of Amos 9:7–10. Israel cannot expect God to deal with it by standards different from those by which other nations are treated. The final words of the book, however, are positive notes of encouragement; the house of David will be restored in a wonderful new age (9:11–15).

Isaiah

The prophet named Isaiah, from whom the whole book takes its name, was connected with the late days of the southern monarchy during the reign of Hezekiah (see Theme 6, Session 2). Most of Isaiah 1–39 is concerned with his ministry. Isaiah, chapters 40–55, were proclaimed principally by an anonymous prophet during the period of the Exile. In this time, the unknown prophet proclaimed words of comfort to the people for all they had suffered and promised that the Exile would be ended. Isaiah 56–66 is believed to be the work of another anonymous prophet during the time of Ezra and Nehemiah. All of Isaiah deals with the righteousness of God's people—or its lack.

The first chapter launches into a denunciation of the sins of Judah (for example, see **Isaiah 1:16–20**). The prophet deals often in specifics: idolatry, ill treatment of the poor, drunkenness, greed, lying, bad leadership, treachery, insincere worship. In Isaiah 5:1–7, Judah is depicted as a vineyard, but the harvest is wild grapes. In 5:24, the summary of evil is "they have spurned the law of the LORD of hosts." The women of Judah are singled out for their share in the wickedness (see 3:16–4:1 and 32:9–13). There are also strong denunciations of Judah's enemies in chapters 13–23.

The content of Second Isaiah (40–56) is markedly different. It is clear that the Jewish exiles are addressed (see 45:1, where Cyrus is mentioned). God's people are not righteous, but God is intent upon restoring them (see 40:2; 44:22). A figure called "my servant" is prominent in God's purpose, for example, 42:1–4. In **Isaiah 52:13–53:12,** the servant suffers in place of God's people to restore them to righteousness; note especially 53:5–6, 11. Christian interpreters have appropriated many of these passages to describe Jesus Christ. Jesus himself was possibly strongly influenced by these "servant songs." The lyric call to repentance in **Isaiah 55:6–9** is memorable.

Jeremiah

From the outset, Jeremiah's words assail the wickedness of Jerusalem and Judah (which he sometimes calls "Israel"). In Jeremiah 2 and 3, God's people appear as the Lord's "bride," a figure of speech common in scripture. Jeremiah 4 begins a series of appeals for righteousness interspersed with threats of punishment and laments for Judah's wickedness. In 5:1, the prophet intimates that if only one righteous person could be found, Jerusalem would be pardoned. (See Gn 18:22–23 for a story with a similar theme.) Verses 4:2 and 5:2 reflect the second commandment.

Jeremiah 7 contains a sermon delivered in the temple. It deals with righteous and unrighteous conduct. Read **Jeremiah 7:1–11.** Chapters 8–10 contain a collection of oracles, mostly lamenting Judah's wicked ways. There are many notable, quotable lines, for example, 8:20, 22a; 9:22–23; 10:5. The figure of the fruitful tree,

which appears in Psalm 1, is also in Jeremiah 17:7–8.

In the days of Zedekiah, the last king of Israel before the Exile, the ancient covenant of sabbatical granting of freedom for Hebrew slaves was invoked,[4] but the owners reneged. Jeremiah then threatened the owners with the fate of the covenant-sacrificial animals (see Jer 34:8–20). Chapter 35 recounts the example of the Rechabites, who kept their unique tradition intact, lived righteously, and became a sign of judgment to Judah. These references are only a sampling of Jeremiah's call for righteousness.

Minor Prophets[5]

Hosea was nearly contemporary with Amos. We have seen in Theme 2, Session 2, how he dramatized the covenant relationship between God and the people by his own domestic tragedy. Chapters 5–8 show the harsh side of his message; 7:8b and 8:7 are notable barbs.

Micah lived in roughly the same time as Isaiah ben-Amoz (the prophet of Isaiah 1–39). Micah's denunciation of the wickedness of Judah is scathing (see Mi 2:1–11; 3:1–12; 7:1–7). Perhaps his best-known passage is **Micah 6:6–8.** As with most of the prophets, he was not completely negative, but we shall return to that point in Theme 10.

Habakkuk's writing is poetic in form. Chapters 1:2–2:5 deal with the problem of evil. We have seen in Theme 3, Session 2, the problem that is pinpointed in 1:13. Habakkuk 2:6–20 is a catalog of woes against wickedness. Chapter 3 is a prayer-psalm. Probably the best-known words from the book are **Habakkuk 2:4,** "but the just man, because of his faith, shall live" which became a very important text for Paul (Rom 1:17, Gal 3:11). See also Habakkuk 2:20.

Zechariah addresses times after the Exile. The literary form is "apocalyptic" (to be studied further in Theme 10). The Lord gives the prophet a call to righteousness, which is required as urgently in the restoration period as it was formerly (see Zec 1:1–6; 7:8–14; and 8:16–17).

Malachi's name means "my messenger." It is uncertain whether this is the prophet's actual name or a pseudonym for anonymity. Malachi writes during the post-exilic restoration and is particularly concerned for the righteousness of the priesthood (1:6–8, 13–14). The question-and-answer literary form is unusual. Read chapter 3; note **Malachi 3:16–18.**

Ezra-Nehemiah

In the restoration efforts led by Nehemiah and Ezra, the law plays a very important and explicit part. In Nehemiah 8:2–3, an assembly listens to the public reading of the law. Ezra's qualification as an authority on the law of Moses is noted in Ezra 7:6, 10. The restoration of altar-centered worship is related to the law of Moses in Ezra 3:2. Ezra 7:11–26 cites a letter of Persian king Artaxerxes covering the return to Jerusalem. It makes several references to God's law, which the king is supporting. Among the returnees, mixed marriages and resulting evils are a serious problem. See part of Ezra's prayer, 9:6–7, 10–11. Ezra's response is in terms of law and covenant. See Ezra 10:3. Ezra is seen as the father of latter-day worship in Jerusalem, with its emphasis on law and exclusiveness.

Psalms

The Book of Psalms provides a prime witness to the place of the law in the lives of God's people. We have already referred to Psalm 1, which can be understood as a preface to Israel's worship book. The motif of righteousness and law declares that a person will be blessed who delights and meditates on God's Law. **Psalm 19:8–15** praises the Law and prays for righteousness. Psalm 119 is the supreme poem about the Law: every verse (two-line couplet) has some reference to an aspect of the Law! In a poetic form called an "acrostic," each group of eight verses begins with a letter of the Hebrew alphabet—twenty-two sections in all. Note **Psalm 119:9–11, 18**, 97, **105**, 165, 176.

Suggestions for Further Study

Research

1. Review Exodus 20:1–17; 1 Samuel 12:13–25; Ezra 9:6–7, 10–11. How do these passages reflect the purposes of God's laws in the establishment of right relations

   • between God and the people?
   • among individual Israelites?
   • between individual Israelites and the nation?
   • between Israel and other peoples?

2. Read the article, "The Biblical Concept of Justice" found in Appendix 3. What does this article tell us about the ways in which God has acted toward the people? About the ways the people are to act toward one another?

3. Review 1 Kings 2:1–4. If you were a ruler like David, what kind of parting words would you give your heir under similar circumstances? How does David connect God's covenant promise and the law?

4. Read an article on the prophets in a Bible dictionary or in the introduction to the prophetic books in the NAB. What is the role of the prophet in calling God's people to righteousness?

5. Read Psalms 1, 19, 119. What attitudes towards the law are illustrated in these psalms?

Reflection

1. What difference, if any, do you see between the call to be "holy" and the demand for "righteousness"? Explain.

2. The prophets called for behavior that their times required. Do we receive such messages today? If so, where do they come from? If we don't, why not?

3. In what respect(s) does God's demand for a righteous people differ today from what the prophets proclaimed? How is it the same?

4. You may want to master the following verses:

   • Isaiah 1:18; 53:5–6; 55:6–9

   • Amos 5:24
   • Micah 6:8
   • Habakkuk 2:4b

Notes

1. John L. McKenzie, *Dictionary of the Bible*, 499b.

2. Theme 5, Section 1. See 2 Samuel 12:1–15.

3. This passage is emphasized in Theme 2, where "covenant" is studied.

4. See Exodus 21:2 and Deuteronomy 15:1, 2.

5. This designation is sometimes applied to the last twelve books of the Old Testament. It is only appropriate, of course, with regard to the length of the prophetic books. We have observed that Amos is a "major" prophet in every other sense.

SESSION 3

Jesus and the Law

Session Overview

The Law played a prominent role in New Testament times. The prophetic call to righteousness so often found in the Old Testament was revived by John the Baptist. Jesus' ethical teaching was consistent with the spirit of Torah but reinterpreted it. His approach was simple and direct, yet at the same time complex and open-ended. He was notably compassionate toward sinners and outcasts. The gospels proclaim that Jesus came to fulfill the Law.

Key Bible Readings

Mark 7:1–13
John 1:17
Luke 3:7–18
Matthew 5:17–48;
  22:34–40
Luke 10:30–37
Matthew 7:12; 11:28–
  30
John 3:1–21
Acts 3:12–26; 7:51–53

Key Words

fulfill
repentance

Law and Old Testament Scriptures

Torah, the first five books of the Pentateuch, has remained central in Jewish life throughout Jewish history. The developments of history, however, affected the interpretation of Torah. The understanding of Torah became the commentary on the written word, enhancing the importance of a literate elite who could read and interpret the text. Daily life was filled with ritual observances that helped the people to fulfill the intent of the Law. Other books and collections of writings came to be accepted as sacred, that is, they were in some sense canonized. By Jesus' day, the prophetic books and the Psalms were generally received as sacred scripture, and other writings, including most of the rest of our Old Testament, were widely used.

In addition to these written books there was developing a body of oral tradition that Pharisaic Judaism accepted as authoritative. See **Mark 7:1–13**. The Pharisees interpreted how the Law could be lived out in daily life. The intention was to "put a fence about the Torah" to guard the person from violating the Law. The result, however, seems to have been a multiplication of regulations the average Jew could not hope to keep. Only a "professional" student of the Law had the knowledge and time to do this. It is important to note that the gospels were written at a time in which the early Church was in bitter conflict with the Pharisees over the interpretation of the meaning of the scriptures and the place of Jesus in the history of salvation. These conflicts are reflected in the negative portrait of the Pharisees in the gospels and thus do not give a fair representation of their views and teachings (see Lk 11:46; Mt 23:2–4, 23–24).

All the Jewish people of the early first century doubtless thought of themselves as God's people, and they revered God's law. The Pharisees, scribes, and lawyers were responsible for transcribing and interpreting the written text of the law for the people. The Sadducees were made up of the conservative priests, aristocrats, and landowners. They were proud that they accepted only the Torah and rejected the oral law, which might put limitations on their power.[1] The Essene people of the Dead Sea Scrolls had their own interpretations of the scriptures. They accepted the authority of additional writings, such as their *Manual of Discipline*. The Samaritans accepted as scripture only the Pentateuch, and they had their own version of it. The beliefs of the rest of the people known as the '*am ha arets*' or "the people of the land"—clearly the large majority[2]—can only be surmised from the comments of the others who did write.

Law and the Gospels

The Christian Church came into existence to proclaim the mission and victory of Jesus. In its first years, the Church developed within the Jewish faith; but there were soon conflicts over the application of the Law to gentile converts. It must be noted again that Torah means "instruction" and is not limited to the legal codes studied in Session 1 of this theme. The Passover deliverance described in the Torah is the central event of the Jewish faith and the model for the Christian celebration of the Eucharist. It is advisable to avoid generalizing about "law in the New Testament."

The New Testament emphasizes Jesus Christ: **John 1:17.** The narrative of Jesus' life, death, and resurrection made him the unique and essential center of the new faith. It was natural that his followers wanted to know more and more about him. What did he have to say? How did he live? How did he deal with people? What was his family background? The gospels give some answers to such questions; but, as we have seen in Theme 6, Session 3, the gospels are not biographies of Jesus but proclamations. As such, the gospels give us four portraits of Jesus that proclaim his saving mission.[3]

As portraits, the gospels teach what the earliest Church proclaimed about Jesus. They were the end product of a generation of reflection on the meaning of Jesus' life, teaching, death, and resurrection written under the inspiration of the Holy Spirit. First, there were the events of Jesus' earthly career. Then there were the oral reports and the spreading proclamation based on the reports. Finally, there were the gospels, the documentation of the Church's revered traditions. The closest we come to an organized summary of this whole process is in the two-volume work Luke-Acts.

John the Baptist

The gospel story, other than birth narratives and prologues, begins with the ministry of John the Baptist. This is presented as the immediate backdrop of Jesus' public career. Through the preaching of John the Baptist, the gospels stress "repentance for the forgiveness of sins" (Luke 3:3). Luke gives us a summary of how John spelled out the detailed implications of this call for righteousness. See **Luke 3:7–18.** When we analyze this passage, we see that the Baptist is saying that true repentance would be reflected practically in the lives of those who profess it. John calls this producing "good fruits"; persons must be righteous in the individual circumstances of their life. Repentance was the necessary first step toward the forgiveness made available in Jesus Christ.

Jesus on the Law

Matthew's gospel contains many specific comments of Jesus on the relationship of the Hebrew law to the new life being offered by Jesus. The most striking and sustained passage is part of the Sermon on the Mount, **Matthew 5:17–48.** At least six of the Ten Commandments are commented upon, though not in the original order. In Matthew 5:17–20, Jesus speaks of fulfilling the Law. Matthew presents Jesus as reinterpreting the Torah with a righteousness that surpasses that of the Pharisees. This means that Jesus interprets the law according to God's original intention of love.

When Jesus is asked explicitly about the relative importance of the commandments, he gives a twofold reply. See **Matthew 22:34–40** and review it against the background of the two great commandments in Session 1 of this theme. In Luke's version of this incident, 10:26–28, the dialogue with Jesus' interrogator leads to the parable of the good Samaritan, **Luke 10:30–37.** What we call the "golden rule" Jesus describes as the epitome of "the law and the prophets": **Matthew 7:12**. Note that the NAB places the parallel teaching in Luke 6:27–31 in the context of the "sermon on the plain."

Jesus on Righteousness

In the Gospels of Matthew and Luke, the proclamation of Jesus has strong ethical content. When Jesus speaks about the Law, he invariably goes on to demand right conduct (note Mt 5:20, 48). The "beatitudes" (Mt 5:3–12; compare Lk 6:20–23) describe how Jesus' followers are to live if they expect to be "blessed." He calls his followers "the salt of the earth" and "the light of the world" (Mt 5:13–16). In Luke's "sermon on the plain" (Lk 6:17–49), the beatitudes are followed by "woes." Both Matthew's and Luke's collections are from Jesus' proclamation. The differences reflect the fact that they were written for two different communities. These "sermons" contain a summary of Jesus' ethical teaching, and you should become thoroughly familiar with them. Jesus' ethic presents the demand that "God's law calls for a righteous people."

Matthew notes that Jesus taught with uncommon authority (Mt 7:28–29). **Matthew 11:28–30** shows that Jesus invites the tired and the burdened to follow him, learning to serve God and humanity in love.

Jesus on Interpreting the Law

John's gospel portrays the laws regarding the Sabbath as principal cause of the clash between Jesus and Jewish authorities. See John 5:10–11, 16–18; 7:23; 9:13–16. Jesus, however, does not think that he is breaking Jewish law; we have noted above that he speaks rather of "fulfillment." He strongly suggests, moreover, that his antagonists are the lawbreakers (see Jn 7:19; also Mk 7:9; Lk 13:14–17).

Jesus maintains a fine line between himself and the substance of his proclamation. He explicitly refuses the role of legal judge (Lk 12:14), but he constantly confronts people with the law's demands. Jesus is presented as having no doubt that his interpretation of the demands is right ("but I say to you"), yet he focuses the hearers' attention on God as the ultimate authority of the Law (see, for example, the discussion of divorce in Mk 10:2–12).

The most striking thing that Jesus says about law is probably the "new commandment" given to his disciples: "that you love one another." Obedience to this commandment is to be the mark of his followers (see Jn 13:34–35; also 15:12–14). There is beautiful exposition of this in the First Letter of John 2:7–11; 3:11–18; 4:7–12, 20–21; 5:1.

Jesus and "Sinners"

Jesus' association with those who in his day were commonly known as sinners is repeatedly noted in the gospels (for example, Mk 2:15–17). Jesus does not want to exclude anyone from his call to discipleship, so the statement that he did not come "to call the righteous" may imply that these are indeed scarce. Read the parable in Luke 18:9–14.[4]

In the gospels Jesus is criticized because he associated with sinners and the ordinary people in Galilee, where most of his ministry took place. In response, Jesus directed some of his harshest words against religious leaders who behave as though they have a corner on righteousness (see Mt 23:13 and the parallel Lk 11:52). The whole of Matthew 23 is a scathing denunciation, with a series of dire woes against the "scribes and Pharisees, you hypocrites." We should again note that the criticism of the Pharisees and scribes in this passage and similar passages in John 7:53–8:11 reflect the conflict between the early Church and Jewish leaders of the synagogues at the time the gospels were written. As mentioned above, the harsh criticism of the Jews does not represent a fair portrayal of the Pharisees and scribes and their teachings.

The criticisms in this light also give no excuse for the anti-Semitic behavior that has marred the Church's treatment of the Jews historically nor any excuse for anti-Semitic behavior today. In the Second Vatican Council's *Declaration on the Relation of the Church to Non-Christian Religions,* the Church teaches:

> Even though Jewish authorities and those who followed their lead pressed for the death of Christ (cf. John 19:6), neither all Jews indiscriminately at that time, nor Jews today, can be charged with the crimes committed during his passion. It is true that the Church is the new people of God, yet the Jews should not be spoken of as rejected or accursed as if this followed from holy Scripture. Consequently, all must take care, lest in catechizing or in preaching the Word of God, they teach anything which is not in accord with the truth of the Gospel message or the spirit of Christ.

> Indeed, the Church reproves every form of persecution against whomsoever it may be directed. Remembering, then, her common heritage with the Jews and moved not by any political consideration, but solely by the religious motivation of Christian charity, she deplores all hatreds, persecutions, displays of antisemitism, leveled at any time or from any source against the Jews.[5]

The New Testament Church believed that Jesus himself provided the way for his followers to become righteous. One very well-known attempt to make this clear is **John 3:1–21.** The passage recounts a meeting between Jesus and Nicodemus and their discussion about how to have eternal life. The author of John uses Nicodemus as a foil to prompt Jesus to explain more deeply the meaning of the life of grace brought by Jesus. Here new life, God's reign, the Spirit of God, the saving history of God and the people, believing, light versus darkness, and God's determined favor toward the people are all combined in the one magnificent presentation. John 3:16 is a well known verse in the New Testament. Remember that in John's gospel "believing" is a moving, active force. The noun "belief/faith" never occurs in John's gospel; but always the verb "believe/have faith (in)" (see Jn 6:28–29).

Jesus' Good News

The gospels proclaim that in Jesus' mission and message a new era is breaking out. The period of "the law and the prophets" extends to John the Baptist (Lk 16:16), who is portrayed as Jesus' forerunner (Mt 11:11–15). Jesus' presence is the evidence of something greater than the preaching of Jonah or the wisdom of Solomon (Mt 12:40–42; Lk 11:30–32). Therefore, Jesus proclaims, "But I say to you," and issues a "new commandment."

The early leaders of the Church work out the ramifications of the new life offered by Jesus. In Acts 3:6, Peter and John invoke Jesus' name to heal a lame man. In an ensuing address, **Acts 3:12–26,** Peter connects Hebrew history with the new power of Jesus Christ. In Acts 6:11–14, Stephen is charged with opposing the law; but in his defense he reviews Jewish history and declares that his accusers do not understand the scriptures. He connects this to their rejection of "the Righteous One" (Jesus Christ). Read **Acts 7:51–53.** In Session 4, we will note how Paul develops a similar line of thought.

Suggestions for Further Study

Research

1. Review the word "repentance" in a Bible dictionary. How does John's call to repentance fit into the context of the Old Testament teaching on repentance? How does John's differ from the Old Testament?

2. Review the Sermon on the Mount (Matthew 5–7). How does the Sermon describe Jesus' attitude toward the Law?

3. Review Matthew 7:12 and 22:34–40. How does Jesus summarize the Law in these passages?

4. Review John 3:1–21. How does the dialogue between Jesus and Nicodemus describe how Jesus provides for his followers to become righteous?

Reflection

1. Imagine that you are asked to explain to someone what it means to live as a Christian in everyday life. What would you say are the important things a person should do?

2. How ready are you to hear the call of repentance and to be ready for God's forgiveness in Jesus Christ?

3. You may want to master the following texts:
   • Matthew 5–7, the "Sermon on the Mount"; 5:3–12, the "Beatitudes"; 7:12, the "Golden Rule"; 11:28–30; 22:37–40
   • Luke 10:30–37, the "Good Samaritan"
   • John 3:14–17 (at least verse 16); 13:34–35

Notes

1. See John Drane, IOT 35.

2. See Amos 1:2; 7:14–15.

3. See "Four portraits of Jesus" in John Drane, IOT 181–97.

4. The words "righteous," "righteousness," "just," and "justification" usually represent the same word-root in the Greek New Testament.

5. Vatican Council II, *Declaration on the Relation of the Church to Non-Christian Religions* 4.

SESSION 4

Righteousness in the Church

Session Overview

Jesus left no legal code, but his teachings were treasured, and the demand for repentance and righteousness continued in the Church. The Jerusalem Church held the law in great respect. Paul opposed applying Jewish law to Gentile converts, though he had a place for law. He insisted that righteousness results not from obeying laws but from faith. The development of this new focus is traced through New Testament letters.

Key Bible Readings

Acts 15:1–35
Galatians 5:1, 13–14,
   22–23
Romans 1:16; 2:12–16
1 Corinthians 8:11; 13
Ephesians 6:10–17
Colossians 3:18–24
1 Timothy 6:9–10
James 1:22; 2:14–26

Key Words

legalism
fruit of the Spirit
second great
   Commandment

Jesus' Legacy

Jesus mandated no laws in the sense of the Old Testament legal codes. In a manner of speaking, however, he did leave new Torah, for his teaching established guidelines for the lives of his followers. This teaching was collected and became authoritative because the first Christians believed that through Jesus God had effected a radical, new deliverance.

The two-volume work of Luke-Acts brings together a collection of the teachings of Jesus and attendant events. It is a kind of history of the people and times when Jesus' teaching became a formative influence in the earliest Church. In keeping with Jesus' nonlegal approach, there is almost no concern with laws as such in Acts. Only a few exceptions can be noted.

Apostolic Witness

The preaching of the apostles maintained the demand for a right relationship with God that had been an important implication of Jesus' message. Peter's sermon on Pentecost led up to the climax, "Repent and be baptized." He exhorted his hearers to save themselves "from this corrupt generation" (Acts 2:38–40). Repentance in the New Testament requires a complete re-orientation of life.

The story of Ananias and Sapphira, Acts 5:1–11, is a startling example of the total commitment expected from members of the early Church. Jesus was sometimes referred to as "the righteous (or just) one" (see 3:14; 7:52; 22:14).[1] Peter learned from his experience with the conversion of the household of Cornelius that God impartially accepts "whoever fears him and acts uprightly is acceptable to him"—even Gentiles (see 10:34–35; 11:17).

The early Church developed in many directions. The Christian congregation centered in Jerusalem was led by some of the original apostolic group and tended to have a conservative, Jewish outlook. The preaching in this setting, as reported in Acts, stressed the continuity from the Old Testament to Jesus as the Messiah (see Acts 2:22–31; 3:13; 10:36–38).

On the other hand, a number of groups with Hellenistic backgrounds (that is, from Greek-speaking Judaism) developed a broader outlook. The first deacons of the Church were from this circle (6:1–6). Their attitude of openness displeased some Jewish-Christian leaders and raised problems for the Jerusalem-centered Church. Scan the activities of Stephen and Philip in Acts 6:8–8:40. From this movement and from Peter's example in dealing with Cornelius came the impetus for Paul's great missionary efforts. The Church at Antioch in Syria became the center for this activity (see 11:19–26; 13:1–3).

Enter Paul

Paul became the apostle to the Gentiles, and this made him the focal point for a struggle within the Church. The very nature of the Christian movement was at stake. Its relation with Judaism had to be clarified. Read Galatians 1 and 2. Note how important Paul considered the problem to be. The confrontation with Peter is a capsule illustration of what was taking place.

One dimension of the disagreement may be seen in **Acts 15:1–35.** The requirements placed upon Gentile converts are certainly derived from some laws in Torah, but Paul's relationship to such regulations is not easy to delineate. In Acts 21:17–26, he participates in a move to conciliate Christians of Jewish background, and verse 25 refers to the letter from the Jerusalem council. His effort, however, leads to conflict with some Asian Jews (21:27–40). He defends himself (22:1–22) and tells about his religious background. Elsewhere in Paul's writings, and in the stories in Acts, the decision of the council does not seem to play a part.

When you study Paul, three factors should be kept in balance: his emphasis on the Gentiles not being bound by the details of Jewish regulations, for example, the case of circumcision; his insistence on regulations for Christian living; and his demand for righteousness, which is both a gift of God and a response to God's goodness. In the first sermon of Paul recorded in Acts, his main point is that Jesus uniquely brings about a right relationship with God for humanity; faith in Jesus makes possible what Mosaic law could not achieve (Acts 13:38–39). This message is also central in the letters to the Galatians and to the Romans.

Galatians

The radical limit to which Paul moves away from the conservative tendencies of the Jerusalem Church is seen in Galatians 3 through 5. Here he contrasts "faith" and "works of law," and he implies that faithful Christians are moved beyond the old law. **Galatians 5:1** puts the principle succinctly. In **5:13–14** he echoes Jesus' "second great commandment" and quotes Leviticus 19:18. His ninefold "fruit of the Spirit,"

5:22–23, begins with "love" and is a noteworthy summary of Paul's ethical emphasis.

This means, of course, that Paul did not intend to do away with the law altogether. Indeed, from 5:16 to the end of the letter he gives directions how the Galatian Church should regulate its life. It becomes clear that he is ordering priorities. If one puts obedience to law first, depending on one's own strength to fulfill the requirements of the law, one is doomed to failure. In Christian living, one begins with faith in God, accepting the grace offered in Jesus Christ, and responding in love by living in accord with Jesus' revelation of God's will. This is certainly a disciplined life, and Paul does not hesitate to pronounce what such discipline involves.

Paul is not neatly consistent in his use of the term "law." This is not new to us, for we have observed how "Torah" means "instruction" and is not simply a list of regulations. Sometimes Paul treats the law as a good thing, as in Galatians 3:24, where the law is compared with the guardian or monitor who escorted the child to school. Sometimes it is downright bad, as in 5:4, when it gives the impression that righteousness can be achieved through human effort or adhering to human rituals. At other times he clarifies the law as Jesus did by highlighting the law's intention to assist the life of faith as fulfilled in love (Gal 5:14). Paul is not unclear in his thinking; his complex reasoning, rather, defies oversimplification. We must exercise care, therefore, in dealing with Paul's thought, and we should in all cases be wary of generalizations.

Romans

Paul's letter to the Romans also deals with his views about law. It is the most orderly presentation of his theological reflection. Paul wrote the letter to a Church that had already been founded by other Christians. This is probably the reason why he tries to be more comprehensive. It is helpful to read the letter at one sitting. Several clearly marked sections help to outline the contents.

Romans 1:1–17 is an introduction. **Romans 1:16** proclaims "the power of God for the salvation of everyone who believes" and is practically a theme text for the letter.

Chapter 1:18–3:20 describes the condition of humanity trapped in sin. Although law should foster faithfulness to God and provide a yardstick for measuring conformity to God's will, it really becomes the evidence of humanity's inability to liberate itself from sin. In **Romans 2:12–16,** Paul shows that those who have not heard the Lord are still accountable because the law of God is written in their hearts.

Romans 3:21–4:25 shows how righteousness becomes effective through Jesus Christ. Abraham's faithfulness is presented as an elaborate example.

Romans 5:1–8:39 describes and reflects the many facets of life freed from sin by a faith-relationship with Jesus Christ. Jesus' life provides patterns of assurance for our life. We live by God's "grace," not "under law" (6:14). Paul is careful to avoid equating the law with sin, but the law provides "opportunity" for sin to take over, 7:7–12. The psychology of law and sin is analyzed in 7:13–25. The final words of this section, 8:35–39, are a memorable declaration of the power of God's love in Christ.

Romans 9–11 are probably the most difficult chapters in the book. They deal with the special place of Israel (the Jews) in God's plan for humanity. The relation between the old Israel and God's new people is not easy to formulate. Paul is quite sure that God still has a saving destiny for the Jews. God's purpose is merciful (11:26, 32), but Paul does not know its detail (11:33–36).

Romans 12:1–5 and 13, like the final section of Galatians, deal with specifics of Christian living. Though Christians do not live under law, there are certain things they ought to do. These reflect some Old Testament precepts and also show appreciation of Jesus' interpretation of law. Some of the Ten Commandments as well as the "love" commandment are referred to in Romans 13:8–11. God's people constitute "one body," in which the action of each person is of highest importance (12:4–6). A corollary of this principle is that interpersonal responsibility outweighs individual freedom (14:1–15:7).

Romans 15:14–33 and 16:1–23 are two personal postscripts. They contribute to our knowledge of Paul's career and of the history of the early Church.

First Corinthians

The Corinthian correspondence also tells a lot about Paul's Churches, for he deals with practical pastoral problems. These in turn prompt many comments and commands about living in a right relationship with God and one another. Since Corinth was a seaport town, and many members of the Church evidently were drawn from paganism, it was probably inevitable that morality and ethics should be prominent in Paul's letters.

In one instance, it appears Paul received inside information reporting serious irregularities of conduct (see 1 Cor 1:10–11; 5:1). The basic flaw in this Church is a divisive spirit that destroys its effectiveness as a Christian community and its relationship with other Christian influences (notably Paul's!). Paul feels a personal responsibility to address these problems (see 1 Cor 4:14–21). In chapters 5 and 6, he deals specifically with immorality.

In 1 Corinthians 7, we find a complicated discussion of sex and marriage. Paul's principle of mutuality (verse 4) is remarkably advanced for his day. This passage is the first of a series of responses to queries communicated from the Church. Chapter 8 responds to problems raised by meat sold in the public markets; it was routinely "sacrificed to idols" as part of its preparation—a kind of pagan "kosher." The meat was then cheaper to buy. The principle of Christian responsibility for each individual member of the community prevails, Paul writes (recall Rom 14:1–15:7). Christians today may not face the same problem of eating food offered to idols, but there are other divisions in the Church in which the same principles of love can be applied. Notice the basis in **1 Corinthians 8:11,** "the brother for whom Christ died."

In 1 Corinthians 12, Paul develops the idea of the Christian, corporate "body" and its relationship to Christ and the Holy Spirit. Paul pays special attention to describing the diversity of gifts available to the members of the Church, emphasizing that they are all "different forms of service but the same Lord" (12:5). Paul uses the analogy of the body, which is a unity though it has many parts. He emphasizes that each of the manifestations of the Spirit is meant to build up the Church, and all are of equal merit. The one gift giver is God, who calls all members of the Church to a special vocation. In chapter 12, we have the earliest description of the Eucharist, written about twenty years after the Last Supper (recall also Rom 12). Paul interrupts the discussion with his famous hymn declaring that love is the supreme aim and gift in all Christian living in **chapter 13,** and the discussion of corporate life and liturgical practice continues in chapter 14.

Contained in 1 Corinthians 15 is an early Christian creed (15:3–7) that outlines the common ground of the Church's teaching on the resurrection. There are those in the Christian community who would deny the resurrection of the dead. Paul strongly condemns such teaching and outlines the consequences of the disbelief

(15:16–19). Christ, through the resurrection, has defeated death and in Christ "shall all be brought to life" (15:22).

Other Pauline Material

Other letters written by Paul or associated with his mission spell out how God's law demands righteousness. Examples are 2 Corinthians 6:14–7:1; Philippians 3:17–21; and 1 Thessalonians 4:1–8.

In Ephesians,[1] a magnificent prayer (Eph 3:13–21) is followed by so-called practical aspects of the gospel.[2] Note how chapters 4–6 give everyday advice with a doctrinal turn. The summary, **6:10–17,** is especially eloquent.

Colossians somewhat resembles Ephesians 3:1–4:6. It is a comprehensive collection of precepts for Christian living. **Colossians 3:18–24** lists "household" responsibilities. Such lists in this literary form were fairly common in first-century literature. A longer version appears in Ephesians 5:21–6:9, and there is a non-Pauline example in 1 Peter 2:13–3:7.

The "pastoral" letters, 1 and 2 Timothy and Titus, reflect details of Church life somewhat differently from the other letters. Exhortations to righteousness, however, are abundant. There are specific admonitions for Church officials. See 1 Timothy 3:1–13. Titus 2:1–10 is a kind of household list. Discord is wrong, harmony is good: 1 Timothy 6:3–8. See also 2 Timothy 2:23–26; Titus 3:9; also Philippians 4:11–13. Jesus warned about the dangers of wealth (as in Mk 10:23–31), but probably the best-known quotation about money is from **1 Timothy 6:9–10.**

James and Hebrews

The Book of James is a kind of collection of Christian "laws." It is really a sermonic essay beginning as a letter, but it does not end as one. There are nearly sixty imperatives in the book. The "second great commandment" is quoted in 2:8 and called "the royal law." James 2:11 quotes two of the Ten Commandments, and 2:12 (and 1:25) may remind one of Galatians 5:1. James emphasizes action in **1:22.** Sometimes **2:14–26** is thought to be a polemic against Paul's emphasis on salvation by faith apart from deeds, but careful study of both Paul and James suggests that they differ more in emphasis than in substance. James's exhortation to Christians to become actively involved in the needs of the poor still must be heard today. Other ethics passages are James 4:1–12 and 5:1–6.

The Book of Hebrews focuses elsewhere than law and righteousness. See, however, Hebrews 12:1–2, 14–16; 13:1–5, 16–17. Even Revelation refers to the value of righteous deeds. See 14:13, which is often quoted in funeral liturgies. The everlasting effect of righteousness is marked in Hebrews 22:10–15.

Suggestions for Further Study

Research

1. The meeting in Acts 15 is often referred to as the first general council of the Christian Church. The date is usually placed at AD 49. Try to relate Paul's biographical comments in Galatians 1 and 2 to the Acts chronology (note also Acts 11:27–30).

2. Review Galatians and Romans 1–8. Summarize Paul's teaching on the Christian's relationship to the law and Christian liberty.

3. Review Colossians 3:1–17, Ephesians 6:1–9, 1 Peter 2:13–25. What qualities do they teach that a Christian should embody?

4. Review Galatians 5:16–24. What qualities does Paul list that the Christian practices? How do these compare to the qualities of the person who has not accepted God's grace?

5. Study the following for convenience of reference:

   - Lists of virtues in the Pauline letters are in Galatians 5:22–24; Philippians 4:8; Colossians 3:12–15
   - Lists of vices are in Romans 1:29–31; 1 Corinthians 5:11; 6:9–10; 2 Corinthians 12:20; Galatians 5:19–21; Ephesians 4:31; 5:3–5; Colossians 3:5–9.

Reflection

1. What experiences have shown you that the saving grace of God has entered into your life?

2. If Paul were writing to your group today, what would he likely say about law? About freedom? About righteousness? Could he address God's people as a whole on these topics today? Why or why not?

3. You may want to master the following verses:

   - Romans 1:16; 8:35–39
   - 1 Corinthians 13
   - Galatians 5:1; 5:22–23
   - James 1:22
   - Revelation 14:13

Notes

1. In John 17:25 Jesus addresses God as "righteous Father."

2. Scholars differ as to whether this letter is (1) a letter written by Paul to the Ephesian Church; (2) a letter written by Paul to several Churches; or (3) a summary of Paul's teaching written by a disciple under the apostle's name.

THEME 8

God's People Learn Wisdom

SESSION 1

Wisdom in Jewish Scriptures

Session Overview

Jewish scriptures shared the widespread interest of the ancient world in what was called wisdom. This included insights about the natural world, advice on diverse aspects of meaningful human life and conduct, and a variety of expressions of good judgment. Solomon was regarded as the patron of practical and literary wisdom in the biblical tradition. After the Exile, a wisdom movement became very important in Judaism and produced significant literature.

Key Bible Readings

1 Kings 5:9–14
Proverbs 1:1–7
Ecclesiastes 3:1–9
Job 28:12–28
Sirach 44
Wisdom 3:1; 7:13–22

Key Words

wisdom literature
Ben Sirach
Book of Wisdom
Sirach/Ecclesiasticus

Wisdom in the Ancient World

Wisdom was highly regarded throughout the ancient world. Wise persons were sought out for their insight into the meaning of life and the conduct of affairs. The courts of kings drew advisors who could be consulted on difficult matters. Villages and clans also held in high esteem those whose judgment was regarded as worthy of acceptance by the community.

These persons were the kind we would expect of the culture of Egypt and Babylon. In the court of the Egyptian pharaoh the wise men were magicians (Ex 7:8–13), akin to the scientific advisors of our day. Daniel 2 portrays the Babylonian king as seeking the interpretation of troubling dreams from "magicians and enchanters, sorcerers and Chaldeans." We should feel more at home with the wisdom of Moses' father-in-law, Jethro, whose wise counsel helped strengthen Moses' leadership (see Ex 18:10–24).

Wisdom enabled persons to cope effectively with their particular environments. Wisdom was common sense and skill, and these know no national boundaries. Wisdom included not only political ability but the fine crafts of artisans. It covered knowledge of animal life as well as of the heavens. It was a keen observer of human weaknesses and was concerned for the stability of the coming generation. In general, wisdom was optimistic; for human nature could be guided and could learn to live in kind and just relationships.

Wisdom in Israel

It should be no surprise that God's people shared in this concern for wisdom. Well-adjusted living was a common goal of those who shaped Israel's thought and practice. Certainly, this was one of the ends of Torah (Dt 4:5–6), and the prophets shared the aim (Mi 6:8). Although Torah regulated much of Israel's life, this does not mean that sages couched all their counsel in religious terms. In fact, much of it is common-sense advice (as the words of Jethro).

The people of Israel and Judah, however, put a distinctive stamp on the wisdom writings. This came about because of the unique religious, cultural, and social environment of Israel. So Psalm 111:10 declares, "The fear of the LORD is the beginning of wisdom"—that is, the awe a person has standing before God and the law of the covenant constitutes "true religion," a principle reiterated by other writers. A number of the Psalms, including 1, 32, 34, 49, 112, and 128, may also be considered wisdom literature (see Theme 9, Session 2, for more detail on the psalms). Magicians and sorcerers were banned by Torah (Ex 22:17; Lv 19:31; Dt 18:9–14); so there were clear limits to where Israelites should seek advice.

Solomon

The name of Solomon stands out in Israel's wisdom tradition. His prestige was so great that he became the patron-figure for wisdom much as Moses was the model of the lawgiver and David was the psalmist par excellence. As we shall see, Solomon's name was associated with a number of wisdom writings.

Solomon's sagacity in resolving difficult problems was celebrated (see, for example, 1 Kgs 3:16–28). His reputation is elaborately described in **1 Kings 5:9–14.** The queen of Sheba made a long journey to test his wisdom (10:1–7). His extraordinary endowment is attributed to the gift of God (3:5–13). Understanding that wisdom came from God was a distinct stamp of Israelite wisdom.

Wisdom as a Movement

Wisdom sayings and thoughts are scattered among Old Testament books. The wisdom tradition evidently had a lengthy development in the oral tradition of parents telling their children what they needed to know to be successful in the world, and played a large part in Israel's everyday life and thought. It also shows the influence of the wisdom traditions of the surrounding cultures of the Ancient Near East. Skill at crafts is attributed to wisdom from the Lord in Exodus 31:1–6. "A gifted woman" plays a key role in a story in 2 Samuel 14:1–21, and another appears in a somewhat gory episode in 2 Samuel 20:16–22.

In the period from Elijah to Ezekiel (c. 850–571 BC), the prophets were the predominant witnesses of God's word in the national life of Israel and Judah. At the end of that period, the prophet, priest, and wise figure were sometimes rivals. In Jeremiah 8:8–11, the prophet bitterly denounces the wise men for perverting the Torah for the sake of their interpretations of the law. He also criticizes the peace they offer because it neglected the true foundations of peace based on justice, covenant fidelity, and compassion for those in need.

Following the return from Exile, the prophetic influence declined, and the priestly guardians of the law and the teachers of wisdom were the principal influences in the life of the people. They had to teach the people how to live according to God's will in this difficult time. Evidence that wisdom was a distinctive movement is to be seen in literature that became a part of the writings in the Jewish canon and in several deuterocanonical books.

The Book of Proverbs

Proverbs is a collection of collections. Most of the divisions are identified by introductory markers. A simple survey-outline of the book may help you manage its structure:

Chapter 1:1–7: Prologue to the collection.

Chapters 1:8–9:18: Discourses on wisdom, many addressed to "my son."

Chapters 10:1–22:16: Miscellaneous proverbs, attributed to Solomon.

Chapters 22:17–24:34: A collection with parallels to Amen-em-ope.

Chapters 24:23–34: is called "sayings of the wise."

Chapters 25–29: Attributed to Solomon, but collected by "the men of Hezekiah" (which would be about 715–687 BC).

Chapters 30–31: Two collections bearing the names of otherwise unknown wise men, Agur and Lemuel, plus a poem in praise of "a worthy wife" (31:10–31).

Proverbs 1:1 may appear to refer to the whole book, but this is not really appropriate. Some sections are attributed to Solomon; but some are clearly not intended to be his. Even if some of the sayings are ancient, the collections are meant for the instruction of young Jews in the post-exilic period. Wisdom by this time was conventionally attributed to Solomon, and even pre-exilic editors are noted in 25:1.

Proverbs 22:17–24:22 bears close resemblance to an Egyptian wisdom writing, *Instruction of Amen-em-ope,* which may be dated some time after 1000 BC. Chapter 30 contains the words of Agur and a series of sayings that involve numbers. Chapter 31 begins with the words of Lemuel, which he learned from his queen-mother. Chapter 31:10–31 is well known for its praise of an ideal wife-mother. The role of the teacher and the function of moral precepts are emphasized throughout the book and become a prominent motif in Jewish education.

Except for this general outline, the study of Proverbs is hard to systematize. The writing is in poetic form, mostly as couplets or series of interrelated verses. A common feature of Hebrew poetry is parallelism. In Proverbs, two lines are most often either synonymous, with the second building on the first, or they are antithetical, with the second contrasting to the first (see, for example, 4:12 and 10:1). Striking figures of speech are frequent (6:27–28). There is a strong interest in the world of nature (6:6–8). Numbers are used to add force to the point being made (6:16–19).

In Jewish life, the family was of central importance and instruction by parents was a backbone of society (see 6:20). The sanctity of marriage is often implied by warnings against infidelity (see 6:23–29). The instruction of faithful courtiers follows similar principles, and proverbs about the king and his people are mixed in with instruction for family and community life (see 20:7–8).

In three passages, wisdom becomes a woman, addressing all who will hear and proclaiming the urgency of her message: read Proverbs 1:20–33, 8:1–36, and 9:1–6. (The Greek word for wisdom, *sophia,* is a feminine noun.) In Proverbs 7:4–5, woman-wisdom is contrasted to the evil woman who figures so often in this section. Since so much of the book (and of other Old Testament literature) is male-dominated, these passages call for special attention. We should emphasize how important the role model of mother-wife is elsewhere in the book. The book closes with the description of "a worthy wife" because she makes her husband rich (Proverbs 31:10–31).

As we have said, the proverbs were told to the young to teach them how to be faithful to God. The optimistic promise of Proverbs reflects a theology similar to that of Deuteronomy. Thus the emphasis is on obedience to God as the way to be rewarded in this life. There is no mention of Israel's covenant relation with the Lord. For the wise Israelite, however, life was not compartmentalized; so common sense, good living, and the divine will appear in a comfortable mix in Proverbs.

Ecclesiastes

The wisdom of Ecclesiastes, however, is not so optimistic. The book was written around 180 BC by an instructor of wealthy youth. The author writes like a worldly wise and somewhat cynical philosopher, but he is really a Jewish sage who deals with main themes of the wisdom movement. His Greek title, Qoheleth, means "one who convokes the assembly" which the RSV translates as "preacher" (1:1) although the precise office of the person is unclear. He has tried everything life has to offer and finds it all disappointing; so he concludes that "all is vanity" (1:13–14).

The negative skepticism of the book may cause surprise that it is in scripture at all. The writer attacks the traditional optimistic pieties like those in Proverbs because all human aspiration ends in death. Thus all that we strive for is vanity. The quality of human frustration is depicted in **Ecclesiastes 3:1–9,** which depicts an existence in which life is ultimately frustrated. In this, the writer sounds like the existentialist philosopher Jean-Paul Sartre, whose basic phi-

losophy is that life is ultimately absurd because all human striving and building is frustrated by death. The preacher, however, sees more deeply into the unknown qualities of human existence and of God who is a total mystery. Instead of the God of Proverbs, who is expected to reward on the demand of human performance, the preacher acknowledges that God is inscrutable and beyond the limits of human thinking and aspiration (Eccl 9:1). The proper attitude toward God is not expectation of performance but fear, which is understood as respectful awe in the presence of mystery (Eccl 12:13–14). Kathleen O'Connor elaborates, "To be a human creature is not to know. Mortality and unknowing define human existence. To draw near to the Living God, humans must embrace the truth of creaturehood, and in awe and wonder, surrender to the surprising and disturbing love of the Creator."[1]

Job

This wrestling with the problems of life should remind us of the experience of Job. In Theme 3, Section 2, we found Job struggling to understand how God could be just and still allow him to become so miserable. Ultimately, Job discovers that God's justice is a gift. Read **28:12–28,** where Job speaks at length about the nature of wisdom.

Concern for the individual is characteristic of wisdom. In Torah and the prophets, God's people are mostly treated in collective relationships, that is, in a corporate covenant with God. Proverbs speaks often of "my son," and Ecclesiastes is mostly concerned with the welfare of "a man." Here Job focuses on one person and his individual misery: "Why has this happened to me?"

Job is also akin to Ecclesiastes in that the glib answers the friends give to Job's questions are rejected though they claim to be the response of wisdom. They have assumed that one gets about what one deserves in this life. "Not in my case," Job retorts; and the nature of human life is argued out. Finally, Job finds his answer in the speeches of the Lord, which are full of nature questions Job cannot answer. Thus, the ultimate wisdom of God is vindicated.

Like the final words of Ecclesiastes, it is the explanatory prologue that has made the difficult discussions of Job palatable to most readers of the book (see 1, 2, and 42:7–17). In 42:1–6, Job responds to a direct encounter with God by rejecting the notion that he has a right to God's justice and accepts it as a gift.

The Song of Songs

The Song of Songs gets its title from the Hebrew word that means "the greatest song." The book is really a collection of lyric love poems with no explicitly religious content. The connection with Solomon is literary, made perhaps because of his reputation as a composer of songs (1 Kgs 5:12) plus the tradition about his prolific marriages (1 Kgs 11:3). The description of a wedding procession of Solomon in Song of Songs 3:6–11 is usually understood as a figurative poem celebrating a (much later) bridegroom's arrival at his wedding.

There is no certainty about the date of the collection; but it is usually placed after the Exile. Thus, it falls in the period of the wisdom movement and it is regularly listed with the wisdom books, though it is quite different from the ones we have just studied. It has maintained its place in the Jewish and Christian canons largely because it has been interpreted as figurative of the relationship between God and people—the Lord and Israel, Christ and the Church.

When you read the book without a conscious attempt to make a religious analysis, you will find that it is full of very beautiful expressions of human love including the erotic. The poetry presents dialogues between a man and a woman; and there is also a kind of chorus, the "daughters of Jerusalem," who are repeatedly addressed and who sometimes respond. You may note words that have found their way into our literary vocabulary; for example: "a flower of Sharon, a lily among thorns" (2:1), "the song of the dove" (2:12), "the little foxes that damage the vineyards" (2:15), "deep waters cannot quench love" (8:7).

Sirach

The author of Sirach is identified (50:27) as "Jesus the Son of Sirach"; and the book is often referred to as The Wisdom of Ben Sirach. (*Ben* is Hebrew for "son of".) It is also known as Ecclesiasticus. The book was first written in Hebrew, but was translated into Greek about fifty years later by Ben Sirach's grandson. Perhaps the author was a teacher in a wisdom school (see 51:23). Information in chapter 50 fixes the date of the book as around 180 BC.[2] The best-known chapter is **Sirach 44**. It begins a survey of Hebrew history that continues through chapter 49.

If you sample the book, you fill find much of the contents similar to Proverbs. There is an important difference, however: The separation of wisdom from covenant law, which we have observed, has given way to their union (see 24:22–23). Wisdom is now neither secular common sense nor is it secret (as we find suggested in Book of Wisdom). Wisdom is at last at home in the temple (24:1–12).

The Book of Wisdom

The Book of Wisdom is not like the other wisdom books you have read. Although there is some wisdom language, the style is more flowing; and the content shows its contact with Hellenistic Greek culture. Indeed, scholars find its closeness to Greek philosophy a problem when they try to discover its origin. The book received its traditional name because the author relates himself to Solomon's prayer for wisdom (see chapter 9). The author was a pious, somewhat traditional Jew; but he is influenced by cultural change. He wrote in Greek, probably in Alexandria shortly before the Christian era. Sample his writing by reading **7:13–22.**

The book is theologically significant because it identifies God's Spirit with wisdom (7:7; 9:17), it affirms a future life (**3:1;** 5:15–16), and it attempts to blend Hebrew and Greek wisdom (6:12, 24; 10:1–3). In 15:18–19:21 there is an elaborate series of contrasts related to the Exodus; God helps the Israelites and plagues the Egyptians.

Summary

We have seen a wide variety of literature all included under the umbrella of wisdom literature. We read the sanctified common sense of Proverbs and Sirach, the skeptical questions of Ecclesiastes and the painful probing of Job, the beautiful poetry of The Song of Solomon, and the elaborate reflections of The Book of Wisdom. All are seeking the deeper meaning in life, and they find that meaning closely connected with the creator God.

Suggestions for Further Study

Research

1. Using a Bible dictionary, review the major types of wisdom literature. What are the characteristic traits of the literature?

2. Argue for and against the proposition: The author of Ecclesiastes is inconsistent in the presentation of his thought.

3. Review the articles on the Song of Songs, Sirach, and Wisdom of Solomon in a Bible dictionary. What are the major points of these books? How would you describe them to a friend?

Reflection

1. Which wisdom book do you think is most congenial to popular thinking today? Does anything function as "wisdom" or wisdom literature today?

2. What do you think people mean today when they say that we have to be "realistic" about life? How would you respond to their point of view from the perspective of wisdom literature?

3. Try your hand at writing an original proverb.

4. You may wish to select three sayings from Proverbs, learn them, and be prepared to share them in the group session.

Notes

1. Kathleen O'Connor, *The Wisdom Literature*, 128.

2. For more information about this complicated period in Jewish history, consult a study Bible or HBD. It is just before the Maccabean revolt, which is mentioned in Theme 1, Session 2.

SESSION 2

Wisdom in the New Testament

Session Overview

The role of wisdom changed in New Testament times. Jesus used wisdom-like sayings and was portrayed as a wise man. The influence of the wisdom literature may be seen in the prologue to the fourth gospel. The movement of the Church into the Greco-Roman world brought a confrontation with new kinds of wisdom, and Paul meets this challenge. He is familiar with Greek philosophy, but his emphasis on wisdom that comes from the Holy Spirit is carefully related to Jesus Christ. Among the New Testament writings, James is closest to Jewish wisdom; but there are some other references.

Key Bible Readings

Matthew 11:28–30;
  16:1–3
Luke 7:31–35;
  12:54–56
John 1:1–18
1 Corinthians 1:17–31;
  2:6–13
James 1:5–11; 3:13–18

Key Words

signs
the Word

The Nature of Wisdom

Wisdom in the Jewish scriptures means first of all the sensible and consistent handling of contemporary life in one's environment. Much of this is similar and sometimes related to the thought of the surrounding cultures, but there is an emphasis on the creator God and the Torah as the ultimate sources of wisdom.

There is no wisdom movement as such in the New Testament, but wisdom is present in several important ways. In the gospels, there are passages that show a definite connection with aspects of Jewish wisdom. We should expect this, since the teaching of Jesus was so deeply rooted in the Old Testament. When the Christian movement spread beyond Palestine, however, the intellectual and religious environment was mostly rooted in Greek thought. The influence that we saw in The Book of Wisdom is everywhere, and wisdom in an international garb becomes a challenge to Christian faith. What we have learned about wisdom is a helpful bridge as we try to sort out what is distinctive in Christian wisdom.

154

Wisdom in the Gospels

Wisdom appears in the gospels in several forms. The simplest kind occurs in sayings of Jesus that we might call "folk wisdom." Jesus points out in **Matthew 16:1–3** that his listeners are able to forecast the weather from various observations, yet they miss the more serious "signs of the times." In the parallel **Luke 12:54–56,** the weather signs are different. Often his terse comments are very similar to sayings in Proverbs (see Mk 3:24–25; 7:15).

Upon occasion, Jesus mentioned wisdom; read **Luke 7:31–35.** Here Jesus uses a homely picture of children's play to make a point about his contemporaries. In verses 29–30, Luke observes how Jesus' hearers are divided over John the Baptist. Now their antagonism is extended to Jesus' own ministry. Luke concludes that Jesus and his followers are wisdom's "children" and are thereby "vindicated." In Matthew's parallel, 11:19, it is "works" that justify wisdom; but the point is not different. Read the familiar words in **Matthew 11:28–30.** You will recall how wisdom was portrayed in Proverbs as calling to those who would hear. See also Sirach 51:23–27. On the other hand, Jesus' pronouncement of woes is reminiscent of the wisdom strictures against folly (see Luke 11:45–52). In 11:49, "the Wisdom of God" is mentioned as though it were a quotation, but no definite literary source can be identified. In the parallel Matthew 23:34, almost the same words are attributed to Jesus himself; so perhaps Luke means "God's wisdom." We have seen how wisdom is considered to be a gift of God;[1] so Jesus would here be claiming to have that gift.

The tradition and substance of the wisdom forms used by Jesus and the gospel writers were already present in first-century Judaism. Luke tells how the twelve-year-old Jesus "astounded" those who heard his conversations in the temple, and wisdom is mentioned twice as a char-

acteristic of Jesus' childhood development (Lk 2:40, 47, 52). Later, many of his Galilean audience "were astonished" at his wisdom (Mk 6:2). He did not pose as a sage, but his mastery of the scriptures clearly included the wisdom lore.

In discussing his mission and message on one occasion, Jesus said, "there is something greater than Solomon here," and he cites the visit of the queen of Sheba "to hear the wisdom of Solomon" (Mt 12:42). Jesus' interview with the Syrophoenician woman (Mk 7:24–30) and his decision about taxes paid to Caesar (12:13–17) may remind one of Solomon's wisdom; but Jesus' good news is more important than any reference to wisdom sayings, however great.

In Theme 3, Session 3, we looked at how Jesus revealed God in the prologue of the fourth gospel, **John 1:1–18.** Jesus embodies "the Word" (Greek, *logos*), and this we connected with God's word in creation (Gn 1:1, 3). Now we may see further how this is related to Jewish wisdom thought. "The Word" reminds us of the role of wisdom as the expression of God's being and the agent of God's creating and communicating; compare Psalms 33:6, 9; Proverbs 8:22–31; Sirach 1:4, 9–10.

All that God seeks to communicate, "the Word" is. We should not think of wisdom as a separate being when she is personified as she seems to be in Sirach and the Book of Wisdom. John 1:1 seems to risk this when it states that "the Word was with God"; but having distinguished the identity of "the Word," it affirms that "the Word was God." In 1:14, however, there is a radical move: "the Word became flesh" declares God's ultimate communication with humankind. The rest of the gospel will seek to show that Jesus is not a created spirit but "the son of God" (20:31). Thus he can say of his unique relationship to "the Father" (the term he usually uses for God), "The Father and I are one" (10:30).

Paul and Wisdom

Paul mentions wisdom twenty-eight times in his letters. Each of Paul's references must be studied within its complete passage, for there are different shades of meaning. Keep in mind that it was a drastic move when Paul traveled from the Near East to Europe. The traditions of the great Greek philosophers were already five hundred years old, and their thought world was quite different from that of the Old Testament. In Greek and Roman thinking, God was totally outside of human experience and completely unaffected by human concerns. The Jewish idea that God was involved in human affairs and the Christian teaching that God became human in Jesus Christ were totally repugnant to Greek and Roman philosophers. This was not totally new to Paul. He was a native of Tarsus, a university town in southeastern Asia Minor (Acts 22:3), and the training that he received in Jerusalem had already exposed him to Greek thinking. His speech in Athens shows his ability to deal with such philosophy (Acts 17:16–34).[2] He is quite convinced, however, that philosophical wisdom is too speculative and secular for God's people.

Paul's most sustained treatment of wisdom is woven through the early chapters of 1 Corinthians. Read **1 Corinthians 1:17–25; 2:6–13.** Note that "wisdom" is used in more than one sense. Human wisdom is contrasted to God's wisdom and is sometimes negative, sometimes neutral. The Greeks especially look for wisdom. God's wisdom may come to humans as a gift "according to the same Spirit" (1 Cor 12:8). Many people, however, will consider God's wisdom to be foolishness.

The effective center of this whole treatment is Christ crucified. This is a stumbling block to Jews because they could not think of their messiah coming to such an end (Dt 21:23). Besides, it is "foolishness to Gentiles," a term interchangeable in this context with Greeks; they cannot make sense of worshiping a God who is capable of suffering and who appears impotent to prevent such an unjust and cruel event. Paul is writing of wisdom and quoting from Isaiah (Is 19; 13; 64:3), a prophet who was closely connected to the wisdom movement. In Romans 11:33–36 Paul enthusiastically expresses praises of God's wisdom and knowledge to celebrate how God's plan of salvation works in the world.

Several times in Colossians the phrase "in all wisdom" occurs, but the meaning goes beyond the wisdom-literature background. Read Colossians 2:1–3, where "all the treasures of wisdom and knowledge" are hidden in Christ. This is *God's* mystery. In Paul's day, there were pagan religions that made much of "mysteries" and initiated persons into those mysteries. In Colossians 2:20–23, "a semblance of wisdom" is related to ascetic taboos, but Christ separates one from all of this. With Christ one dies "to the elemental powers of the world," a phrase that may be taken to refer to earth, air, water, and fire.

In Ephesians 5:15–17, Christians are urged to be wise, not foolish. Timothy is told that "[the] sacred scriptures . . . are capable of giving you wisdom for salvation" (2 Tm 3:15). In 2 Peter 3:15–16, we find reference to the wisdom given our beloved brother Paul and the reflection that wisdom is somewhat difficult to understand!

What a challenge for Paul! Here he was, a chief advocate of a new manner of understanding God's wisdom in an unfamiliar environment. A measure of the success of his undertaking is recorded in the history of Christian thought in the West, where the old and the new were fused into the worldwide mission of God's people.

James

One book of the New Testament comes close to being wisdom literature: the Book of James. The book begins like a letter, but it has no epistolary ending. In its question-and-answer sections, and in some other ways, it resembles a Greek literary form known as *diatribe,* a "discourse conducted in a familiar conversational style, which developed often by lively argument with a fictitious opponent."[3] (This does not have the extremely negative meaning that the word "diatribe" has today; the form was used by the Stoic philosopher Epictetus, and often by Paul.)

There are only five explicit references to wisdom. Read **James 1:5–11** and **3:13–18.** You will sense that the author uses wisdom illustrations and offers practical advice. Control of the tongue is emphasized; in 3:3 it is compared to bridling a horse (see also 1:26; 3:6–12; 4:11; 5:12). In James 4:6, there is a similarity to Proverbs 3:34; and 4:8 echoes Psalm 145:18.

The passage found in James 2:14–26, which deals with the relationship between faith and works, is sometimes cited as being in theological controversy with Paul's views (as, for example, in Rom 3:20–22; Gal 3:9-10). James, however, is approaching life from a wisdom-like, practical viewpoint of how a person activates the grace received from the Holy Spirit. Paul would not dispute that a do-nothing faith is ineffective (see Rom 13:13; 15:17; and Gal 6:4, 7).

In Conclusion

Wisdom is mentioned in Revelation in two ways. In 5:12 and 7:12, it is included in sevenfold ascriptions of praise to God and to the Lamb. In 13:18 and 17:9, it functions as a kind of signal that what follows is in a sort of code that requires a key to understand. The word mystery is used in a similar way. We shall examine these matters in Theme 10, Session 4.

In the development of liturgy in the Church, wisdom as a title of the Holy Spirit has played a prominent role in the Eastern branches. In the Eastern Churches in union with Rome and the Russian Orthodox church today one will hear solemn invocations of wisdom.

In review, we may conclude that the theme of wisdom is not as plain as other themes we have followed through the Bible. It is important, however, for three reasons. First, there is a body of literature that we must classify in this way. The more general term "poetry" does not distinguish it sufficiently. Second, wisdom literature provides a significant point of contact with nonbiblical religion and secular thought. Third, the Church in the liturgy uses personified wisdom as a reference to the separate persons of the Trinity and to Mary, predestined to be the mother of the incarnate Son of God. We stress what is unique in the biblical tradition, and that is fundamental for our study, but we must remember that there is truth outside our scriptures. Recognizing what is common to several traditions will serve to isolate and highlight what is different and distinct.

Suggestions for Further Study

Research

1. Review an article on wisdom in a Bible dictionary. In what ways is Jesus identified with the wisdom tradition? How do the other New Testament writings reflect wisdom?

2. Review John 1:1–18 in HBC 1046–48. What links does your commentary help to explain between John's theology of the *logos* and the wisdom tradition?

3. Look up the word "fool" in a Bible dictionary. What characteristics does the "fool" have in the Bible? How do you think a "fool" in the Bible's sense of the word would act today?

4. Review the letter of James. What message do you think he has for the Church today? Copy out the sayings you think are most relevant for your parish.

Reflection

1. Think of some modern wisdom-type sayings. In what way do they influence behavior?

2. Respond to the interpretation of the relationship between biblical and secular wisdom presented at the end of this session. Do you agree or disagree? In what ways?

3. You may want to thoroughly master the prologue of the Gospel of John and memorize 1:1–5, 14.

Notes

1. See Proverbs 2:6; Ecclesiastes 2:26. This is also mentioned in Ephesians 1:16–18; James 1:5.

2. See the NAB footnote to Acts 17:22–31.

3. *Jerome Biblical Commentary*, 79:11.

THEME 9

God's People Worship

SESSION 1

Early Backgrounds and National Rites

Session Overview

Worship is at the center of life for the Jewish people. From the patriarchs through Passover at the Exodus to the Temple in Jerusalem, worship experience is vital to Jewish identity. Exile and restoration brought changes, but the major festivals marked the cycle of the year and are essential to an understanding of the Bible.

Key Bible Readings

Genesis 22:1–14;
  28:10–22
2 Samuel 6:1–19
1 Kings 2:6–7, 22–30;
  8:4–11, 22–30
Isaiah 6:1–13
Psalm 137:1–6
Ezra 3:1–13
Leviticus 23:1–44
Esther 9:2–32

Key Words

Rosh Hashanah
tabernacle
Yom Kippur
Succoth
Levite
Hanukkah
Temple
Purim
synagogue
Feast of Weeks

Worship and Beginnings

When Moses first appeared before the pharaoh, he requested that the Hebrews might go to "celebrate a feast" in the desert in honor of the Lord (Ex 5:1). This led to the series of events that overshadow all of Israel's subsequent experiences as God's people. The Passover celebration, with all its overtones of memory and meaning, became central in the Hebrew national religious consciousness. The Hebrews celebrated in worship the covenant relationship between God and the people.

Worship was a part of their earliest traditions. In the prehistory, the anger of Cain against his brother Abel is said to have stemmed from God's regard for Abel's offering rather than for Cain's (Gn 4:3–5). Noah's first act when he left the ark was to build an altar and offer burnt offerings to God (8:18–21a).

The story of Abraham's willingness to sacrifice Isaac is a notable high point in the patriarchal traditions. Read **Genesis 22:1–14.** Verse 5 introduces the word "worship"; the Hebrew word means "bow oneself down." Much later extrabiblical tradition located the event on the low mountain where the Jerusalem Temple eventually was built. Later Abraham sent a servant to find a wife for Isaac, and several times that servant worshiped God because of success in his mission (24:26, 48, 52).

Jacob's dream-experience at Bethel, **Genesis 28:10–22,** includes details that are repeated in other occasions of Israelite worship. His sense of the presence of God is reflected in the common experience of Israel's "dwelling." The erection of memorial stones, the pouring of oil, the making of vows, and the promise of the tithe all are practiced again and again.

From Moses to Samuel

The call of Moses from the burning bush (Ex 3) reiterates two features from Jacob's experience: the identification of holy ground and the revelation of God. The spot was made holy by the presence of God, and Moses learned something about who God is when the Lord revealed the sacred name. Moses was the initiator of Israel's understanding of a special relationship to God and how this was to be worked out in life, and particularly in worship.

When God met Moses on Sinai and gave directions for the corporate life of the people, the text recounting this event contains extensive details for the equipment, personnel, and practice of Israel's worship. The first item is the "dwelling," which was translated into the Latin word *tabernacle*, meaning "a portable place of worship." In Exodus 25–30, there are more details than we need to remember, but they include many interesting matters that reflect the later history of worship. A nomadic lifestyle is implied throughout. This wilderness period is seen as Israel's ideal time (see, for example, Stephen's speech in Acts 7:44–50). The text, however, was composed after the people were settled in Palestine, and it shows the theological and ritual concerns of the later writers.

Note the role played by the priests and Levites in Israel's worship. These groups are not identical, but at times they are not distinguished in the texts. See Numbers 3:5–10; Deuteronomy 33:8–11. There is a curious story in Judges 17 where Micah (not the prophet) has a shrine with an idol. This was certainly not an orthodox practice in Israel, and it indicates the religious state of the period of the judges. When Micah finds a way to employ a Levite, he considers his enterprise orthodox. The whole thrust of the story reflects the later deuteronomist theological concern to show the corrupt nature of worship at Dan which was established as an alternative to Temple worship in Jerusalem.

The prerogatives of the Levites are spelled out in Deuteronomy 18:1–8. They served at worship centers throughout the promised land, and they resided there. As it turned out, their principal place of service was Jerusalem.

The story of Samuel includes interesting glimpses of worship practiced in his time. From early boyhood he serves as an attendant in the sanctuary at Shiloh under the priest Eli (see 1 Sm 1:21–28; 2:11, 18–20). The call of Samuel in this setting is a familiar story which may be reviewed in 1 Samuel 3. In later life he performs priestly functions (see 7:8–10; 9:14; 10:8). An unhappy part of the story is what happened to Eli's sons (see 2:12–17, 22–36; 4:10–11).

The Ark and the Temple

In the battle in which Eli's sons died, the "Ark of God" was captured by the Philistines. This Ark was a chest that became a focus of Israelite worship. Read about its construction in Exodus 25:10–22. The people evidently believed that God "sat" invisible upon the "propitiatory" atop the Ark. Thus the Ark was evidence of God's presence. The places where it was kept during the settlement of the promised land became worship centers: Gilgal (Jos 5:10; 7:6; 9:6); Bethel (Jgs 20:26–27); Shiloh (1 Sm 3:3); Kiriath-jearim (5:1–7:2). When David brought the Ark to Jerusalem, it marked the settling of central worship in that city. See **2 Samuel 6:1–19.**

The building of the Temple in Jerusalem was of far-reaching importance for Israel and the history of Jewish worship. The story is told in 1 Kings 5–7 and is repeated with additional material in 1 Chronicles 28:11–29:22 and 2 Chronicles 2–4. The dedication of the Temple was a very great occasion. The dedicatory prayer of King Solomon is featured. See 1 Kings 8 and 2 Chronicles 5:2–7:10. See **1 Kings 6:2–7, 22–30; 8:4–11, 22–30.**

This sketchy survey should indicate how much of the Old Testament is concerned with matters of cultic practice and belief. From the time of Solomon, concern is directed to the encroachment of alien religious cults. Recall the contest between Elijah and the prophets of Baal and the subsequent conflict of Jehu and other devotees of Baal (1 Kgs 18). Some foreign deities and their worship left marks on Jewish worship. Solomon's Temple had architectural features borrowed from the Phoenicians—not surprising, since Hiram, the architect, was a Phoenician.

Details of the construction of the Ark and the Temple need not be studied here. We shall note as we go along the worship practices that have lasting importance. The reforms under Josash, Hezekiah, and Josiah are important and have been noted in Theme 6, Section 2.

The Prophets

Threats to Israel from outside powers were more than political and social. The prophets saw clearly the drastic danger from disruption of Israelite worship, particularly as it affected the central Jerusalem Temple. Worship in Jerusalem "proclaimed the eternal promise of protection to the house of David prophesied by Nathan in 2 Samuel 7 as the cornerstone of God's covenant with Israel."[1] The establishment of Temple treasures figured in negotiations with enemies (2 Kgs 18:13–16). When envoys from Babylon visited Hezekiah and he showed them the treasures, Isaiah reproved him and predicted that captivity in Babylon was coming (2 Kgs 20:12–19).

The call of Isaiah includes one of the classic passages on worship in the Bible. Study **Isaiah 6:1–13** carefully. This is sometimes referred to as a pattern for the experience of worship. Try to identify the parts of this pattern.

Other prophets complained about faults in worship and the attendant responsibilities. There are examples from both Jewish kingdoms. Review Amos 5:21–27. See also Hosea 8:11–13; 6:6; Zephaniah 3:4; Malachi 1:6–3:4.

Exile and Restoration

The Exile posed particular problems for Jewish worship. How could worship be maintained without its physical focus, the Temple, which had been destroyed? **Psalm 137:1–6** reflects this dilemma in a poignant way. Some scholars think that the synagogue began to develop during this time as a response to the situation. *Synagogue* is a Greek word meaning an "assembly of people." It was used to denote a gathering of Jews who pray, hear scripture, and hear teaching and preaching based on scripture. Synagogue also means the place where the congregation assembles. Certainly the lack of the Temple was important in this change of worship practice.

Ezekiel ministered to exiles in Babylon. As early as Theme 1, we noted his encouraging message. In 39:25–29, he prophesies the restoration to the Jewish homeland. From 40:1 through 47:2, he recounts visions of the rebuilding of the Temple. Although details are idealized, the description is reminiscent of the Temple of Solomon, where Ezekiel may have served before the Exile.

The rebuilding of the Temple after the exiles returned is treated in Ezra and Haggai. Read **Ezra 3:1–13** (see also Neh 12:40–13:22, 28–31). This second Temple is important to Christians because in it were developed the practices that influenced Judaism in the period of independence (165–63 BC) and on into the beginning of the Christian era until the final destruction of Herod's Temple in AD 70.

Features of Worship

The Temple was the focal point of Jewish national religion, and the sacrificial system was one of the major activities of the Temple. Sacrifice was the principal medium of worship of God. Offerings of several kinds and for various purposes are specified in Leviticus, Numbers, and Deuteronomy. In a sense, all of them are in acknowledgement that "The LORD's are the earth and its fullness" (Ps 24:1, note the liturgical content of verses 7–10). Life is a gift from God. The people belong to God. Although the whole sacrificial system came to an abrupt end with the final destruction of the Temple, the spiritual ideas that underlay it and have sprung from it still endure. They run through the New Testament and help to explain Jesus and the sacrificial aspects of his death.

An equally notable feature of the worship of Israel is its calendar of holy days. A modern rabbi has said that "the catechism of the Jew is his calendar." The appointed feasts are outlined in **Leviticus 23:1–44,** and to this list were added later a number of other festivals that are still observed in Judaism. Several other aspects of Jewish worship are also important. The celebration of the Sabbath, daily prayer, and the observance and study of the law, including household and dietary customs continue to be a regular part of modern Judaism.

Major Festivals

The most visible of all the recurring observances is the Sabbath. Recall the commandment that requires its hallowing. In Leviticus 19:1–4, the Sabbath is given a central place. In Nehemiah 9:13–14, the Sabbath law is the only one mentioned specifically in a passage about God's commands. Jeremiah complains particularly about the profanation of the Sabbath (see 17:19–27). Isaiah 58:13–14 declares how the sabbath ought to be kept and enjoyed.

Along with the weekly recurrence of the Sabbath, there was a monthly observance of the new moon. The official calendar of Judaism is lunar, so the annual cycle is regulated by this event. See the instruction for its observance in Numbers 28:11–15; also 10:10. Some of Israel's neighbors worshiped the moon (Dt 4:19; 2 Kgs 23:5); but since it was one of God's creations, the people of Israel thought of it only in relation to the worship of the Lord. Apparently, there were special observances of a family nature (1 Sm 20:5), and the time was considered propitious for consulting prophets (2 Kgs 4:22, 23). The Sabbath and new moon are mentioned together (as in 2 Chr 2:3 and Ez 46:1). The prophets denounced those who observe these times improperly (see Is 1:13–14; Hos 2:13; Am 8:5).

The Old Testament prescribes no special observance for the beginning of a new year. Later Judaism placed this day, *Rosh Hashanah,* immediately before the Day of Atonement, in Hebrew, *Yom Kippur.* Read the data in Exodus 30:10 and Leviticus 16. Blowing the ram's horn and a connection with Abraham's offering of Isaac are later developments. The order of the festivals was maintained from early times, but the numbering of the months changed. In the Torah, the year began in the spring at Passover time; later, it began in the fall after the Day of Atonement.

Five days after Yom Kippur the Feast of Booths was observed (see Lv 23:26–43). This has become known by the Hebrew word for booths, *Succoth*. The people lived for eight days in rustic booths in memory of the temporary shelters their ancestors had inhabited during the Exodus. The period also prompted thanksgiving, and offerings were presented in connection with the grape and olive harvests.

At about the time Christians celebrate Christmas, Jews observe *Hanukkah*. In John 10:22 this is called the Feast of the Dedication. Its origin is described in first Maccabees (see Theme 1, Session 2) in connection with the successful Jewish revolt against Antiochus IV. When the Temple was rededicated, an oil lamp was lit, and it is said to have burned eight days although there had been oil enough for only one day. So the celebration is sometimes called Feast of Lights, and a candle is lighted on eight successive days. Traditionally, the "Hallel," Psalms 113–118, is sung.

The next festival in the calendar is *Purim*. It is traced to events in the story of Esther. See **Esther 9:2–32.** This is a nationalist more than a religious holiday, and it was celebrated in the villages. The gaiety of the occasion has been preserved and accentuated in later times. The Book of Esther will not be used again in this course, so you may want to read it in its entirety now.

Passover was given considerable attention in Theme 1; only a brief review should be necessary now. The intimate connection between Hebrew history and worship is nowhere more evident than in this celebration.

Seven weeks after Passover, the harvest festival was held. In Exodus 34:22, it is called the Feast of Weeks because of the way the date was determined. Deuteronomy 16:9 counts the seven weeks from the beginning of the harvest, which comes after the Feast of Unleavened Bread, which includes Passover. Leviticus 23:15–16 makes the interval fifty days, whence the Greek designation, Pentecost. The Christian Pentecost takes its name from this Jewish feast. It was one of the three prime festivals of the Jewish nation from its early days (see Ex 23:14–17; 2 Chr 8:12–13). In later Judaism, the day commemorated God's giving of the law to Moses, and the Book of Ruth was also read.

Thus, the worship of Israel is one including history, praise, and festivals. It is the genius of the Jewish people that they combined their life experiences in such unity. Whenever they lost this sense, their identity was in peril. Precisely this ability to hold all life as holy has given Judaism its ageless continuity. This is also an important legacy from Judaism to Christianity.

Suggestions for Further Study

Research

1. Review Genesis 22:1–14; 28:10–22; 2 Samuel 6:1–19; 1 Kings 8:22–30. What attitudes toward worship are present in the characters in these stories?

2. Using a Bible dictionary, find the meaning of the following: priests, Levites, the Tent of Meeting or Tabernacle, worship, temple, synagogue. Be prepared to discuss them in the class session.

3. Review an article on worship and synagogue in a Bible dictionary. What are the similarities between these forms of worship and the celebration of the Liturgy of the Word? What are some of the significant differences?

4. Review the meaning of the Jewish festivals.

Reflection

1. Details of liturgy from Old Testament sources imply certain things about how the participants or the writers understood God. How do our forms of worship reflect our understanding of God?

2. In what ways has Christian worship been influenced by Jewish practices?

3. You may want to master the following:

- Isaiah 6:3

- Psalm 137:1–6 (note its reference to worship in despair)

- the cycle of Jewish festivals

Note

1. Lawrence Boadt, *Reading the Old Testament* (Mahwah, NJ: Paulist, 1984), 270.

SESSION 2

Devotional Life, Public and Personal

Session Overview

From early times, Israel prayed in poetry; the Psalms are the collection of this literature. The Psalms include a wide variety of devotional expression couched in poems of simple beauty and complex form. Familiarity with many of them nurtures religious development, for they continue to be a fundamental resource for prayer.

Key Bible Readings

Psalms	1	Psalms	90
	2		91
	8		95
	19		100
	22		103
	23		110
	24		121
	27		122
	46		136
	51		137
	72		139
	84		150

Key Words

antithetic parallelism
climactic parallelism
synonymous parallelism
synthetic parallelism

The Role of the Psalms

While the regulations for Temple offerings and the observance of religious festivals are extensive and detailed in the Old Testament, our principal source for an understanding of the spirit of Israel's prayer is the Book of Psalms. The Psalter can fairly be described as the prayer book of Israel, particularly in the second Temple (c. 520–37 BC).

Other Near Eastern peoples also expressed their religious beliefs in poetry, but Israel outstripped them in the development and intensity of expression. Scholars are convinced that the collection grew across the years as Israel's religious experience evolved. Many of the psalms must have had their origin during the period of the monarchy. Tradition attached David's name to the whole Psalter; and although he had nothing to do with many of the psalms, the inspiration for such a collection may well go back to him. For psalms specifically ascribed to writers other than David, see Psalms 73–83. We noted in Session 1 that **Psalm 137** is clearly from the Exile.

166

Liturgical Poetry in Israel

The Book of Psalms is not the only biblical material that contains liturgical praise. Other examples may be found in 2 Samuel 6:5 and Amos 5:23. From the earliest times the Israelites had expressed themselves in poetry, as in Exodus 15:20–21; Genesis 49:1–27; Judges 5. Probably certain persons became cantors or choirmasters (see the superscriptions on Ps 4–6; 44–47).

A number of the psalms reflects the hymn's used in public liturgy, such as 20:2–4; 26:6–8; 27:4–6; 81:2–4; **84;** 134; **136;** and especially **24,** which we noted in Session 1. Some are related to the monarchy, so that the term "royal" psalms is often used by scholars. Among such are **2** and **110,** which are frequently quoted in the New Testament. Psalms 20; 61; **72;** 89; and 132 may be considered prayers for the king, and 144 is a hymn for the king. Psalm 45 seems to be a bridal ode for a royal marriage.

Organization of the Psalter

There are various ways of dividing the Psalter. As finally edited, it is in five "books," probably in imitation of the Torah. The divisions are: (I) 2–41; (II) 42–72; (III) 73–89; (IV) 90–106; (V) 107–150. Psalm **1** is an introduction to the whole, and **150** is a final paean of praise. Psalms 42–83 and 108 use the Hebrew word for "God," whereas the rest prefer the divine name, "Lord." Some psalms occur twice; for example, 14 = 53; 40:14–18 = 70; 108 = 57:8–12 and 60:8–14. Recall also that Psalm 18 = 2 Samuel 22:2–51.

Psalm 71:20 indicates the end of David's "prayers," and some scholars see in this one indication of how the whole Psalter developed. First there were collections early attributed to David's hand; then psalms of Asaph and of the sons of Korah were added; and still later additional groups were included. In the last section two important groups may be noted: the "songs of ascent," or pilgrim psalms (120–134), which were evidently sung on the way to Jerusalem festivals (read **121** and **122**) and the *Hallel* or praise psalms, which were also sung at festival times (105–107, 113–118, 135, 136, 146–150). Jesus and his disciples probably sang some of this latter group at the Last Supper (Mk 14:26).

Other classifications usually include: hymns (**95–100**); thanksgivings (92–118); laments or entreaties, which may be collective (83, 137) or individual (**22**, 31, 42, **51**); historical (78, 105, 106); nature (**8, 19,** 29, 104); personal meditation and reflection (**23, 27, 90, 91, 139**). A few are unique and belong to no class. One of these is 119, an elaborate acrostic with an eight-line stanza for each letter of the Hebrew alphabet, each line of each stanza beginning with the same letter.

Literary and Poetic Characteristics

The psalms have two other important characteristics. One, they employ much literary adornment, particularly simile and metaphor, found in nearly every psalm. Two, they reflect the deep questions people ask about their lives and about God, including the ethical question, "What is right?" (24:3–4; 51:8–9; 119:9–11); the theological question, "Given the justice of God, why...?" (13; 74:1–11); philosophical inquiry of a sort (77:8–11; 139:1–18); and the search for faith (22; 73:25–28). Many psalms contain affirmations of faith (**46; 103**).

Our chief interest is in the meaning and content of the psalms, but we also need to give some attention to the form of Hebrew poetry, already introduced in Theme 8, Session 1. Unlike most English poetry, Hebrew poetry does not have meter or rhyme. It does, however, have rhythm. A more evident feature is parallelism, which also occurs in other ancient Near Eastern literatures.

In this stylistic device, "lines" of poetry (usually clauses or their equivalents in length) are balanced in sequence in various ways. For example, Psalm 27:1 says

> The LORD is my light and my salvation;
>   whom should I fear?
> The LORD is my life's refuge;
>   of whom should I be afraid?

In synonymous parallelism, an idea is repeated in approximately similar words, as in 19:2. Synthetic parallelism adds to the thought of one line with a similar but different line, as in 23:1–3. These two forms are skillfully combined in 27:1 above. Antithetic parallelism presents contrasting lines or half lines, as in 1:6. Least common is climactic or step parallelism, where the initial line is added to in a step-by-step progression, as in 29:3–9 and 150.

Significance of the Psalms

For this study, perhaps the greatest value of the psalms is the insight they provide into the devotional life of the people who first created and used them. Their real feelings find utterance here, feelings of grief and joy, of despair and hope, of anger and penitence, of passionate entreaty for help or calm assurance of trust. Here are prayers and praises to suit the changing needs of the soul.

The psalms help us to appreciate the religious pilgrimage of Israel in a way that the national cult or the Temple could never do. They help us to understand why the prophets often criticized the formal religious ceremonies because they were out of touch with the needs of the common people and with the righteous requirements of God (Am 5:21–24; Mi 6:6–8).

The psalms also made it evident that a good deal of Hebrew worship was carried on where the people lived—in the family, in the village, and later on in the local synagogue. It is sig-nificant that the psalms are quoted in the New Testament more frequently than any other Old Testament book except Isaiah. The records of the New Testament Church make it evident that the psalms were a vital part of the religious experience and expression of first-century Christians (see Acts 1:20; 2:25, 34–35).

People in the Hebrew and Christian traditions through the ages have found that the psalms beautifully and accurately reflect their spiritual history. Though some of the psalms are hardly usable for Christian worship (58; 109; 137:8–9), most of us will concur with the French scholar André Robert, who wrote, "The Book of Psalms enables us to hear an echo of the entire Bible whose doctrine it expresses in prayer."[1]

In the Liturgy of the Hours, the psalms are a part of the daily prayer life of the Church. They are prayed by the clergy and religious every day either individually or in community. The laity are encouraged also to make the Liturgy of the Hours a part of daily prayer so they may be reminded "that through public worship and prayer they are in touch with all . . . and can contribute in no small degree to the salvation of the whole world."[2]

Suggestions for Further Study

Research

1. Begin your own survey of the Psalter by noting key phrases or ideas in the following well-known psalms:

1	24	90	121
2	27	91	122
8	46	95	136
19	51	100	137
22	72	103	139
23	84	110	150

2. Review the different classifications of the psalms. Be able to identify at least one of the psalms in each of the classifications.

3. Review five of the psalms that are indicated in bold print. Then answer the following questions:

   • What can you tell about the personality, position, or circumstances of the author?

   • What feelings are expressed in the different parts of the psalm?

   • Who does the psalmist seem to be speaking for? himself? the community? the nation?

   • How might this psalm be used in worship?

4. The Key Word list notes four kinds of parallelism in the psalms. Review the examples of each. Create your own examples.

5. Can you think of ways the psalms are used as themes for new music in the Church to-day? At Sunday Mass, review the songs in your parish hymnbook to discover some examples.

6. Each Sunday or weekday at Mass, take note how the Responsorial Psalm that follows the first reading is actually an echo of or response to that reading.

Reflection

In what ways have the psalms influenced your personal prayer life? What themes in reading the psalms for this session are most meaningful for you?

Notes

1. Quoted in Carrol Stuhlmeuller, *Psalms 1*, p. 16.

2. *General Instruction of the Liturgy of the Hours* 27.

SESSION 3

Liturgical Prayer in the New Testament Setting

Session Overview

Christian liturgy was influenced by the Jewish synagogue, temple, and festivals. A number of events in Jesus' life relate to these influences. Jesus formed the Eucharist from the familiar rituals of the Jewish home. Through baptism Christians are united with Christ in the life of the Spirit.

Key Bible Readings

Luke 1:46–56; 2:22–
   32, 41–42; 4:14–30
John 4:19–24
Acts 3:1–11; 7:44–51
Hebrews 9:1–14
Acts 16:13, 25
1 Corinthians 11:17–34
Acts 20:7–12
Ephesians 3:14–21
1 Corinthians 14:15–
   16, 24–33
Revelation 4:8–11;
   5:9–12

Key Words

Eucharist
proselyte
prophesying
speaking in tongues
sacrifice

Backgrounds of Christian Liturgy

Liturgical prayer was a constant feature of life in the early Christian Church (Acts 2:46–47; 12:12). The records present frequent injunctions and promises in this regard (see Mt 18:20; Heb 10:25; Rv 19:10; 22:8–9). There are many other references. This emphasis came naturally from the backgrounds of the Christian movement.

Among the influences on Christian worship, certainly none is as important as Judaism. The lines of development are sometimes complex, for some New Testament elements come from Jewish faith and practice that are not reflected in the Old Testament literature. Nevertheless, the relationships are deep and pervasive.

A few areas of Christian liturgy show connections with non-Jewish sources, but in almost every instance such connections are through the prior contact of Judaism with those other religious traditions. So when Paul speaks of "mystery," as in 1 Corinthians 13:2, he may reflect some awareness of the "mystery religions" of the Middle East (see also Eph 5:32; Col 1:26–27; 1 Tm 3:16). This vocabulary of Paul's, however, was likely developed from his religious training.

Influences on Christian Worship

The synagogue was a principal influence on Christian liturgy. Since Jesus ministered primarily outside Jerusalem, and since Paul carried his mission far beyond Palestine, we should expect this synagogue connection. Emphasis on the reading and expounding of scripture, together with prayers and hymns, comes from the practices common to the synagogue.

Church liturgy in the Gentile world often had a direct foundation in the synagogues that were established throughout the Roman empire (see Acts 15:21). Paul used local synagogues as springboards for his mission in cities new to him. Acts implies a conscious, even if hesitant, continuity between Jewish and Christian worship (see 13:14–15, 42–49).

The influence of the Temple is indirect. Its role changes several times in the relatively short New Testament period. We shall mark later its place in Jesus' career. His followers began the life of the early Church in an active relation to the Temple but gradually moved away from it. The destruction of the Temple was a turning point in the history of early Christianity (as well as Judaism).

Although the Church did not embrace any of the Jewish festivals directly, their mark on the New Testament is indelible. The progress and length of Jesus' public ministry is closely tied to the mention of festivals he attended in Jerusalem. The Pentecost experience of Acts 2 is sometimes called the "birthday" of the Church. Some of Paul's movements are related to the festival cycle, as in 1 Corinthians 16:8.

Jesus

From his birth and childhood, Jesus is related to the Temple, as is seen in **Luke 2:22–32, 41–42.** The families of John the Baptist and of Jesus were pious Jewish folk. In connection with the offering mentioned in Luke 2:24, see Leviticus 12:8. The stories about Simeon and Anna (Lk 2:36–38) suggest Temple activity not apparent elsewhere in the New Testament.

Jesus' experience in the Nazareth synagogue has been noted in other themes. Read **Luke 4:14–30.** Note the continuation of "his custom" in 4:31–32, and see Matthew 13:53–54. Whatever antagonism arose between Jesus and Jewish religious leaders, he could not be charged with abandoning the places of worship of his people.

In Mark there is no indication that Jesus attended any Jerusalem festivals except the Passover during his last days. John, however, mentions several other visits, but a fixed outline is difficult to set. John certainly understands the ministry to have lasted several years, and this allows for the development of events better than does a one-year period. Because John mentions three Passovers, we usually refer to Jesus' public ministry as covering three years.

As we have seen, John for his own theological reasons places Jesus' cleansing of the Temple at the beginning of Jesus' ministry, whereas the synoptics put it at the close (see Theme 5, Session 3). Jesus' conflict with the authorities centered around the Temple at other points too. A statement he made about destroying the Temple (Jn 2:19–22) was brought out at his trial (Mk 14:58), and he had explicitly prophesied the destruction of the Temple in another connection (Mk 13:1–2). The dialogues with Jewish leaders during Jesus' last week took place mostly in the Temple precincts. See Matthew 21:23.

The evangelists frequently mention Jesus praying alone (see Mk 1:35; Lk 6:12; Mt 14:23; Jn 17). Also read the story of his conversation with a Samaritan woman at Jacob's well, **John 4:19–24.**

Early Church Transition

After the crucifixion and resurrection in Jerusalem, Christians continued to go to the Temple, and there is no indication that there was any immediate rift between Jesus' followers and Jewish ways of worship. Judaism allowed some flexibility in liturgical assemblies. Peter and John find the locale for their early ministry in the Temple (see **Acts 3:1–11;** 5:12–13, 21). Not until Paul is there a clear break with the parent religion (see 13:46; 18:6). Only Stephen makes an open, verbal attack on the Temple liturgy. Read **7:44–51.** Stephen's opposition to the Temple may reflect some Jewish hostility at that time. He had been arraigned on a charge reminiscent of Jesus' trial (6:8–15). A similar view emerges in Hebrews. See Hebrews 4:14–5:10; 7:11–8:6; **9:1–14,** 9:15–10:25. Thus the Temple and Jerusalem, the center of first-century Judaism, continue for some time to draw the first Christians.

Although the Temple and its liturgy lost its immediate influence, the vocabulary associated with the Temple passed into Christian tradition. The Eucharist was celebrated in the early Church in the houses of the faithful, making each table on which the sacrifice was made an altar. Eventually, the ones who led the Eucharistic sacrifice were called priests. Jesus mentions the altar in his teaching (Mt 5:23–24; 23:18–22). The Book of Hebrews makes a connection between Jesus' sacrifice and an altar (Heb 13:10–15). Sacrifice, without specific reference to an altar, appears widely (see Rom 12:1; Phil 4:18; Heb 10:12, 14; 1 Pt 2:5, among many texts). It is in this context that references to blood, specifically the blood of Jesus in his sacrifice, are to be understood (see Rom 3:24–25; 5:8–9; Eph 4:7; Col 1:20; Heb 9:12–14; 1 Pt 1:2, 18–19; 1 Jn 1:7). Occasionally the idea of cleansing implies purification by water (see 2 Cor 7:1; Eph 5:25–26; Jas 4:8). Baptism will be considered below. Revelation is crammed with such symbolism (see 5:8, 10; 7:14; 11:1–2; 19:13; 22:1–2).

Paul

Paul moved out of but never completely severed his ties to Judaism. His embassy to Damascus, during which he was converted, was addressed to the synagogues there, and these were to have been his channel for getting at the Christians. In a remarkable reversal, he makes the synagogues and assemblies of Jews the first targets of his evangelistic endeavors (see Acts 13:5, 14, 42–43; 14:1; 17:1, 10, 17; 18:4, 19, 26; 19:8). Note also his statements about his career, given in his defense before the Roman governor Felix in Acts 24:10–21.

In **Acts 16:13,** Paul finds an unusual "place of prayer" in Philippi. The whole story, 16:11–40, has interesting movement and details. Note the remarkable liturgical scene in **16:25.** Twice we read of Paul undertaking unusual acts of Jewish devotion: 18:18 and 21:17–26. The second instance leads to his final arrest, which takes place in the Temple area. See 21:27–36.

The Eucharist

Just as the Passover is of central importance in the Old Testament, so the Eucharist or Lord's Supper is central to New Testament worship. It was in the celebration of the Eucharist that the Church remembered what Jesus said the night before he died. We have seen in the discussion of Passover that the biblical meaning of memory means to make present again, to take a stand for God in the present day (see Theme 1, Session 2). In celebrating the Eucharist, the Church represents in the sacrifice of the Mass the saving acts of Jesus Christ. This is not just the recollection of a past event, but the representation of the sacrifice of Jesus Christ in the midst of the Church. The feeding of the five thousand, which prefigures the Eucharist, is recorded in all four gospels. Remember also our special notice of Luke 24:30–31; and see Acts 2:42. Read the accounts of the Last Supper: Matthew 26:20–29; Mark 14:1–26; Luke 22:14–38; and **1 Corinthians 11:17–34.** It is clear that the Eucharist has come out of a Passover setting.

Baptism

Baptism played an important part in the development of Christian worship. The immediate background is found in the baptism of John which was a call to repentance, but the antecedents of John's rite are not certain. Judaism did baptize proselytes, and the people of the Dead Sea Scrolls practiced regular ceremonial washings. Already in the teaching of Jesus, baptism is referred to figuratively (see Mk 10:35–40). It is mentioned fairly frequently in Acts (see 2:38 41; 8:12 16; 10:44 48; 19:1–6). The theological symbolism is used by Paul in Romans 6:3–5 (see also Colossians 2:12). A practical problem is discussed in 1 Corinthians 1:13–17. There is some reason to think that 1 Peter contains material originally used as baptismal catechesis (note 3:21).

The Lord's Day

Change of the principal day of liturgy from the seventh day (the "Sabbath") to the first day of the week (our Sunday) may only be inferred from the New Testament. Paul exhorts a Church to make a collection "on the first day of the week" (1 Cor 16:2). In Revelation 1:10, there is an explicit reference to "the Lord's day," which may be the new day of Christian worship (see also Acts 10:7). Supporting these references are statements of the "apostolic fathers" of the Church, who wrote during the years and decades just following those when the New Testament was produced. They make it plain that the Christian day of public liturgy was set because the resurrection was "on the first day."

Other Details of New Testament Worship

What were liturgical services like in New Testament times? Since there are no explicit descriptions, we must read between the lines. The meal setting with the celebration of the Eucharist was most typical, but there were certainly other worship occasions. The first recorded instance of someone falling asleep in church is in **Acts 20:7–12** ("on the first day of the week"). The meeting was probably in a house (see also 2:46; Rom 16:5; Phlm 2). The sermon appears to have been longer than usual. There was breaking of bread, but in Acts 13:1–3 this element is not included.

The Jewish scripture was regularly read and expounded (see Acts 17:2–3, 11; 18:24, 28; Rom 15:4; 2 Tm 3:16). Scripture also figured in private worship (see Acts 8:26–35). We may assume that traditional material from and about Jesus was used (Acts 20:35; 2 Tm 2:8), and occasionally apostolic letters were read (Col 4:16; 1 Thes 5:27).

Prayers were certainly said on all occasions of worship, and there was strong precedent for this from Jesus himself. One of the most beautiful prayers in the New Testament outside of Jesus' words is **Ephesians 3:14–21.** Note the posture, but see also 1 Corinthians 14:25; 1 Timothy 2:8. Benedictions or prayers for God's blessings were well-known from synagogue practice, and a number are recorded in the New Testament. The best known is 2 Corinthians 13:13, often referred to as the "apostolic" benediction. But the central feature of worship was the Eucharist, or doing what Jesus did at the Last Supper: the offering, changing, and receiving of bread and wine converted into the body and blood of the Lord Jesus (see 1 Cor 11:17–22, the earliest description of the Eucharist).

The Pastoral Epistles give a number of details about worship. Several aspects of prayer are mentioned in 1 Timothy 2:1–2, 8. In the early congregation, as in Judaism, women did not always have privileges equal with men (2:9–12). In 1 Corinthians 11:5, however, Paul mentions the praying and prophesying of women in public worship.

The principal activities of early Christian liturgy were thus similar, at least superficially, to those of the synagogue (see 1 Tm 4:12–16; also 2 Tm 4:1–5).

Other information is scattered throughout the New Testament. First Corinthians is a specially valuable resource, as it details a time when the Church was having difficulties in its public liturgy. The common meal that was observed in connection with the Eucharistic celebration became an occasion for factions. This is the earliest description of the common meal and was recorded about seventeen years after the Last Supper.

Apparently, some specific liturgical practice in the Corinthian Church divided the members of the Church who were rich from those who were poor. Paul criticizes these social divisions as offensive to the body of Christ (see 1 Cor 11:17–22). Certainly, the more formal kinds of liturgical practice in specially appointed buildings came later (see also 2 Tm 2:14–17, 23–25; 3:1–5; Jas 2:24; and Acts 18:13).

Paul strongly approves of prophecy, which seems to be a kind of informal, spontaneous preaching with emphasis on the gospel challenge, but he emphasizes that speaking in "tongues" must have the goal of building up the community (see **1 Corinthians 14:15–16, 24–33**).

James 5:13–16 refers to a practice of anointing the sick with the accompanying prayer, a practice continued in the Church in the Sacrament of Anointing. Perhaps this recalls healings by Jesus, as in Mark 7:32–35; 8:22–25; and John 9:1–11.

The Book of Revelation is rich in liturgical symbolism. It is difficult to know how much of it reflects practices in the first-century Church, but it certainly has colored the later language of Christian worship. Chapters 4 and 5 present dramatic scenes of liturgy in heaven and are in some respects an epitome of the central message of the book. Read at least **Revelation 4:8–11.** Theme 10, Session 4, looks at Revelation in more detail.

The prevalence of hymns in New Testament liturgy is certainly indicated, though detail of their use is not as clear. Probably they were chanted, following the precedent of the psalms. (see Eph 5:19; Col 3:16; 1 Cor 14:26). Jesus and his disciples sang a hymn (probably a Hallel psalm) after the Last Supper (see Mk 14:26; Mt 26:30). The poetry in Luke 1 and 2 is probably to be understood as hymnic. Sometimes it is hard to distinguish whether a passage is a hymn or a confession or a creed; as in Philippians 2:5–11; 1 Timothy 3:16. In Theme 7, Session 4, 1 Corinthians 13 is called a hymn. Revelation is loaded with fine hymns, for example, 4:8–11 (mentioned above); **5:9–12;** 7:12; 19:4–6. A number of these hymns appear in Handel's *Messiah*.

Suggestions for Further Study

Research

1. Review Luke 2:22–32; 2:41–42; 4:14–30; and Mark 13:1–2. What do these readings tell you about Jesus' attitude towards the Temple?

2. Review the scriptures under the heading Early Church Transition. What do these read-

ings illustrate about the attitudes of the early Church toward the Temple?

3. Read through the order of the Eucharistic celebration in the Sunday Missal or Missalette. List all the allusions to the Old Testament you can find.

4. Review an article on the synagogue in a Bible dictionary. In what way are the function and the order of liturgy in the synagogue similar with the activities in your parish?

Reflection

1. How has what you have learned about the early Christian liturgy influenced the way you see the practice of liturgy in your parish?

2. You may want to master the following verses word for word:

   • 1 Corinthians 13

   • 2 Corinthians 13:13

   • Ephesians 3:14–21

THEME 10

God's People Have Hope

SESSION 1

The Hope of Israel

Session Overview

The concept of hope has been woven throughout the themes. It often has been national with a focus on the Davidic dynasty. The Exile produced a hope aimed towards the future, and was expressed often in apocalyptic form. Hope found in life after death is not treated much; the nether world was the abode of the dead. The prophecies of Isaiah often look to the future with hope.

Key Bible Readings

Genesis 17:1–8, 15–21
Lamentations 5:19–22
Haggai
Jeremiah 33:14–16
Deuteronomy 32:45–47
Job 17:13–16;
   19:23–27
Isaiah 7:10–25; 9:1–7;
   11:1–9; 25:6–8;
   40:25–31; 42:1–4;
   52:13–53:12;
   60:1–3
Jeremiah 29:10–14

Key Words

apocalyptic
the nether world
messianic hope
shoot/servant
eschatology

Images of Hope in the Bible

There may have been times in your life when you have been told to "face reality," to "be real," to "get your head out of the clouds." Facing reality in terms of the situation you are in usually means to take what you can get and not dream of possible futures. In this theme, we will be looking at some of the dreams of the people of God in terms of the possible futures revealed to them in times of despair and defeat. We may be uncomfortable with these writings because their visions and symbols are difficult to understand by rational examination. As we read them, however, we will discover that the faith that is our heritage was born in the dreams and visions of the people. We will also discover that these visions will feed our own faith as we create our own visions of the possibilities God is calling us to as we grow and share in the life of grace we have received.

Review: The Promised Land

Themes 1 through 9 have touched on topics related to the theme of hope. While this theme is concerned with a particular kind of development in the Bible, let us first do some reviewing.

The conviction that God is the creator and sustainer of the world and ultimately is sovereign should be a basis for firm hope. That is indeed expressed in some of the psalms. The whole matter of hope, however, is much more complicated. In the Old Testament, God's people face the future mostly concerned with the survival of their families, clans, or nation. They did not believe in life after death so their expectations were related to this world in material terms.

God's promise, then, as written into the early records, elicited hope for land and ancestors. People lived on in family and nation. This hope was already part of the prehistory in the story of Noah (Gn 9). In the covenant with Abraham, **Genesis 17:1–8, 15–21,** this promise was repeated. In the Exodus story and often during the wilderness period, hope was revealed in terms of images of the promised land of milk and honey (Ex 3:17); but that generation did not experience the fulfillment. Their children did, and the land became the long-awaited home of the nation.

Review: The Promise to David

Another form of hope was expressed in the promise to the house of David: God would perpetually provide for a ruler on David's throne. With the loss of the kingdom of Judah and the experience of Exile, this hope turned to despair. The Jewish people were forced to look to the far future, and they grasped at any possible evidence that the promise was coming to pass. The Maccabean victory is an example. The New Testament finally provided a startling new direction for this hope.

"Messianic hope" is a general term often applied to this image of expectation in the Old Testament. Remember that "messiah" comes from a Hebrew word meaning "anointed." It was applied to the king. As long as the Davidic line survived, expectation was that the kingdom founded by David would endure, a view which was supported by the theology. The despair that was engendered by the fall of Jerusalem and the monarchy is reflected in Lamentations 4:18–20 and 5:15–18. **Lamentations 5:19–22** ends with a desperate plea for restoration based on the Lord's sovereignty, but the tone remains grave.

After the Exile, two prophets, Haggai and Zechariah, led a futile attempt to recover the glory of the kingdom. They did this with the cooperation of Joshua, a priest, and Zerubbabel, a political leader who claimed a relationship with David. See Ezra 5:1–2; **Haggai;** Zechariah 6:9–14. Zechariah's language indicates that he considers this an "end-time" fulfillment, a thought to which we shall return. The restoration was unsuccessful. In this instance, "messiah" is not applied to the king expected at the end of time.

Expectations

The climate of despair engendered by the Exile and succeeding failures in reestablishing a new Jewish kingdom led to the development of new images of expectation. It is a mistake to define the meaning of Jewish messianic expectation solely in terms of fulfillment in Jesus Christ. The very term "messiah" is used in a variety of contexts. The foreign king, Cyrus, is referred to as "his anointed" in Isaiah 45:1. Elijah is commissioned to anoint not only a king, but also his own successor (see 1 Kgs 19:15–16). The patriarchs are referred to as "anointed ones" in Psalm 105:12–15. There is evidence that priests were anointed (see Ex 30:30; 40:12–15). There is expectation of both an anointed prince and an anointed priest (see Jer 33:17–18; Zec 4:6–14). This latter idea occurs in the Dead Sea

Scrolls, which speak of "the messiahs of Aaron and of Israel."

Zechariah refers to a future figure he calls the "shoot" (6:12). The name also occurs in Isaiah 11:1; Jeremiah 23:5; **33:14–16;** Zechariah 3:8. In Isaiah 40–55, the "servant" of God appears, and in Ezekiel and Daniel there is the term "son of man." Both of these have a future dimension.

Eschatology and Apocalyptic

At this point, we need to consider two technical terms (neither of which appears in the Bible): "eschatology" and "apocalyptic." Both words are derived from the Greek. Eschatology refers to any matter having to do with the end-time or "last things." Apocalyptic is a special genre of literature concerning eschatology. Throughout the early years of Israel's history, the end-time was an individual's death or, what was worse, the termination of a family line. Only when there was trouble or danger that threatened the existence of the nation did concern with the future become sharply focused. Thus, when the prophets preached in critical situations, they tried to place the future over against the present, and they sought hope in what the Lord might do to set the difficulty right. Most of the Old Testament prophets viewed future hope almost entirely in terms of recovery or restoration within the bounds of human history. When the hope of success in this world seemed impossible, a different kind of outlook sometimes appeared. This different outlook is found in the writings of a seer, a person who received divine messages in visions or dreams. A seer looked beyond this world and envisioned renewal through outside intervention from the supernatural world. The literature that records this latter variety of hope is apocalyptic.

The apocalyptic seer deals with ideas and events beyond the scope of everyday life, so these writings were usually cast in a form filled with visionary details, elaborate imagery, and supernatural beings. One or more of these heavenly beings could interpret the visions to the seer. Sometimes the intended message was deliberately written in coded language to be understood only by the intended hearers. The shrouded meaning would be incomprehensible to outsiders or enemies. Contemporary historical events and political figures would be disguised in symbolic language. The persons for whom the writing was intended would recognize that their own situation was being addressed and could hear the message of hope being proclaimed.

We see then that apocalyptic developed after prophecy ceased. It developed during the crisis-ridden 200 BC–AD 200 period. The Jewish apocalyptic literary form has been adopted by Christians and there exist some one hundred apocalyptic works. Of these, the Bible only includes Daniel 7–12, Zechariah, Revelation, and parts of the gospels, such as Mark 13:5–13.

Life after Death

There is really very little written in the Old Testament about life after death. Because the Israelites in the early periods of their history thought of themselves as surviving in the family on the ancestral land, they were intensely eager for children. Recall the story of Abraham, Ishmael, and Isaac. There was also a kind of survival in the permanence of the nation (see Nm 14:16; **Dt 32:45–47**). Since the people of Israel were considered God's children, there were statements about living with God, as Psalm 23:6, but there is no indication that this implied any notion of what we call heaven.

In most of the Old Testament the abode of the dead is known as "the nether world." This is sometimes translated "hell" or sometimes "the grave," but it does not really have the connotations of those two words. The nether world was a shadowy place where departed persons might continue to exist in a kind of ghostly state, but the precise intention of each reference is not always easy to determine. It was not a place of reward or punishment. It seems rather to have been an alternative to total extinction, and perhaps not a very appealing choice. In Hannah's song, 1 Samuel 2:6, there is one hint that the Lord could retrieve lives from the nether world. Usually it was a final destiny (see Gn 37:35; Ps 18:6; 55:16; Is 14:11). The Spirit of God was present there (Ps 139:8), but God derives no praise from the nether world (Is 38:18).

The Book of Job provides a number of references to the nether world (see 14:13; **17:13–16;** 26:5–6). A declaration of faith in life after death is often read out of **19:23–27,** but the statement is not very clear. In 42:5, Job professes to see God, and this after all is what he hoped for in 19:26–27. There is also some indication in the Book of Daniel of faith in survival (see 7:18 and 12:1–3). Only a selective future is intimated, and again the picture is unclear.

Isaiah

For the remainder of this session and all of the next we shall consider parts of books that deal with images of future hope. Here we look at Isaiah. In Session 2 we shall turn to books with an apocalyptic bent: Ezekiel, Daniel, and Zechariah.

The pre-exilic part of Isaiah, chapters 1–39, contains many passages that look to the future, and some of these are quite well-known. Read **Isaiah 7:10–25.** Verse 14 is quoted in Matthew 1:23 as a prophecy about the birth of Jesus. The context in the passage does not support such an interpretation, however, Matthew has given this text an inspired interpretation. The word translated "virgin" in the NAB is "young woman" in the RSV, and the latter more accurately reflects

the Hebrew original (see also NJB, including the footnote).

The coming ideal king is described in **Isaiah 9:1–7.** It is easy to see why Christians adopted this text with its messianic overtones. An idyllic description of the messianic rule appears in **11:1–9,** but the image really portrays Eden regained. Other lesser-known passages set forth the prophet's hope. Some foretell gloom and destruction (see 31:1; 32:1–4).

Most of these passages do not show characteristics of apocalyptic. Chapters 24–27 are different. See 24:4, 17–23; **25:6–8.** These passages contain images of apocalyptic expectation. 26:19 speaks poetically of a limited resurrection. Note the trumpet in 27:13; it often figures in scenes of final judgment.

The exilic portion of Isaiah, 40–66, is different from anything else in the Old Testament. The sustained beauty of its language and the profound scope of its hope are unparalleled. It has been mentioned in other themes, but this is a good time to read the entire section. The prominence of the "servant" figure has already been noted. There are four so-called "servant songs": **42:1–4;** 49:1–6; 50:4–11; **52:13–53:12.** Quite probably, these influenced Jesus' understanding of his mission. The servant in these passages, however, is not uniformly an individual. Sometimes one person seems to be implied, but there is also room to interpret the figure as Israel itself (49:3) or as a remnant of Israel (49:5). Probably the prophet was content to allow for this ambiguity. The fourth song so vividly suggests the passion of Jesus that Christian faith has always adopted it; 53:10–11 may imply resurrection.

The whole Book of Isaiah is really a collection of oracles and other material, and this is readily evident throughout the book. Chapters 55–66 are quite miscellaneous and probably date from just after the return from Exile. They are called Third Isaiah by many scholars. The concerns of the prophet in these chapters are more sweeping than those in Ezra-Nehemiah or even Haggai. Isaiah 58:3–7 sets forth a sharp program for "social action." **Isaiah 60:1–3** is a particularly beautiful plea to God's people to measure up to their appointed destiny. God is called "our Father" in 63:16, a rare occurrence in the Old Testament of the address Jesus taught his followers. God is anxious for the people to seek God even though they do not respond: see 65:1–2. A wonderful future is described in 65:17–25 that includes an apocalyptic new creation.

Jeremiah

Jeremiah has appeared prominently in Themes 2, 5, and 7. We have seen that he expresses the kind of hope that looks for restoration of the fortunes of God's people in this world's terms. He writes of the return of a remnant, and he mentions the "shoot" of David (see 23:3–8). He tells of the Lord's promise that the exiles will return after seventy years (see **Jer 29:10–14**). Further words about this are found in chapters 30 and 31. He buys a field at Anathoth as a witness that there is a future in the land (see 32:5–25). Chapter 33 picks up several of these ideas.

Suggestions for Further Study

Research

1. Review Genesis 17:1–8, 15–21 and 2 Samuel 7:8–16. What hopes do these passages describe for the people? List the ways you think these hopes were fulfilled in Israel's history. In what ways were they not fulfilled?

2. Read an article on the word "messiah" in a Bible dictionary. List the different meanings the word has in the Old Testament. What kinds of meanings do you think were in the minds of people when they asked Jesus if he was the Messiah?

3. Review an article on apocalyptic literature in a Bible dictionary. What are the characteristics of this literary genre?

4. Review 1 Samuel 2:6; Genesis 37:35; Psalms 55:15; 139:8; Isaiah 38:18; Job 17:13–16; 19:23–27; and Daniel 12:1–3. What images of life after death do these scriptures show? How do they compare to your own image of life after death?

5. Review Isaiah 40–55. List all the examples of hope which you find described in these chapters.

Reflection

1. Contrast the nether world as described in the Old Testament with popular ideas of heaven today.

2. How do you regard the Old Testament hope of a future through family and nation? What other bases for hope are there? What is it that you hope for your own future? How about for those who will follow after you?

SESSION 2

Hope in the Prophets

Session Overview

Ezekiel's prophecies are unusual, partly because of his personality, partly because of their sweep from the early exile to visions of the coming restoration. Zechariah's book is largely apocalyptic, and his visions are diverse. The Book of Daniel combines lesson-like stories and apocalyptic visions that look toward the end-time.

Key Bible Readings

Ezekiel 3:25–27;
   24:24–27; 34;
   47:22–23
Zechariah 1:7–17;
   4:1–14; 9:9–17
Daniel 7:13–18, 27

Key Words

prophecy
visions
restoration

Ezekiel

The prophet Ezekiel was one of the people taken into Exile about a decade before the fall of Jerusalem in 586 BC (see Ezl 1:2–3). It appears that he was of an aristocratic family, perhaps priestly (see 2 Kgs 24:10–14). His call bears some similarity to those of Isaiah and Jeremiah, but it is at once evident that Ezekiel's personality and career are quite different (see Ezl 1–3; note especially **3:25–27**). There is much more symbolism and drama in this book, and many of the images appear again in Revelation.

Jerusalem was still standing when Ezekiel began to have his visions, and the first half of his prophecies pronounces doom against Judah and its capital (4–24). In his prophetic ministry he employs dramatic actions that are bound to catch interest. Descriptions of his behavior lead us to conclude that his personality was eccentric, but his message seems clear enough. He claims that God has made him a "sign"; Ezekiel is the Lord's designated spokesperson (see **24:24–27;** also 3:16–21; 33:1–9). Like Jeremiah, Obadiah, Nahum, and others, Ezekiel delivers prophecies against neighboring nations (25–32).

Beginning in chapter 33, the message of the prophet turns to hope. Ezekiel watches faithfully, declaring what he sees is coming. The turning point is 33:21: the announcement arrives that Jerusalem has fallen. Now scolding and doom no longer are dominant; it is time for hope (see 33:11, 14–16, 32–33). He speaks against the false "shepherds" of Israel, but then he declares that the Lord God will now become the shepherd, seeking out and caring for the flock, "the house of Israel . . . my people." Read **Ezekiel 34.** In 20:33, there is a declaration that God "will be king over" the house of Israel. The two passages contain the same intent. This restoration will be in the land of Israel (see, for example, 36:8–12).

Notice the refrain, "thus you shall know that I am the LORD" (36:11, and so on). The restoration will come about, not because of the conduct of Israel, but for the sake of the great and holy name of God (36:22–24). The people will have a new heart and Spirit. See 36:25–28, and notice the similarity to Jeremiah 31:31–34.

As noted in Theme 1, the promise of restoration of the "dry bones" in Ezekiel 37 is justly famous. Go over the chapter again, and note the new dimensions our further study has added. Verses 11 and 12 pinpoint Ezekiel's message: the people have despaired, and the prophet declares hope from the Lord. This is somewhat of a reversal of the prophet's earlier approach: there he proclaimed doom in the face of false hope. Now the prophet proclaims an expectation of a Davidic messiah. His promises are elaborate and include a renewed sanctuary.

Most of the material in the second half of Ezekiel anticipates fulfillment in the near future. It is not certain, however, that the prophet is thinking of the end of history, for 39:25–29 speaks again in terms of national rehabilitation.

Chapters 40–46 contain a vision of the restored Temple. The structure is idealized, of course, and the vision passes from physical characteristics of the Temple to the glory of the Lord's presence and to the ordinances that are to prevail in the Temple.

The last two chapters are visions of the future of Israel's land. There is a description of a river that will profoundly affect both land and sea. There is an accounting of the future boundaries of the land that details fair distribution among the twelve tribes, which are to be reunited. Resident aliens are to participate in the inheritance (**47:22–23**). Finally, twelve gates of "the city" are to be named after the tribes. The city is to be some five miles in circumference! And it is to have a new name: "The Lord is there."

Zechariah

Zechariah was a contemporary of Haggai and Ezra (see Ezr 5:1; 6:14), but his book is quite different from theirs. After a brief introduction calling for repentance (1:1–7), there is a series of eight visions in apocalyptic form. An outline will be useful.

Chapter 1:7–17: Vision 1: Four horsemen and a message of hope for Jerusalem. As is common in such writings there is an interpreting angel. The length of the exile is given as seventy years (see also Jer 25:11; 29:10).

Chapter 2:1–4: Vision 2: Four horns and four smiths. The horns represent nations.

Chapter 2:5–9: Vision 3: The man with the measuring line. The purpose of the vision is Jerusalem's protection.

Chapter 2:10–13: Not a vision: Call for the return of exiles. Two phrases, "the apple of my eye" and "the holy land," have passed into common modern use.

Chapter 3:1–10: Vision 4: A message for Joshua the high priest. Satan appears here in the role of prosecutor/accuser in the heavenly "court." The "shoot" is presented in 3:8.

Chapter 4:1–14: Vision 5: The lampstand and the two olive trees. The passage provides much of the interpretation necessary to understand it. 4:6 is a resonant principle.

Chapter 5:1–4: Vision 6: The flying scroll. This may remind one of Ezekiel 2:9–3:3.

Chapter 5:5–11: Vision 7: The woman in a barrel. The land of Shinar is further identified in Daniel 1:1–2.

Chapter 6:1–8: Vision 8: The four chariots. "The land of the north" is Babylon (see Jer 3:18).

Chapter 6:9–15: Deals with the messianic person who will rebuild the temple. Scholars have found this passage very difficult to interpret.

Chapter 7: Proclaims the Lord's displeasure with a fixed feast and the hardheartedness of the people.

Chapter 8: Reiterates promises of restoration.

Chapters 9–14: A miscellaneous collection of oracles. Although they seem to be directed to a later time, they are in the spirit of Zechariah. **9:9–17:** expresses joy in the arrival of a peaceful king. 9:13 places this vision in a situation facing Greek opposition. In chapter 11 the figure of the shepherd appears; in 13:7–9 God's shepherd is stricken, but a remnant of his sheep is saved. Chapter 14 is loaded with apocalyptic imagery and action.

Readers who are familiar with Revelation will notice many echoes of Zechariah.

Daniel

Daniel is the only book in the Old Testament which is a thoroughgoing apocalypse. One mark of apocalyptic writing is the use of the name of some important historical figure as the author. This kind of pseudonymity, the use of a fictitious or assumed name, was really a literary device and not an intention to deceive. Daniel was an historical character. Ezekiel refers to him along with Noah and Job (14:14, 20; see also 28:3), so that the reference is evidently to an early time. Ezra 8:2 and Nehemiah 10:6 indicate that a Daniel lived in the time of Nebuchadnezzar, but they do not allude to any fame or position of power. Other than this, we know nothing except that in nonbiblical North Canaanite literature a person named Daniel is well-known.

Careful study of apocalyptic literature has shown that it really deals with situations in history other than those it claims to portray. If one has the key, one can discover that the visions and mysterious details refer for the most part to the historical situation leading up to the time of the actual composition or editing of the text. Then this description is used as the basis for projecting what is shortly to happen. The events envisioned usually involve the end of historical time.

In the case of Daniel, the "coded" details indicate that the book was written toward the end of the career of Antiochus IV (called "Epiphanes") but before the Maccabean rebellion (175–164 BC). The stories and visions in Daniel are intended, then, to give incentive for loyal pious Jews (the "hasidim") to withstand Antiochus's radical efforts to Hellenize them. The visions may be shown to follow the course of Palestinian history from the Babylonian empire to Antiochus IV, some of it in remarkable detail, some of it not so precise.

The Book of Daniel can be divided into two parts. The first part tells the stories of Daniel and his companions in Exile who are seeking specifically to obey God's will. Three stories with this implicit point are famous: faithfulness to prescribed Jewish diet, Daniel 1:8–20; the fiery furnace, 3:8–30; the den of lions, 6:1–28. In another well-known story about Belshazzar's feast, the foreign king is judged for not honoring the God Daniel worships (see 5:23). An apparition of a man's hand writes a mysterious message on the wall, and Daniel interprets it. Daniel 5:27, "you have been weighed on the scales and found wanting," has become a literary byword for a condemnatory verdict. Daniel 13 tells the story of Susanna and the attempts of two magistrates to seduce her. She is condemned to death only to be saved by the young Daniel. Chapter 14 has two brief stories in which Daniel shows the foolishness of idol worship.

The second half of the book has four visions that tell in strange, sometimes bizarre detail what is to come after the time of Exile in Babylon. A running outline will be useful for study:

Chapter 1 Story 1: Daniel and his friends manage to keep Jewish dietary laws under pagan cultural pressure. They are skilled in wisdom. The timespan in 1:21 would be almost seventy years and may be dated approximately 606–538 BC, the span of the Babylonian Captivity.

Chapter 2, Story 2: Nebuchadnezzar's dream of coming kingdoms. God's wisdom is supreme, so Daniel knows the content of the dream without being told by any human. The kingdoms represent Babylon, Media, Persia, Greece (with the Seleucid and Ptolemaic divisions), and God's coming kingdom.

Chapter 3, Story 3: The three young men in the fiery furnace. Challenge to apostasy is to be met, if necessary, by martyrdom.

Chapter 4, Story 4: Nebuchadnezzar's dream of his future. He learns the meaning from Daniel. God's power is sovereign and endures no usurpation. Consequently, Nebuchadnezzar goes mad but is later restored.

Chapter 5, Story 5: Belshazzar's feast. This story is a kind of sequel to the preceding one, but here there is an overt act of sacrilege. The Aramaic words refer to weights but have additional meanings. See notes in NAB.

Chapter 6, Story 6: Daniel in the lion's den. God saves faithful individuals. There is no need to mention the popularity of this story!

Chapters 7:1–12:13 is a separate book that is fully apocalyptic.

Chapter 7, Vision 1: The four beasts. The interpretation has parallels to Nebuchadnezzar's dream in chapter 2. The vision within the vision, **7:13–18, 27,** requires careful attention. Note that the "one like a son of man" is directly related to "the holy ones of the Most High." The "little horn" is probably Antiochus Epiphanes (7:8). Those familiar with Revelation will see Daniel 7 as a forerunner of Revelation.

Chapter 8, Vision 2: A ram and a he-goat. An interpretation is provided (8:19–26).

Chapter 9, Vision 3: Seventy weeks. The chronology is hard to work through. The career of Antiochus may be forecast as three-and-a-half years, and there are allusions to the "abomination of desolation," his desecration of the temple.

Chapters 10–12, Vision 4: The end-time. Details can be paralleled in known events of Near Eastern history as far as 11:40. Chapter 12 deals with the final end beyond the "coded" history. Note that Michael is Israel's "guardian angel" (see 10:21).

Chapters 13–14: Short stories that were written in the Greek but are not found in the Hebrew.

One of the clearest Old Testament statements anticipating a resurrection is in 12:2. Although the text speaks of "many resurrections," both happy and unhappy destinies are anticipated, so there is an implication of the general resurrection. Note the qualifications that merit special reward (12:3). Daniel is promised a particular place in "the end time."

A number of other apocalyptic writings are known from the period just before the Christian era. These are valuable for studying Judaism of that time, and several are important as extra-canonical sources for the background of the New Testament. One such is the Book of Enoch. It is one of the "pseudepigrapha" (pseudony-mous writings).

Suggestions for Further Study

Research

1. Review an article on apocalyptic literature in a Bible dictionary. What was the historical and social situation of the Jewish people at the time in which apocalyptic literature was popular? How do these situations relate to the popularity of apocalyptic literature today?

2. Review the introductions to the Books of Ezekiel, Zechariah, and Daniel. What are the historical backgrounds of these books? What is the principal message they teach?

3. Many of the images and figures in these books appear again in the New Testament. Start a list of any that sound familiar.

Reflection

1. What kind of prophetic message do you find most fitting for our modern world?

2. You may want to master the following verses:

   • Ezekiel 34:15; 37:4, 14

   • Zechariah 4:6; 9:9

   • Daniel 12:2–3

SESSION 3

The New Hope in Christ

Session Overview

Hope in the New Testament grows out of the Old Testament but is of quite a new kind. In the gospels, Jesus' view of the future was colored by apocalyptic forms of expression, but did not lose touch with this world. John's gospel emphasizes this. The early Church related the new age of the Holy Spirit to the eschatological time. Accordingly, Jesus' resurrection becomes a central datum for the Church, and Paul writes much about it. Other New Testament letters also deal with hope.

Key Bible Readings

Mark 12:18–27, 13
John 11:1–44
Matthew 25:31–46
John 14:15–26; 16:7–
    15; 15:18–27
Romans 5:1–5;
    8:10–39
1 Corinthians 15:3–28,
    51–58
1 Thessalonians 4:13–
    5:11
Hebrews 9:23–28; 11:1
1 Peter 1:3–21
2 Peter 3:1–13

Key Words

synoptic apocalypse
resurrection of the dead

A New Kind of Hope

In a broad sense, hope in the New Testament follows naturally upon hope in the Old Testament. Yet the Christian situation is different, and the images of hope have changed. Several factors contribute to this. Messianic expectation was different after the Exile, as the hope for a kingdom of Davidic descent faded. Apocalyptic expectations had become a firm and popular part of theological reflection. Thought about God and the people led to the conclusion that the relationship must involve more than land and progeny in the future.

Jesus says in John 5:45 that Old Testament hope was centered in Moses and the Torah. With Jesus a new mission and message had entered the picture: a new quality of life was being realized. Mosaic religion centered upon law; Jesus' way centers upon the possibility of a new relationship with God. The very nature of this relationship is freedom and hope. Late Judaism must have left the "people of the land" with deep insecurity about the future, for their chance of meeting the requirements of the Torah was shaky indeed.

Israel's hope was in one respect nationalistic. Some of the prophets understood a wider dimension of God's plan for all of humanity, and Jesus worked to broaden this hope. In Matthew 12:21, the evangelist quotes Isaiah 42:4 (according to the Septuagint text), where the "servant" is described as one in whom the Gentiles will hope. An expanding of messianic expectation is one reason for Jesus' popularity among the people (see Mk 12:35–37). Even so, he was mostly misunderstood in this regard. Occasionally, he was called "son of David" with messianic intent (see Mt 21:9; Mk 10:47; also Jn 7:41–42). John records an abortive attempt to force Jesus into a kingly role (see 6:15).

Jesus and the Future

The noun "hope" never occurs in the gospels, and the term appears only five times in the New Testament. Images of hope, however, are everywhere. Consider the discussion in **Mark 12:18–27** and its parallels. Jesus replaces a crude materialistic interpretation of the resurrection with the image of those who rise from the dead as spiritual beings living in God's presence. Read the story of the raising of Lazarus, **John 11:1–44.** The point of the whole passage is to reveal Jesus as the resurrection and the life (verse 25).

Even after the resurrection there seems to have been some lack of agreement in interpreting sayings and events related to the future. Compare Mark 9:1 with the parallels in Matthew 16:28 and Luke 9:27. Bible students today debate how "otherworldly" was Jesus' view of the future. The influence of apocalyptic forms of thought upon Jesus and his interpreters is a chief element in conclusively solving the problem. There is no doubt that Jesus knew and assimilated apocalyptic ideas. There is evidence that he was acquainted with some apocalyptic literature not included in our canon.

The phrase "kingdom of God" was considered in Theme 6, but it also relevant here. Two other synoptic passages are important in

this context. **Matthew 25:31–46** is a remarkably vivid image of the future. Notice that future life with God is influenced by present actions, especially in the area of justice.

Mark 13 (parallels: Mt 24:1–36; Lk 21:5–36) is often referred to as the synoptic apocalypse. When these verses were written, the early Church had already seen the destruction of the Temple (70 AD) and interpreted it as the imminent sign of the end of the world. The verses were also written at a time when the Church was experiencing persecution, and they linked the fate of Jesus' suffering and death with their own suffering. In the apocalyptic imagery of this chapter, Mark is telling the early Church to persevere in spite of the tragic events that have already taken place and the promise of further suffering. The message is to persevere vigilantly in faith.

Jesus is quoted as using typical or traditional apocalyptic elements. Noted above, and from the parenthetical remark in Mark 13:14 (Mt 24:15), is that the passage is editorially directed to a succeeding generation. Note also how Luke 21:20 differs at this point. In Matthew 24:22–27, signs of the approaching end contrast with its final suddenness. According to Mark 13:30, fulfillment is imminent. The ending of the discourse is different in each gospel, but all emphasize the need for watchful preparedness.

The farewell discourses in John are quite different in content and tone (see Jn 14–16). Elements of hope and expectation are strong, but apocalyptic details are missing. Many words refer to the future, but most are concerned with the action of God in this world (see **John 14:15–26;** 16:16–20). Jesus talks about his "coming," presumably a return, but this seems to be inextricably involved with the promise of "another Advocate" (see 14:16–17, 26, 28; **16:7–15**). These discourses are realistic; they speak of trouble for Jesus' followers as in **John 15:18–27** (see also 16:1–4, 20–22, 32–33). The images in apocalyptic passages are vivid and gripping. The words of hope in John are deep and sustaining. Each kind of hope is helpful. It is important to understand how these two kinds of proclamation helped the Church face the future in differing circumstances.

Jesus' resurrection was the focal point and guarantee of hope in the early Church. The difficulty the early Church had in adjusting this to traditional messianic expectations shows plainly in the reaction of the disciples who met the risen Lord on the way to Emmaus (see Lk 24:13–36 and note verse 21). Mark indicates that Jesus warned about his suffering and death (8:31; 9:31–32; 10:32–34), but the gospel writers candidly show that Jesus was not really understood until after the resurrection.

Hope in the Early Church

Acts, Paul's letters, and other New Testament writings also show this alternation between a far-off future and a near future, between an apocalyptic expectation and a more immediate experience of God's reassuring love as understood in Jesus Christ and guaranteed by the Holy Spirit. The Pentecost story in Acts 2 emphasizes the role of the Holy Spirit, and Peter proposes that this is an eschatological event. The quotation from Joel contains some apocalyptic detail, but this does not stop the preacher from applying it to the immediate experience (note 2:16, 33). There is some similarity to the near expectation contained in the Johannine discourses.

The future life at once became an element of the apostolic preaching. "The resurrection from the dead" is given as the principal cause of conflict between Peter and John and the religious authorities at the Jerusalem Temple (see Acts 4:1–2). This opposition evidently reflects the influence of the Sadducees, but it makes clear how central the resurrection is to the the-

ology of the early Church. Paul is evidently in accord with this emphasis. The summary of his sermon in Athens is a case in point (see 17:18). Some of his hearers even seem to have thought that "resurrection" was a god he was preaching about. Paul's defense addresses this matter, and again it is the matter of the resurrection that leads to the termination of the assembly.

Twice during Paul's official hearings in Palestine the resurrection becomes crucial. Before "the council" (the Sanhedrin) he takes advantage of the Pharisee-Sadducee antagonism about the resurrection and declares that the examination centers on "hope in the resurrection of the dead" (see 23:1–10). Later, in his defense before King Agrippa, Paul connects the hope in God's promise to Israel with the hope of God's raising the dead (see 26:1–8, 22, 23).

Resurrection and the Future in Paul's Letters

In the light of these passages in Acts, it is not surprising to find many references to resurrection hope in Paul's letters. It is particularly important in four of the letters. Romans is usually considered to be Paul's most "theological" letter, probably because he wanted to make his faith plain to a Church he had not visited. In **Romans 5:1–5,** see how hope plays an important part in the development of the apostle's thought. Chapter **8:10–39** also focuses on this theme. Notice how many ways Paul deals with hope. "The one who raised Christ from the dead will give life to your mortal bodies also" (verse 11); "heirs" will be glorified (17); "creation . . . would be set free" (21); God's people will be "conformed to the image of his Son" (29); etc.

The Corinthian Church evidently has many problems, and Paul deals with them in his correspondence. In 1 Corinthians 12–14, Paul discusses spiritual gifts and proposes that love is the greatest spiritual gift of all. In chapter 13, a hymn in praise of love, he says that love is even greater than faith and hope! But love "hopes all things," and in chapter 15 Paul turns to the chief element of Christian hope, the resurrection. This is the most extended discussion of the topic anywhere in the Bible. Paul insists that what he writes is central to the gospel (15:1–2).

He begins by recounting the tradition about Jesus' death and resurrection and the witness to them. The words "received" and "delivered" indicate that this is a fundamental part of the accepted tradition of the Church. Read **1 Corinthians 15:3–11.** Now Paul counters an argument that there is no resurrection (verses **12–19**). Next is a projection of how God's rule will come to final triumph through Christ's conquest over death. Then God will be "all in all" (**20–28**). In 29–34, the apostle adds some arguments to support his line of reasoning. Verses 35–50 present a somewhat involved discussion of the nature of the resurrection. Verses 36 and 37 are very much like some things Jesus said (can you trace them?). Verse 50 is one of Paul's infrequent references to "the kingdom of God." Verses **51–57** are a magnificent doxology. Finally, verse **58** places this eschatological discussion in an ethical dimension.

Of all the Churches in Paul's sphere of influence, the Thessalonians seem to have been the most concerned about "last things." His first letter to them begins by recalling their relationship while he was establishing the Church there (see 1:2–2:16). Then he outlines what has happened since and includes references to a mission by Timothy (2:17–3:10). A prayer, 3:11–13, makes a bridge to the teaching sections that follow. Chapter 4:1–8 deals with morality (for those converted from paganism, 1:9); and 4:9–12 discusses how love works.

In **1 Thessalonians 4:13–5:11,** Paul takes up Christian hope. Here the expected return of the Lord has created a special concern among the Thessalonians. Apparently, they thought that those who were dying before the great event would be at some disadvantage—perhaps they would miss it altogether! With apocalyptic embellishment, Paul writes about the resurrection as a comfort and reassurance to his readers. He warns them, however, that they should always live with imminent awareness of this end. This ought to have a positive effect on their way of life. The rest of this letter consists of various exhortations for the life of the church.

In the second letter, after the usual introduction and thanksgiving, the Thessalonians are encouraged in the face of affliction; the Lord will set things right "at the revelation of the Lord Jesus from heaven" (see 2 Thes 1:5–12). Then events associated with "the coming of our Lord Jesus Christ" are considered (see 2:1–12). The readers are assured of the certainty of this, and there is a somewhat cryptic discussion of the lawless, wicked power that is at work in the interim. After various words of praise and exhortation (2:13–3:5), the last section before the conclusion (3:6–13) deals with sloth, a special problem. Apparently, these people thought that since the end of all things was so close, it was not necessary to work. Notice the stern judgment in 3:10. The letter ends as do several others: Paul takes the "pen" from the scribe and adds a personal note and signature.

The General Epistles and Hebrews

The letter to the Hebrews has imported statements on hope and the future. Here again, assurance for the future depends directly and firmly upon what God has already revealed and accomplished. A constant emphasis in the first ten chapters is the superiority of Jesus over other revelation. Read **Hebrews 9:23–28,** and note the stress upon the finality of what Jesus has done: "Once for all he has appeared at the end of the ages." The only explicit reference in the Bible to a "second" coming of Christ is in 9:28. It is worth noting that the text speaks of an appearance rather than a coming. Chapter **11:1** is an often quoted text, as it relates to hope and faith.

Hope is also emphasized in **1 Peter 1:3–21.** The author uses the phrase "the revelation of Jesus Christ" to describe the crisis of the end-time. The sacrifice and resurrection of Christ, however, are inextricably tied in with the revelation, and thus hope is not so much an element in the future as it is a line from the past into the future.

In **2 Peter 3:1–13,** the writer addresses a question that arose among some people who were perplexed about timetables of the end of the age. He explains the delay of the Lord's coming and cites Psalm 90:4 in support. He asserts that the end is sure to come and adds some apocalyptic embellishment. He then moves to an exhortation to circumspect living.

2. In a Bible dictionary, review an article on hope. What are the central themes of hope in the Old Testament and in the New Testament?

3. Compare Mark 13:26 and parallels with Daniel 7:13–14. What significance do you see in this use of Daniel in the synoptic apocalypse?

4. Review 1 Corinthians 15:3–50. Why is the Church's teaching on the resurrection so important to Paul?

5. The Greek-derivative "parousia" is sometimes used in discussions about this present topic. Look up the word in a Bible dictionary and formulate a brief definition.

6. Review 1 Thessalonians 4:13–5:11 and 2 Peter 3:1–13. What difficulties were the writers addressing concerning the second coming of Christ?

7. Do you think 1 Thessalonians 5:1–11 is a "scare tactic"? State the arguments pro and con.

Suggestions for Further Study

Research

1. Review Sessions 1 and 2 of this theme. How are the hopes described in these sections redefined in the New Testament?

Reflection

What is the relationship between hope and love

- in your personal life?
- in the Christian faith?
- in the world today?

SESSION 4

The Book of Revelation

Session Overview

The Book of Revelation is apocalyptic with a prophetic application to first-century Churches. John's visions shift between earth, where God's people are in dire jeopardy from a demonic government, and heaven, where Christ's victory over all opposing powers is celebrated. The Book of Revelation, and the Bible, end with an invitation to the world and a prayer of the Church to the Lord.

Key Bible Readings
Revelation 1; 4; 5;
    12:1–12; 19:6–16;
    20:11–15; 21:1–7;
    22:16–21

Key Words
Apocalypse
Maranatha

Introduction

One book in the New Testament is thoroughly apocalyptic; indeed, it is often known as the Apocalypse. The Book of Revelation was written by a poet to engage the imagination. While careful study will help to decipher some of the cryptic language, it is best appreciated when we let the images and symbols speak to our imaginations. There is much in this book that is hard to interpret, and it demands careful study. Even after our best efforts, some things will still elude us, but we may be sure that we understand the main thrust of the book. The principal mistake in reading the Book of Revelation is to read it as if it contained linear codes which give exact information about the end of our times. For these reasons, and because the message of Revelation is so timely today, we devote this last session to the book.

Several features of this apocalypse distinguish it from other apocalyptic material we have studied. Read **Revelation 1.** It begins in the form of a letter, and we soon meet the individual Churches the book is addressed to. The form we have seen at the beginning of Paul's letters occurs in 1:4–5. The seer of Revelation has a contemporary, first-century name—John (1:4, 9)—unlike most apocalyptic writings, which usually bear a revered name from antiquity. Prophecy is mentioned in 1:3, and a response is expected from the recipient. Very quickly, we become aware that the author is adept at using material from the Old Testament. Although he seldom makes an extended quotation, the whole book is a veritable patchwork of Old Testament allusions. (Try to identify these as you go along.)

Setting on Earth: The Seven Churches

A blessing is invoked in 1:3 upon the one "who reads" and "those who listen," and it is immediately clear that the author is a pastor who has written the book for the Churches. John's first vision begins at 1:12, and 1:20 offers a key to its interpretation. The figure "like a son of man" is identified as the exalted Christ. He is in the midst of the Churches and holds their safety in his hands. All that follows in the Revelation depends upon this initial affirmation; the end is sure from the beginning. We must immediately become adjusted to viewing action that moves easily and quickly between earthly and heavenly characters and images. This is more than a literary device; it is essential to what is being revealed through John.

The Churches that have been addressed in 1:11 are in western Asia Minor. Ephesus is named first, probably because it was the chief city of the area. (Recall how important it was in Paul's ministry.) Reference to a map will show that the Churches are in a kind of circuit, and it is likely that the book was intended to be circulated among these Churches. (See the route of the letter carrier in HAB 178–79.) In chapters 2 and 3, each Church receives a message; as far as we can interpret, the details are appropriate to the particular Church. This indicates that the message of the Revelation meant something specific, applicable, and contemporary to the Churches to which it was first addressed. Thus, it is unfaithful to the book to interpret it as though it were directed entirely to the future. Its meaning for both today and the future depends upon understanding its meaning for the Churches to which it was first sent.

The pattern of each little letter in chapters 2–3 is similar and shows great literary skill. There is much use of pictorial language and imagery, which is true of the whole book. Elements reappear from earlier settings, for example, the lampstand from Revelation 1. There are crowns, swords, the morning star, white garments, the book of life, doors, new Jerusalem, and so on. There are allusions to Old Testament persons: Balaam, Jezebel, David. Nearly every sentence contains some metaphor, and some of the imagery becomes elaborate. It is important, of course, to understand the significance of as much of this as we can.

Setting in Heaven: God, the Lamb, and the Scroll

Revelation 4 and **5** present a dramatic introduction to the rest of the book and in a sense summarize its message. John "in spirit" stands in heaven before a throne, and "on the throne sat one," an indirect way of saying "God." Other imagery is abundant, much of it in apocalyptic tradition with echoes of Ezekiel and Isaiah. There are notable hymns of praise.

In Revelation 5, attention shifts to one who is first called by messianic titles and then "the Lamb." "He" has the status to open the sealed book of destiny precisely because he "was slain." The sacrifice of the Christ-figure thus is presented as the key to the future. God, then, is both ruler and savior.

It is helpful to understand the scenes in Revelation as being cosmic drama. The theater was very important in Greek cities such as Ephesus, so this is a reasonable approach. Revelation has been referred to as the gospel in dramatic form. Think of it as a great cosmic drama, set on a multilevel stage and calling for the audience to become immersed in the drama. Scenes continue to shift between earth and heaven (as chapters 2 and 3 and 4 and 5).

The Seven Seals

The seven seals on the book begin to be opened in chapter 6. The first four seals reveal the four horsemen of the apocalypse, as they are sometimes called. The image is drawn from Zechariah 6. They are figures of destruction here, but the first, on a white horse, may be an anticipatory caricature of the Christ-victor in 19:11. The fifth seal reveals martyrs who are impatient for the final, justifying judgment. They receive white robes as tokens of the victory that is already theirs. The sixth seal is apocalyptic build-up toward the end.

Now there is an interlude in the opening of the seals. John sees great throngs of those whom God will save from the grim events just anticipated. The completeness of the assembly is emphasized in 7:1–8. The number 144,000 is 12 (tribes or apostles?) squared and multiplied by 1,000 (the largest number used in counting in the biblical languages), thus $12 \times 12 \times 1,000 = 144,000$. In 7:9–17, the multitude is innumerable, and they are clothed in white robes. It is the Lamb who has saved them and remains their hope.

Seven Trumpets and Seven Visions

The seventh seal, 8:1–6, reveals a new series of seven; seven new trumpets are sounded by angels. These produce a series of catastrophes reminiscent of the plagues in Egypt. Like Pharaoh, many persons are unmoved by these terrors. The seventh trumpet is delayed until 11:15 by another interlude of two visions.

In chapter 10, a mighty angel brings John a scroll, which he eats. It is a prophetic experience like Ezekiel 2:8–3:3. In Revelation 11:1–13, two "witnesses" appear, are martyred, and receive their heavenly reward. The passage is difficult, for the figures may bear more than one identity. From a background in Zechariah they would be Zerubbabel and Joshua, king and priest, but they also may be identified as Moses and Elijah returned to life. The seventh trumpet announces the fulfillment of God's kingdom, but the end is still delayed by five more visions.

The first "portent" is a conflict of a woman, a child, and a dragon; read **12:1–12.** Michael leads angels who eject Satan from heaven. Note in 12:9 the multiple identification of the dragon; all evil power is viewed as one. The woman and child may represent Eve giving birth to the expected messiah who will fight the devil (see Gn 3:15), or Israel and Christ; the imagery cannot be absolutely identified.

Two beasts appear in chapter 13, continuing the series of symbolized kingdoms first revealed in Daniel. The additional kingdom in the Revelation passage would now be Rome. The second beast seems to describe emperor-worship. The number-code in 13:18 is famous, and although it is impossible to be certain, the beast is possibly Nero.

There are three reassuring visions in chapter 14 with a strange mixture of glory and wrath. By dramatic license, the scenes shift rapidly and not necessarily in time sequence. Some details are flashbacks, some are anticipations. The grim, gory picture at the end recalls strongly Isaiah 63:1–6.

Seven Bowls and Babylon's Fall

A new series of seven in chapters 15 and 16 tells of angels with bowls containing plagues. Before they pour out their terrible wrath, there is a scene of glory in heaven. By now you should be able to make some assessment of many of the details. The plagues in Egypt will come to mind. The seventh bowl seems to announce the final end, and indeed it is near. For John, the resolution of the horrors on earth will usher in the new age.

Chapters 17 and 18 are a vivid vision of the fall of Rome, alluded to as "the great harlot" and "Babylon." The identification becomes certain in 17:9. Unfortunately, the identity of the kings is not as certain, because we do not know which Roman emperors John counts in his seven. Commentaries review the options. The beast who "existed once but exists no longer" and "is headed for destruction" is again possibly Nero, the first emperor to persecute the Christians, who contemporary legend held had not really died and would shortly reappear. The poetry in chapter 18 is like the dirges found in Isaiah, Jeremiah, and Ezekiel: compare Revelation 18:21 and Jeremiah 51:63–64.

Final Victory and Judgment

Chapters 19 and 20 portray the final victory of God's people by the "King of kings and Lord of lords"; read **19:6–16.** The anticipations of this finale, which we have seen since chapter 1, should warn us against trying to construct a rigid time sequence. The messianic banquet, "the marriage supper of the Lamb," is an apocalyptic image that we have seen before. References to 1,000 years, 20:1–8, have been given a wide variety of interpretations. Differing ideas of the "millennium" rose early in Church history and have caused much regrettable dissension. Though fundamentalists accept this as a belief, Catholics are not allowed to believe in the millennium. Since the prophetic sources of much of John's material are full of symbolism, one ought to be wary of reading more into this passage than a dramatic portrayal of the victory of Christ's martyrs and the ultimate defeat of all forces arrayed against God. Into this context,

Gog and Magog are introduced from Ezekiel 38–39, but here the details are changed. The last judgment, described in **20:11–15,** leads into the final vision of the new creation.

All Things New

"A new heaven and a new earth" are an old vision (see Is 65:17; 66:22). The pictorial details are well known; read **Revelation 21:1–7.** The bride figure reappears and other Old Testament imagery makes a final appearance. Identify as much as you can. The book is again called prophecy (22:7), and the details of the visions ought not to be limited by literal interpretations. For example, work out the dimensions of the new Jerusalem and consider how they are to be understood. John evidently thinks of the new as a renewal of the old. In 22:2, the leaves of the tree of life are "medicine for the nations," yet presumably the nations have already been healed when all things are made new. Remember that we began this session by observing that the Book of Revelation had a direct application to the Churches first addressed. It is a serious mistake to interpret this apocalypse as a prophecy of events after the first century AD.

Study the concluding words, **22:16–21.** Verse 17 is set in the worship of the Church. Compare verses 18–20 with 1 Corinthians 16:22 and do not forget that there was no New Testament canon when these words were written. "Come, Lord Jesus!" and "Our Lord, come!" both reflect the Aramaic prayer of the primitive Church, the Maranatha (see 1 Cor 16:22). In the final benediction, remember that all the people in Christ's Church are called saints in the New Testament. The ending of Revelation makes a fitting conclusion to the Bible.

Suggestions for Further Study

Research

1. What is the significance of "Alpha" and "Omega" in Revelation 22:13? Write a paraphrase of this verse, using this information.

2. Locate each of the seven Churches of Revelation 2–3 with the help of an atlas, and review the information about them in a Bible dictionary.

3. For unique and surprising contemporary perspectives on heaven and hell, read C. S. Lewis, *The Great Divorce*.

Reflection

1. What new symbols would you use today to illuminate visions like John's? What signs of hope are there for Christians today?

2. We have reached the conclusion of this study program. It is time for review, summary, and critique. We have studied most of the Bible, but you must be aware how much more there is to learn. You now have a very stable foundation for further study. Be encouraged to continue to enrich your knowledge of the Bible and to teach others who have not yet benefitted from extensive Bible study.

3. You may wish to master the following verses: Revelation 5:12; 14:13; 21:3–6; 22:1–7.

Appendices

APPENDIX 1

The Church in the New Testament

Introduction

In this article, the challenge for me is to be both scholarly and pastoral: to reflect the helpful conclusions of recent scholarly studies, and at the same time to give useful information to anyone having problems with church membership. Is it necessary for a believing Christian to join a church? If so, which Christian Church goes back to the New Testament? Did Jesus start a church, or was the church a later invention? Is nominal church membership sufficient?

The Church Came Long before the New Testament

To many people, especially those of a fundamentalist background, it is a surprise to learn that the Christian Church started at least a century before the New Testament was fully written and at least three or four centuries before the New Testament, as we know it, was collected. The apostles, the early martyrs, the first followers of Jesus—all these had no New Testament. Later believers had at best little stories of Jesus or letters from the apostles. The only Bible the first Christians had was the Bible of the Jewish synagogue. The Church generated the books of the New Testament and defined them as inspired. The Bible depends on the Church, and not vice versa. From the New Testament we can learn something about the Christian Church, but not everything.

The Importance of Tradition

To get a full picture of the Church in New Testament times, we must look carefully at what the New Testament tells us. But we must also look at Tradition, spelled here with a capital T to show its importance. Tradition is faith lived, shared with others, confessed, handed on to others, and in time written down. It was Tradition in this sense that formed the Old Testament. It was Tradition in this sense that sustained the faith of those first followers of Jesus Christ before they had a New Testament. Such Tradition, which is something living and developing, is believed by followers of Christ to be guided by the Holy Spirit of truth (see Jn 15:26). This same Spirit has been promised by the Lord to guide all followers and teach them all truth in the future.

How important is Tradition as a source of information about the message and church of Jesus Christ? The answer to this question stands as a basic difference between the Protestant and Catholic view of the Church. The reformers of the sixteenth century emphasized the Bible so much that "scripture alone" became their theological battle cry. Roman Catholics emphasized that both scripture and Tradition witnessed to God's revelation. Today the two sides are not arguing over this question. Protestants recognize that the Bible is an expression of the Church's Tradition and is to be read and interpreted within a living faith community. Catholics acknowledge that scripture, the Church's Tradition frozen by inspiration at one point in its development, is normative for the Church's faith and doctrine. That developing Tradition of the New Testament Church is usually divided into two periods. First is the Apostolic Age, ranging from Pentecost to the death of the apostles and destruction of Jerusalem, dated as AD 30–70. Second is the Subapostolic Age, from the destruction of Jerusalem to the end of the New Testament writing (AD 70 to perhaps AD 110–140).

Generally speaking, the books of the New Testament were written in the Subapostolic period. Their ideas of church reflect Antioch, Ephesus, and Rome more than Jerusalem. The New Testament shows a steady development of the Christian Church.

The Church in Jerusalem

Of the Jerusalem church we have very little knowledge. Our best source is the book of Acts, written a half century after the event, which gives us an idealized picture of the church in Jerusalem. Nonetheless, the descriptions in Acts help us considerably in understanding the basic characteristic of the Church of Jesus Christ. According to Acts 2:41–42, the Jerusalem church

was a sect within Judaism. However, as this text and the book of Acts show, it had several special qualities: (1) baptism was the entrance; (2) acceptance of the apostles' teaching was normative; (3) a communal life; (4) "breaking of the bread": the eucharistic meal of Jesus' body and blood; (5) praying together; (6) serving the poor of society in the name of Christ. Now, nearly twenty centuries later, those characteristics of the first Christian community continue.

The Role of Peter the Apostle

As shown in the early writings of Paul, and in the gospels of Mark, Matthew, and John, the apostle Peter had special importance. Much more was written about the apostle Peter than about all the other apostles combined. Peter was the first on every list. For Paul, the text of orthodox teaching was Peter's teaching (Gal 1:18). Mark's gospel is heavily influenced by Peter's teaching. In Matthew's gospel, Jesus gives this man the name Peter (Rock), says he will build his Church on that Rock, and promises Peter the very keys of heaven (Mt 16:13–20). In John's gospel, the resurrected Lord assigns to Peter the role of pastor or shepherd of the entire flock of Christ, the Church (Jn 21:15–19).

The gospels mark the written end of a long period of development. They do show the special function of Peter. They do not clearly indicate a continuing office of special authority based on Peter, but neither do they exclude the development of such an office. In theological dialogues between Lutheran and Catholic theologians, there has been agreement that the New Testament provides the trajectory for a Petrine ministry to continue for the service of the entire Christian Church.

The Church beyond Jerusalem

The New Testament gives evidence of various early ministries in the Church (cf. 1 Cor 12), and of the gradual development to presbyter-bishops and deacons (see Phil 1:1; 1 Tm 3), ordained by the laying on of hands. There is, as the New Testament is written, increasing emphasis on sacraments and apostolic succession in the ordination by the laying on of hands. There is, in the Great Commissioning that closes Matthew's gospel, a granting of teaching authority to the apostles (Mt 28:18–20).

So, as the Church grew in Tradition, the New Testament books were written. We cannot now recapture the early forms of the Jerusalem Christian church structure within a Judaism now past. We can but follow the steady development from the Jerusalem church to Antioch and Paul's church, and to that of Rome in the 90s.

The Witness of Clement of Rome and Ignatius of Antioch

Two nonscriptural writings from the Subapostolic age help our investigation. Clement of Rome (c. AD 96) taught apostolic succession and shows the apostolic care of the Church at Rome for other churches. Ignatius of Antioch (c. AD 115) spoke of "the catholic church," and emphasized the roles of the single bishop, assisted by priests and deacons. These two wrote before the New Testament was completed.

The Challenge of Church Membership

In a sense, it is easier to follow Jesus without the Church. The problem of the Church is not its divine head but its human members, which we are. Yet Jesus, as the New Testament tells us, is behind this Spirit-guided Church. Christianity is not a do-it-yourself religion. It is a faith that expects membership in the Church and work to build up the Lord's Church in our times. As the New Testament itself shows, the early Christian communities had their fair share of bickering, mishandling, faithlessness, and struggles for power. We should then not be shocked to find the same in the history of Christianity and in our own times and selves. We stay within the Church and build it up because of Jesus Christ, and not because of its weak members. This Church, so filled with frail humans, remains the body of Christ and always leads us to Jesus Christ.*

* If any reader wishes to pursue these summary ideas, he or she may be interested in several books that helped me in the development of this article. They are *The Roots of the Catholic Tradition*, by Thomas Rausch (Michael Glazier, 1986); *The New Testament Experience of Faith*, Leander Keck (Bethany Press, 1984); *Peter in the New Testament*, by Raymond Brown, *et al,* (Augsburg-Paulist, 1973); and *Where Peter Is*, by Edward Gratsch (Alba House, 1974).

article by the Most Reverend John F. Whealon
Archbishop of Hartford

APPENDIX 2

Women in the Bible

The Old Testament

The story of God's people in a patriarchal society must inevitably be focused on men as leaders in bringing their faith in Yahweh into the historical situation in which they found themselves. There are, however, a few Israelite women whose roles are by no means those of passive helpmates, and who had their own, sometimes sinful, opinions about what God was doing in their world.

Abraham's wife, Sarah, is vindictive and possessive, as her injustice toward Hagar and Ishmael shows (Gn 21). She is also a realist in her approach to God's promise of a son. She can laugh at the impossibility of an old lady's conceiving—as she will later laugh with joy in the birth of her son. She is clearly an independent thinker.

There are Israelite women who fill the role of charismatic leaders. Miriam is called a prophet, that is, a person through whom God speaks to the community. She was also a leader of the opposition to Moses, so a sinner like everyone else (Nm 12). Deborah is one of the judges, a charismatic (God-empowered) leader

who struggles to take possession of the land (Jgs 4–5). During the conquest period, there are other, non-Israelite yet spirit-led women. The prostitute Rahab saves the Israelite spies; she is clearly a woman who could trust her instincts to show a humanity that transcends conventional civic loyalties (Jos 2). Ruth, a convert to Israel, and Naomi, her mother-in-law, are put before us as ordinary believers whose faith and creative assertiveness regarding their rights are rewarded by God. Ruth gains a rich husband and royal descendents.

Among the heroines found in the biblical narratives are three more women whose roles were like that of the judges. They were able to overcome the enemies of God's people. Judith uses the violent means of deception and assassination (Jdt 11–13). Esther uses the feminine means of intercession and truth speaking (Est 5–7). The point is that both took on the responsibility for the safety of their people. The third woman is the mother of the seven sons of 2 Maccabees 7, who encourages and supports her sons as they are killed by the tyranny of a political system attempting to wipe out the religion of the Jews. All three are women of courage and scope, women whom the Spirit can call beyond themselves for the sake of their people and their God. They are "Filled with a noble spirit that stirred . . . [their] womanly heart[s] with manly courage" (2 Mc 7:21).

A final word needs to be said about Eve. Genesis 3 gives us a well-defined psychological portrait of the Israelite woman: the equal of man, taken seriously by the serpent and by God as a moral agent, able to sin and lead others to sin, needing to live with the consequences of her moral decisions. After all this she receives the name that describes her destiny: Mother-of-All-the-Living (Eve).

The New Testament

The Spirit-led women of the New Testament fall into two categories: disciples who are believers (that is, hearers and doers of the Word) and disciples who are prophets. The believers are clearly Elizabeth in Luke's infancy, who finds herself in Sarah's situation but whose confidence in God's promise was much deeper; and Lazarus' sisters, Martha and Mary, who both deeply welcomed Jesus' coming into their lives. Of the two sisters, Mary was the more liberated in her vision of discipleship, as she takes on the role of the masculine disciple who sits at the Lord's feet to hear his teaching.

We see this culture-transcending approach in the prophetic roles of both Mary Magdalen (Lk 8 and the post-resurrection stories) and Priscilla (Acts 18). Both were very active in proclaiming and teaching the good news in their situations. Also, there were apparently women leaders in the church assembly, women whose spirit was not that of Jesus in everything, since Paul has to put limits on their activity (1 Cor 14 and 1 Tm 2).

Mary

The New Testament woman par excellence is Mary the mother of Jesus. Luke calls attention to her as the perfect disciple, she who hears the Word of God and does it (Lk 8). But we get the more developed vision of her discipleship as she hears and does the task God is calling her to as mother of Jesus. She is the highly favored daughter of Zion (Lk 1:28), the recipient of all God's blessings of salvation:

> Say to daughter Zion,
> your savior comes! . . .
> They shall be called the holy people,
> the redeemed of the LORD . . . (Is 62:11–12)

Zechariah's vision:

> Rejoice heartily, O daughter Zion,
> shout for joy, O daughter Jerusalem!
> See, your king shall come to you,
> a just savior is he . . . (Zec 9:9)

Mary is the recipient of the prophetic promise: "I will be with you" (Ex 3:12), the one who will move through her life in faith, led by God. She is the one chosen (blessed among women) to be mother of the long-awaited savior-king.

As the Holy Spirit comes upon her (Lk 1:35), she will receive the charismatic mission. She is assertive in trying to understand how this is to come about her. She is, like the Ark of the Covenant and the holy of holies in the Temple, the one who is protected (overshadowed) by the presence of God (Lk 1:35). Therefore, her child is to be holy with God's own holiness. All of this must have been overwhelming, to say the least. This is why, when the consequences of her wholehearted "yes" begin, her characteristic way of dealing with them is that of treasuring everything in her heart (Lk 2:19). For the Jews, the heart was the center of consciousness and discernment, the deepest center of the true self. The true disciple hears and integrates the call of God and thus finds herself: "What profit is there for one to gain the whole world yet lose or forfeit himself?" (Lk 9:25).

Mary as the embodiment of Israel's prophetic faith shines out as she sings: "My soul proclaims the greatest of the Lord" (Lk 1:46). This song shows her as the spiritual heir of Israel's promises and the one who places herself at God's disposal in everything. It also shows that this woman had interiorized the spirituality of God's poor. The poor were those who were always heard by the Lord, because they cried out to God in their need: "Incline your ear, O LORD; answer me, for I am afflicted and poor." (Ps 86:1)

They were the Lord's true servants (prophets) because they listened to God's word to them day by day (Is 50:4). They were committed to God's will to justice for the poor and God's judgment on those who oppress and exploit their weakness. Mary is the true woman believer. Her faith shows the radicality of Jesus' faith, and her enthusiasm embodies Jesus' spirit in a unique way. In this, she is the feminine counterpart of Paul, both of them burning with joy in their believing.

John's gospel gives us a picture of Mary who believes without having seen the signs that the other disciples need. She has already achieved what Jesus calls all his disciples to: "Blessed are those who have not seen and have believed" (Jn 20:29). She is the woman of the wedding feast (Jn 2) and the redeemed Eve at the foot of the cross, who becomes the mother of all the sons and daughters of God born from the water and blood of Jesus' side (Jn 19). It is from John's vision of the greatness of the mission given her—like Eve, to be the mother of all the living—that forms the basis of her being understood as mother of the Church.

In the Bible, many people do many things. But there are not many who really believe. In the Old Testament, there are some prophets, a few good men and a few good women. In the New Testament, there are some disciples, both men and women. Mary is held up as a model of a believer whose reponsiveness to the Spirit can be life-enhancing for all other disciples. Her mission and spirituality are thus normative for other disciples, women and men, who join Jesus as the Way to God.

article by Carol Cowgill

APPENDIX 3

The Biblical Concept of Justice

The English word "justice" does not have an exact equivalent in Hebrew. *Mishpat* is the justice that is embodied in a concrete act or deed. The more general term is *sedaqah*, which is often translated into English as "righteousness." *Sedaqah* implies a relationship, justice in the same sense of a right relationship between God and the people, or between God and the individual, or among the people themselves.

Sedaqah is often used in the sense of goodness, innocence, and then justice stands for right living (2 Sm 22:21–25; Ps 45:8). But it is a dynamic concept, referring less to the idea of being just and more to the notion of doing justice (Ps 15:2). One can "do justice" on juridical, social, moral, and religious levels, and it is often difficult to distinguish between these levels of *sedaqah*.

The source of all justice is God. Israel's God is a "God of justice" (Is 30:18; Sir 35:12) whose justice is immense (Ps 36:7) and lasts forever (Dn 9:24; Is 51:8; Pss 111:3, 119:142). God's rule is based on justice (Ps 89:15), which reveals God's holiness (Is 5:16).

God brings justice about on earth (Jer 9:23), performing deeds of justice every day (Zep 3:5)

and doing justice for the people (Dt 32:36). God's justice is manifested as judgment and retribution, in the form of just punishment, bringing salvation to the just and ruin to the evil (Ps 11:5–7).

God's justice applies to all (Ps 9:9), since God "neither favors the person of princes, nor respects the rich more than the poor? For they are all the work of his hands" (Jb 34:19). Yet God has a special concern for the needy. "The LORD is a stronghold for the oppressed" (Ps 9:10), bringing about justice for the oppressed (Ps 103:6). The poor especially rejoice in the Lord (Is 29:19), for the God of Israel hears the cries of the poor (Ps 69:34).

The God of justice works first to satisfy the needs of the lowly. God "gives food to the hungry ... sets captives free ... gives sight to the blind ... raises up those that were bowed down ... protects strangers ... [sustains] the fatherless and the widow" (Ps 146:7–9). But in addition, the just God gets rid of the causes of injustice (Ps 10:17–18).

God's people must care for the needy as God does (Dt 10:18–19). Speaking for God the prophet tells them to "Make justice your aim:

redress the wronged, hear the orphan's plea, defend the widow" (Is 1:16). To do otherwise is an affront against God: "He who oppresses the poor blasphemes his Maker" (Prv 14:31). Jerusalem is the "city of justice" only when it cares for the needy (Is 1:21–26).

God's creation of the world, saving of Israel, and promise of justice are all bound together (Is 45:17–19), constituting a free choice by a loving God. "Only in the LORD are just deeds" (Is 45:24); so if there is justice among God's people, it is because the Lord loves them so much as to freely give them a share of God's justice. God communicates justice to us (Is 45:8, 61:11), "guides the humble to justice" (Ps 25:9); and rains down justice upon us (Hos 10:12).

Justice can also be a human achievement (Am 5:23–24), and the law states that "Justice and justice alone shall be your aim" (Dt 16:20). The people, then, are to "Sow for yourselves justice" (Hos 10:12), but they can never match God's justice (Ps 143:2), for God's ways are above their ways (Is 55:9) and God sees things differently from them (1 Sm 16:7).

Human justice concerns the downtrodden (Is 1:17), so it is no wonder that Job identifies justice with helping the needy (Jb 29:14–16). It is the task of the good king to bring justice to the poor and oppressed (Ps 72:1, 4, 12), so the mother of Lemuel, king of Massa, advised him to "decree what is just, defend the needy and the poor!" (Prv 31:9).

One of the causes of poverty is injustice (Prv 13:23); and since God hates injustice (Is 61:8), poverty is contrary to the law: "There should be no one of you in need" (Dt 15:4). The urgency of this law gives it primacy over other expressions of religion. The people are to "Bring no more worthless offerings" (Is 1:13) and are instead to "Make justice your aim" (Is 1:16). They are to forget about sackcloth and ashes, since the fasting that God wants is "releasing those bound unjustly, untying the thongs of the yoke;

setting free the oppressed, breaking every yoke; sharing your bread with the hungry, sheltering the oppressed and the homeless; clothing the naked when you see them, and not turning your back on your own" (Is 58:6–7). God hates their feasts, so they are to stop their "noisy songs" and should instead "let justice surge like water" (cf. Am 5:21–24).

God gets angry with the people when they mistreat the lowly (Ez 22:29–31). This is especially true in the prophecy of Amos, in which God gives the command for the destruction of Israel (6:11) because of its sins against justice. It is important to keep in mind that for Amos, as for the other biblical authors, social justice equals religious justice. A just person is one who takes up the right attitude to God and to other human beings and lives by it. "Biblical justice is more comprehensive than subsequent philosophical definitions. It is not concerned with a strict definition of rights and duties, but with the rightness of the human condition before God and within society." (U.S. Bishops, *Economic Justice for All*, 1986. p. 39.)

God's care for the lowly and afflicted is directly related to the covenant with the people (Ex 2:23–24; Jer 23:5–6, 33:14–18). "They shall be my people, and I will be their God, with faithfulness and justice" (Zec 8:8). God promises in the covenant to care for "the smallest of all nations" (Dt 7:7), so that the very election of Israel was an act on behalf of justice for the lowly. And since God's justice lasts forever, the Lord must of necessity be a "faithful God who keeps his merciful covenant" (Dt 7:9).

Justice and faithfulness, then, go hand in hand (1 Sm 26:23; Is 11:5; 1 Mc 7:18; Ps 119:138). When Jerusalem defends the orphan and hears the widow's plea, it becomes the "city of justice, faithful city" (Is 1:26). Perhaps the clearest linking of justice and faithfulness within the context of covenant is found in Hosea, the prophet married to an unfaithful wife as God was married to an unfaithful people. Through Hosea, God tells the people: "I will espouse you to me forever: I will espouse you in right and in justice, in love and in mercy; I will espouse you in fidelity, and you shall know the LORD." (Hos 2:21–22). Here the covenant becomes the umbrella for a number of concepts, including the two aspects of justice, *sedaqah* and *mishpat,* along with God's special love, unbounding mercy and faithfulness. Once the people experience the God of the covenant as just, loving, merciful, and faithful, then they "know the Lord."

Doing justice, therefore, leads to knowledge of God (Jer 22:16), for God is our justice (Jer 23:6, 33:16). The commands to "seek the LORD" and to "let justice prevail at the gate" are part of the same prophetic message (see Am 5:6, 15).

Doing justice also leads to "the peace of justice" (Bar 5:4), for only "justice will bring about peace" (Is 32:17). When the psalmist sings that "justice and peace shall kiss" (Ps 85:11), the idea is expressed that the Israelite experience of right order (peace) reigns in the world only when there is right order (justice) in the relationships between God and people and within society.

Perhaps the most famous summary of the prophetic view of religion is found in Micah 6:6–8, where we are told that God requires three things of us: the doing of justice, the practice of steadfast love, and walking humbly with God. It is no wonder, then, that the prophets foretell a messiah who will be "a just savior" (Zec 9:9), a servant who "establishes justice on the earth" (Is 42:4).

When Jesus comes, he is welcomed as a gift from the God who lifts the lowly and fills the hungry with good things (Lk 1:52–53). Poor and homeless, Jesus sees his ministry as the fulfillment of Isaiah's prophecy of the messiah sent "to bring glad tidings to the poor" and "to proclaim liberty to captives and recovery of sight to the blind, to let the oppressed go free" (Lk 4:18). As a sign of his messiahship, Jesus uses not the spiritual effects of his ministry but rather its social effects: "the blind regain their sight, the lame walk, lepers are cleansed, the deaf hear, the dead are raised, the poor have the good news proclaimed to them" (Lk 7:22).

Announcing a kingdom in which the last shall be first, Jesus is critical in the parable of the Good Samaritan of religious people who ignore suffering humanity (Lk 10:29–37). And in the story of the judgment of the nations, he goes so far as to locate the source of salvation in concern and help for the needy (Mt 25:31–46).

Paul reflects the same concern for the poor that shows up in the gospels (Gal 2:10), and his message is preached primarily to the lower classes (1 Cor 1:26–29). The Deuteronomic law that "there should be no one of you in need" (Dt 15:4) is fulfilled in the early Christian community: "There was no needy person among them" (Acts 4:34).

The New Testament carries over the concept of *sedaqah* in the form of the Greek word *dikaioo,* translated as "righteousness" or "justification." Justice, especially in the writings of Paul, is presented in terms of salvific grace. This grace, freely bestowed, justifies the one who has faith in Jesus (Rom 3:26), and it is, as it had been in the Old Testament, a gift from God (Eph 2:8). There is a dynamic aspect to the Pauline notion of justice, which is not a state of being just but rather a living out of the justice obtained through baptism.

article by Gerald Darring

APPENDIX 4

Books of the Bible:
A Comparison Chart

Varieties of the Old Testament Canon

THE PROTESTANT BIBLE	THE HEBREW BIBLE	NEW AMERICAN BIBLE
Law	**Torah**	**The Pentateuch**
Genesis	"In-beginning"	Genesis
Exodus	"These (are) the names"	Exodus
Leviticus	"He called"	Leviticus
Numbers	"In the wilderness"	Numbers
Deuteronomy	"These (are) the words"	Deuteronomy
History	**Former Prophets**	Joshua
Joshua	Joshua	Judges
Judges	Judges	Ruth
Ruth	Samuel	
1 & 2 Samuel	Kings	**The Historical Books**
1 & 2 Kings		1 & 2 Samuel
1 & 2 Chronicles	**Latter Prophets**	1 & 2 Kings
Ezra	Isaiah	1 & 2 Chronicles
Nehemiah	Jeremiah	Ezra
Esther	Ezekiel	Nehemiah
	The Twelve	Tobit
	Hosea	Judith
Poetry	Joel	Esther
Job	Amos	1 & 2 Maccabees
Psalms	Obadiah	
Proverbs	Jonah	
Ecclesiastes	Micah	**The Wisdom Books**
Song of Solomon	Nahum	Job
	Habakkuk	Psalms
	Zephaniah	Proverbs
Major Prophets	Haggai	Ecclesiastes
Isaiah	Zechariah	Song of Songs
Jeremiah	Malachi	Wisdom
Lamentations		Sirach (Ecclesiasticus)
Ezekiel		
Daniel	**Writings**	
	Psalms	**The Prophetic Books**
	Job	Isaiah
Minor Prophets	Proverbs	Jeremiah
Hosea	Ruth	Lamentations
Joel	Song of Songs	Baruch
Amos	Qoheleth	Ezekiel
Obadiah	Lamentations	Daniel
Jonah	Esther	Hosea
Micah	Daniel	Joel
Nahum	Ezra-Nehemiah	Amos
Habakkuk	Chronicles	Obadiah
Zephaniah		Jonah
Haggai		Micah
Zechariah		Nahum
Malachi		Habakkuk
		Zephaniah
		Haggai
		Zechariah
		Malachi

The New Testament Canon

GOSPELS

Matthew
sermons, parables,
O.T. testimonies

Mark
shortest;
narratives, sayings

Luke
literary parables;
breadth

John
"signs" and discourses

Acts
of the Apostles
(volume 2 of Luke)

NEW TESTAMENT LETTERS

Romans
most theologically
mature letter

1 & 2 Corinthians
local problems
and statements of faith

Galatians
to a Church disaffected
from Paul's teaching

Ephesians
mature consideration of
the Church and its
people

Philippians
appreciation and
advice for a favorite
Church of Paul's

Colossians
reflects on Christ
and the Church

1 & 2 Thessalonians
Churches stirred by
the future

1 & 2 Timothy
pastoral, for
developing Churches

Titus
pastoral

Philemon
personal letter from
Paul to the owner of
a converted slave

Hebrews
the covenant with Christ
replaces the old
covenant

THE CATHOLIC LETTERS

James
faith and works

1 Peter
an early sermon

2 Peter
discussion of
Church problems

1 John
reflections on
Christian love

2 John
to a favorite
Church

3 John
to "Gaius"

Jude
warning against
false teachers

Revelation
assurance for the
Church under
persecution

APPENDIX 5

Pronunciation Guide

Aaron	air'uhn	'am ha arets'	am-ha'arets
Abihu	ah-bee'ho͞o	Amalekites	uh-mal'uh-kīts
Abimelech	ah-bim'e-lek	Ammonites	am'uh-nīts
Abiram	ah-bī'ruhm	Amorites	am'uh-rīts
Absalom	ab'suh-lohm	Anaias	an'uh-nī'uhs
Adonai	ad'uh-nahī	Antioch	an'tee-ahk
Ahab	ay'hab	Antiochus	an-ti'uh-kuhs
Ahijah	ah-hī'jah	apocrypha	uh-pahk'rif-uh

Aramaic	air-uh-may′ik	Gilgal	gil′gahl
Asa	ay′suh	Gnosticism	nahs′tuh-siz-uhm
Asaph	ay′saf	Gomorrah	guhmor′ah
Assyria	uh-seer′ee-uh	Habakkuk	huh-bak′kuhk
Athaliah	ath-uh-lī′yah	Hagar	hay′gahr
Baal	bay′al	Haggai	hag′ay-ī
Balaam	bay′luhm	Hanukkah	hahn′uh-kuh
Barnabas	bahr′nuh-buhs	Hasidim	has′uh-diz-uhm
Bashan	bay′shuhn	Hasmonean	has-muh-nee′uhn
Beelzebul	bee-el′say-buhl	Hebron	hee′bruhn
Beer-sheba	beer-shee′bah	Herod	hair′uhd
Belshazzar	bel-shaz′uhr	Hexateuch	heks′uh-tōōk
Bildad	bil′dad	Hezekiah	hez-e-kī′uh
Boaz	boh′az	Hosea	hoh-zay′uh
Caesarea	ses-uh-ree′uh	Isaac	ī′zukh
Cain	kayn	Isaiah	ī-zay′uh
Canaan	kay′nan	Jabbok	jay′bukh
Chaldea	kal-dee′uh	Jael	jay′el
Chemosh	kee′mohsh	Jehoahaz	je-hoh′ah-haz
cherubim	chair′yoo-bim	Jehoiachin	je-hoy′ah-kin
Colossians	kuh-lahsh′uhnz	Jehoiada	je-hoy′ah-dah
Cyrus	sī′rus	Jehoiakim	je-hoy′ah-kim
Damascus	duh-mas′kuhs	Jehoshaphat	je-hoh′shuh-fat
Darius	dah-rī′uhs	Jehu	jay′hōō
Dathan	day′than	Jephthah	jef′thuh
Deborah	deb′aw-ruh	Jeremiah	jair-uh-mi′uh
deuterocanonical	dōō-tuh-roh-kuh-nahn′i-kuhl	Jericho	jair′i-koh
Ebenezer	eb-uh-nee′zuhr	Jeroboam	jair-uh-boh′uhm
Ecclesiastes	ee-klee′zee-ast′eez	Jeshua	jesh′ōō-uh
Ecclesiasticus	ee-klee′zee-as′ti-kihs	Jethro	jeth′roh
Elihu	ee-li′hyōō	Jezebel	jez′uh-bel
Elijah	ee-lī′juh	Joash	joh′ash
Eliphaz	el′i-faz	Josiah	joh-sī′uh
Elisha	ee-lī′shuh	Judea	jōō-dee′uh
Elohim	e-oh′him	Kingu	kin′gōō
Emmaus	eh-may′uhs	Kíriath-jearim	kihr′ee-ath-jee′ahr-em
Ephesus	ef′uh-suhs	Korah	koh′rah
Esau	ee′saw	kyrios	kir′ee-ohs
Essenes	eh-seenz′	Laban	lay′buhn
Ezekiel	ee-zee′kee-uhl	Lachish	lay′kish
Galatians	guh-lā′-shuhnz	Laodicea	lay-ahd-i-see′uh
Gamaliel	gah-may′lee-uhl	Leah	lee′uh
Gaza	gah′zah	Lemuel	lem′yōō-el
Gideon	gid′ee-uhn	Levi	lee′vī
Gilboa	gil′boh-uh	Leviathan	li-vī′uh-thuhn
Gilead	gil′ee-ad	Levites	lee′vīts

Leviticus	luh-vit′i-kuhs	Philemon	fi-lee′muhn
Lystra	lis′truh	Philippians	fi-lip′ee-uhnz
Maccabees	mak′uh-beez	Philistines	fil′is-teens
Macedonia	mas-e-doh′nee-uh	Phoenicia	foh-nee′shee-uh
Magog	may′gagh	Pilate, Pontius	pi′luht, pon′shuhs
Maher-shalal-hashbaz	may′uhr-shal′al-hash′bahz	Puah	poo′uh
Malachi	mal′ih-kī	Purim	poor′-m
Manasseh	muh-na′suh	Qumran	koom′rahn
Manna	man′nah	Rabbah	rahb′bah
Marduk	mahr′dook	Ramoth	ram′ohth
Mari	mah′ree	Rehoboam	ree-huh-boh′uhm
Mattathias	mat-uh-thi′uhs	Rosh Hashannah	rohsh hah-shahn′ah
Megiddo	me-gid′doh	Sabaoth	sab′uh-ohth
Melchizedek	mel-kiz′uh-dek	Sadducees	sad′yoo-seez
Mephibosheth	mi-fib′oo-sheth	Samaria	suh-mar′ee-uh
Meribah	mair′ee-bah	Sanhedrin	san-heed′ruhn
Mesha	mee′shah	Sapphira	suh-fī′ruh
Mesopotamia	mes-uh-puh-tay′mee-uh	Sardis	sahr′dis
Methuselah	me-thoo′zuh-luh	Sennacherib	sen-ak′uhr-ib
Micah	mī′kah	Septuagint	sep′too-uh-jint
Micaiah	mi-kī′yah	seraphim	sair′uh-fim
Midian	mid′ee-uhn	Shalmaneser	shal′muhn-ee′zuhr
Mishnah	mish′nuh	Shearjashub	shee′ahr-yay′shuhb
Moab	moh′ab	Shechem	shek′em
Naaman	nay′uh-muhn	Shema	shee′muh
Naboth	nay′buhth	Sheol	shay′ohl
Nadab	nay′dab	Shibboleth	shib′boh-leth
Nag Hammadi	nagh hahm-mah′dee	Shiloh	shī′loh
Nahum	nay′hem	Shiphrah	shif′ruh
Naomi	nay-oh′mee	Siloam	sī-loh′uhm
Naphtali	naf′tuh-lee	Sinai	si′ni
Nebuchadnezzar	ne′buh-kuhd-nez′uhr	Sirach	sī′rak
Nehemiah	nee uh mī′uh	Smyrna	smuhr′nuh
Nicodemus	nik-oh-dee′muhs	Sodom	sah′duhm
Nicolaitans	ni-koh-lay′i-tahns	Succoth	suhk′uhth
Nineveh	nin′e-ve	Syrophoenician	sī′roh-fuh-nee′shuhn
Nuzi	noo′zee	Talmud	tahl′mood
Obadiah	oh-buh-dī′uh	Tamar	tay′mer
Omri	ohm′ree	Thessalonian	thes-uh-loh′nee-uhnz
Onesimus	oh-nes′i-mus	Thyatira	thi′uh-ti′ruh
Paraclete	pair′uh-kleet	Tiamat	tee′ah-maht
Parousia	pah-roo-see′uh	Tiglath-Pileser	tig′lath-pi-lee′suhr
Pentateuch	pen′tah-took	Torah	toh′rah
Pergamum	puhr′guh-muhm	Tyre	tīr
Pharaoh	fair′oh	Uriah	yoo-ri′uh
Pharisees	fair′i-seez	Uzziah	yuh-zī′ah

Yahweh	yah′way	Zephaniah	zef-uh-nī′uh
Yom Kippur	yahm kip′uhr	Zerubbabel	zuhr-ruhb′uh-bl
Zarephath	zah′re-fath	Ziklag	zig′lag
Zechariah	zek-uh-rī′uh	Zion	zī′uhn
Zedekiah	zed-uh-kī′ah	Zophar	zoh′fahr
Zelophehad	ze-loh-fay′had		

APPENDIX 6

History of the Bible:
A Time Line

THE ENGLISH BIBLE: FROM THE EARLIEST TRANSLATIONS TO TODAY

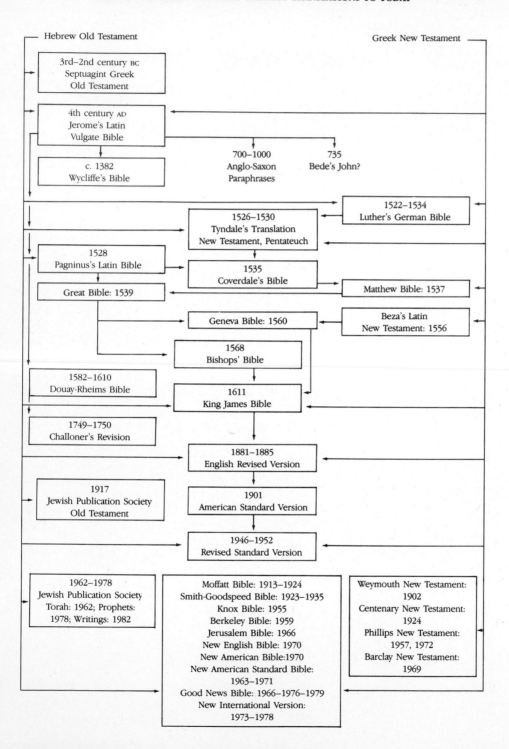

Hebrew Old Testament

Greek New Testament

3rd–2nd century BC
Septuagint Greek
Old Testament

4th century AD
Jerome's Latin
Vulgate Bible

c. 1382
Wycliffe's Bible

700–1000
Anglo-Saxon
Paraphrases

735
Bede's John?

1522–1534
Luther's German Bible

1526–1530
Tyndale's Translation
New Testament, Pentateuch

1528
Pagninus's Latin Bible

1535
Coverdale's Bible

Great Bible: 1539

Matthew Bible: 1537

Geneva Bible: 1560

Beza's Latin
New Testament: 1556

1568
Bishops' Bible

1582–1610
Douay-Rheims Bible

1611
King James Bible

1749–1750
Challoner's Revision

1881–1885
English Revised Version

1917
Jewish Publication Society
Old Testament

1901
American Standard Version

1946–1952
Revised Standard Version

1962–1978
Jewish Publication Society
Torah: 1962; Prophets:
1978; Writings: 1982

Moffatt Bible: 1913–1924
Smith-Goodspeed Bible: 1923–1935
Knox Bible: 1955
Berkeley Bible: 1959
Jerusalem Bible: 1966
New English Bible: 1970
New American Bible:1970
New American Standard Bible:
1963–1971
Good News Bible: 1966–1976–1979
New International Version:
1973–1978

Weymouth New Testament:
1902
Centenary New Testament:
1924
Phillips New Testament:
1957, 1972
Barclay New Testament:
1969

Source: American Bible Society; from *Harper's Bible Dictionary*

APPENDIX 7

Chronology of the Bible

DATE Time scales represent varied number of years.

PREHISTORY	## THE BEGINNINGS: EVENTS IN PREHISTORY

PREHISTORY

THE BEGINNINGS: EVENTS IN PREHISTORY

Creation
Adam and Eve in the Garden
Cain and Abel
Noah and the Flood
The Tower of Babylon

2000 BC

THE ANCESTORS OF THE ISRAELITES

Abraham comes to Palestine. c. 1900
Isaac is born to Abraham.
Jacob is born to Isaac.

1800 BC

Jacob has twelve sons, who become the ancestors of the
    twelve tribes of Israel. The most prominent of these sons is
    Joseph, who becomes adviser to the King of Egypt.

THE ISRAELITES IN EGYPT

The descendants of Jacob are enslaved in Egypt.
    c. 1700–c. 1290

1600 BC

Moses leads the Israelites out of Egypt. c. 1290
The Israelites wander in the wilderness. During this time
    Moses receives the Law on Mount Sinai. c. 1290–c. 1250

1250 BC

THE CONQUEST AND SETTLEMENT OF CANAAN

Joshua leads the first stage of the invasion of Canaan. c. 1250
Israel remains a loose confederation of tribes, and leadership
    is exercised by heroic figures known as the Judges.

THE UNITED ISRAELITE KINGDOM

Reign of Saul c. 1030–c. 1010

1000 BC

Reign of David c. 1010–c. 970

Reign of Solomon c. 970–931

*A circa date is only an approximation. Generally speaking, the earlier the time, the less precise is the dating. From the time of the death of Solomon in 931 BC to the Edict of Cyrus in 538 BC, the dates given are fairly accurate; but even in this epoch a possible error of a year or two must be allowed for.

950 **BC**	

THE TWO ISRAELITE KINGDOMS

JUDAH (Southern Kingdom)   ISRAEL (Northern Kingdom)

Kings   *Kings*

JUDAH (Southern Kingdom)	*Prophets*	ISRAEL (Northern Kingdom)
Rehoboam 931–913		Jeroboam 931–910
Abijah 913–911		Nadab 910–909
Asa 911–870		Baasha 909–886
		Elah 886–885
Jehoshaphat 870–848		Zimri 7 days in 885
		Omri 885–874
	Elijah	Ahab 874–853
Jehoram 848–841		Ahaziah 853–852
Ahaziah 841	Elisha	Joram 852–841
Queen Athaliah 841–835		Jehu 841–814
Joash 835–796		Jehoahaz 814–798
Amaziah 796–781		Jehoash 798–783
Uzziah 781–740		Jeroboam II 783–743
	Amos Jonah	
Jotham 740–736		Zechariah 6 mo. in 743
		Shallum 1 mo. in 743
Ahaz 736–716	Hosea	Menahem 743–738
	Micah Isaiah	Pekahiah 738–737
		Pekah 737–732
Hezekiah 716–687		Hoshea 732–723
		Fall of Samaria 722

THE LAST YEARS OF THE KINGDOM OF JUDAH

Manasseh 687–642

Amon 642–640   *Prophets*

Josiah 640–609   Zephaniah
Joahaz 3 mo. in 609

                           Nahum

Jehoiakim 609–598   Jeremiah
Jehoiachin 3 mo. in 598   Habakkuk?
Zedekiah 598–587   Ezekiel
  Fall of Jerusalem July 587 or 586

Date markers along left margin: 900 BC, 850 BC, 800 BC, 750 BC, 700 BC, 650 BC, 600 BC

550 BC

THE EXILE AND THE RESTORATION

The Jews taken into exile in Babylonia after the fall of Jerusalem

Persian rule begins. 539
Edict of Cyrus allows Jews to return. 538
Foundations of New Temple laid. 520
Restoration of the walls of Jerusalem.
    445–443

Prophets
Haggai   Zechariah
Obadiah   Daniel
Malachi
Joel?

400 BC

THE TIME BETWEEN THE TESTAMENTS

Alexander the Great establishes Greek rule in Palestine. 333

Palestine is ruled by the Ptolemies, descendants of one of
    Alexander's generals, who had been given the position of
    ruler over Egypt. 323–198

200 BC

Palestine is ruled by the Seleucids, descendants of one of
    Alexander's generals, who had acquired the rule of
    Syria. 198–166

Jewish revolt under Judas Maccabeus reestablishes Jewish
    independence. Palestine is ruled by Judas's family and
    descendants, the Hasmoneans. 166–63

The Roman general Pompey takes Jerusalem. 63
    Palestine is ruled by puppet kings appointed by Rome. One of
    these is Herod the Great, who rules from 37–4

THE TIME OF THE NEW TESTAMENT

AD 1

Birth of Jesus*

Ministry of John the Baptist; baptism of Jesus and
    beginning of his public ministry

AD 30

Death and resurrection of Jesus

Conversion of Paul (Saul of Tarsus) *c.* 37

Ministry of Paul *c.* 41–65

Final imprisonment of Paul *c.* 65

*The present era was calculated to begin with the birth of Jesus Christ, that is, in AD 1 (AD standing for *Anno Domini,* "in the year of the Lord"). However, the original calculation was later found to be wrong by a few years, so that the birth of Christ took place perhaps about 6 BC

APPENDIX 8

Maps

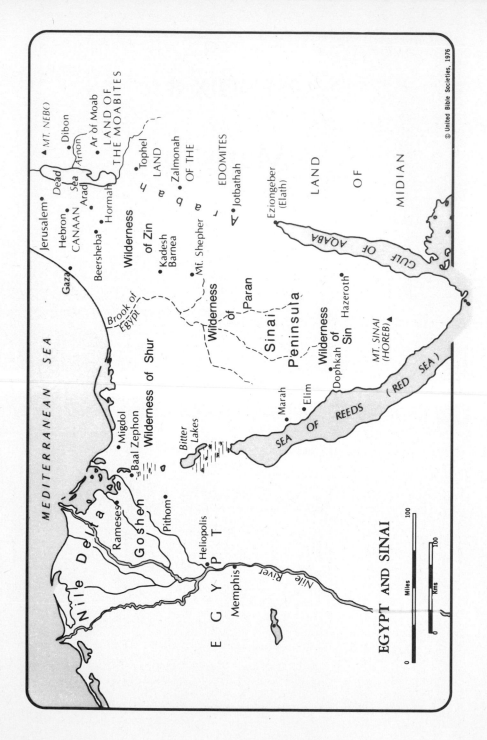

EGYPT AND SINAI

© United Bible Societies, 1976

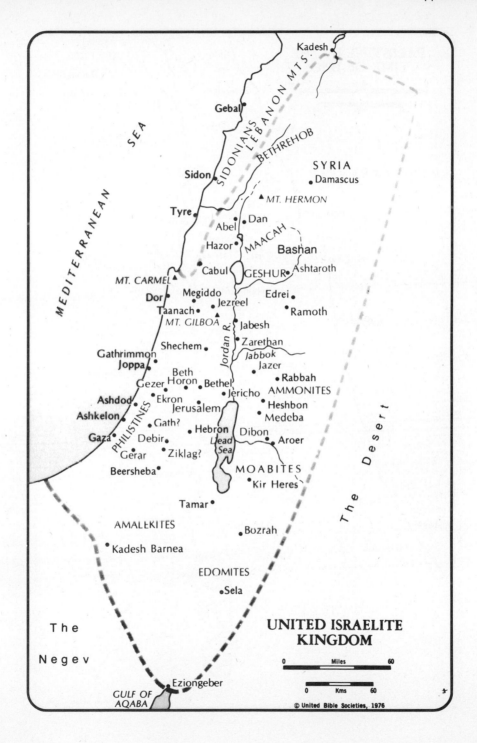

MEDITERRANEAN SEA

Kadesh

Gebal

SIDONIANS

LEBANON MTS.

Sidon

BETHREHOB

SYRIA
Damascus

Tyre

▲ MT. HERMON

Abel   Dan

Hazor   MAACAH

Bashan

Cabul   GESHUR   Ashtaroth

MT. CARMEL ▲

Dor   Megiddo   Edrei

Taanach   Jezreel   Ramoth

MT. GILBOA ▲

Jabesh

Shechem   Zarethan

Gathrimmon   *Jabbok*

Joppa   Jazer

Beth   Rabbah

Gezer   Horon   Bethel

Jordan R.

Jericho   AMMONITES

Ashdod   Ekron   Heshbon

Ashkelon   Jerusalem   Medeba

Gath?

Gaza   Hebron   Dibon

Debir   *Dead Sea*   Aroer

PHILISTINES

Gerar   Ziklag?

Beersheba   MOABITES

Kir Heres

Tamar

AMALEKITES   Bozrah

Kadesh Barnea

EDOMITES

Sela

The

Negev

UNITED ISRAELITE KINGDOM

Eziongeber

GULF OF AQABA

The Desert

| 0 | Miles | 60 |
| 0 | Kms | 60 |

© United Bible Societies, 1976

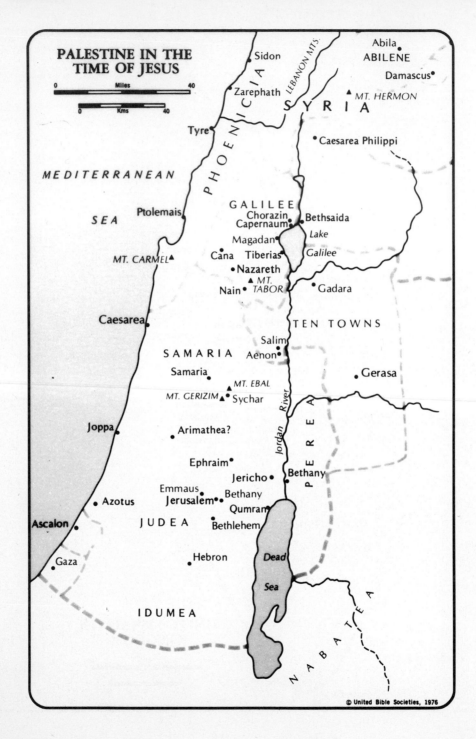

PALESTINE IN THE
TIME OF JESUS

Miles
0   40

Kms
0   40

MEDITERRANEAN

SEA

Sidon

Zarephath

LEBANON MTS.

Tyre

PHOENICIA

SYRIA

Abila
ABILENE

Damascus

MT. HERMON

Caesarea Philippi

Ptolemais

GALILEE

Chorazin   Bethsaida
Capernaum

Magadan   Lake

Cana   Tiberias   Galilee

Nazareth

MT. CARMEL

MT.
TABOR

Nain

Gadara

Caesarea

TEN TOWNS

Salim

SAMARIA   Aenon

Samaria

MT. EBAL

Gerasa

MT. GERIZIM   Sychar

Jordan River

PEREA

Arimathea?

Joppa

Ephraim

Jericho

Bethany

Emmaus

Bethany

Azotus

Jerusalem

Qumran

Ascalon

JUDEA

Bethlehem

Gaza

Hebron

Dead

Sea

IDUMEA

NABATEA

© United Bible Societies, 1976

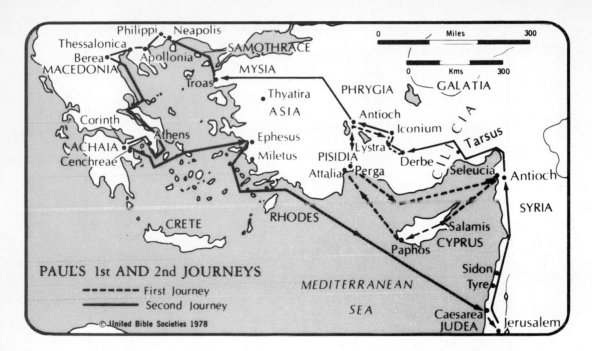

PAUL'S 1st AND 2nd JOURNEYS

- - - - - First Journey
———— Second Journey

© United Bible Societies 1978

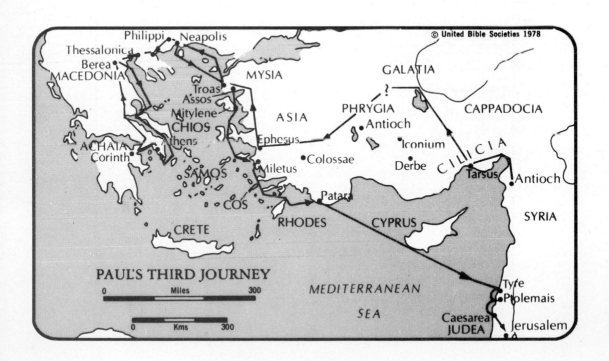

PAUL'S THIRD JOURNEY

© United Bible Societies 1978

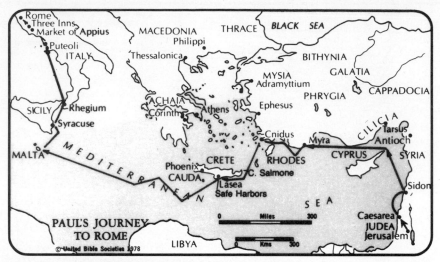

PAUL'S JOURNEY
TO ROME

© United Bible Societies 1978

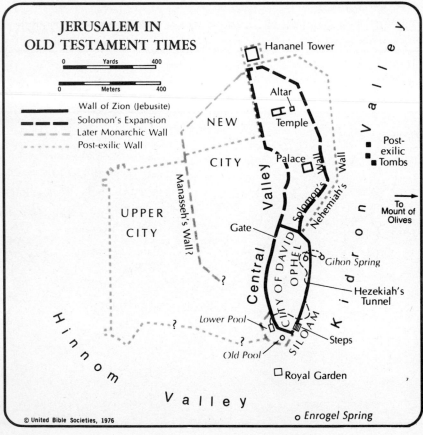

JERUSALEM IN
OLD TESTAMENT TIMES

Wall of Zion (Jebusite)
Solomon's Expansion
Later Monarchic Wall
Post-exilic Wall

© United Bible Societies, 1976

Bibliography

Anderson, Bernhard. *Understanding the Old Testament*. Englewood Cliffs, NJ: Prentice Hall, 1975.

Barton, John. "The Old Testament," in *The Study of Spirituality*. NY: Oxford, 1986.

Boadt, Lawrence. *Reading the Old Testament*. NY: Paulist Press, 1984.

Brown, Raymond. *The Gospel According to John, I–XII*. Garden City, NY: Doubleday, 1966.

Burns, Rita J. *Exodus, Leviticus, Numbers*. Wilmington, DL: Michael Glazier, Inc., 1983.

Caird, G. B. *The Revelation of St. John the Divine*. San Francisco: Harper & Row, 1966.

Collins, Adela. *The Apocalypse*. Wilmington, DL: Michael Glazier, Inc., 1979.

Craghan, John. *Esther, Judith, Tobit, Jonah, Ruth*. Wilmington, DL: Michael Glazier, Inc., 1982.

Donahue, S.J., John R. "Biblical Perspectives on Justice," in *The Faith That Does Justice*, by John Haughey, S.J. ed. NY: Paulist, 1977.

Endres, John, S.J. *Temple, Monarchy and Word of God*. Wilmington, DL: Michael Glazier, Inc., 1988.

Jack Finegan. *Light from the Ancient Past*. Princeton, NJ: Princeton University Press, 1959.

Fitzmeyer, Joseph. *The Gospel According to Luke, I–IX*. Garden City, NY: Doubleday, 1981.

Hanson, Paul. *The People Called*. San Francisco: Harper & Row, 1987.

Heschel, Abraham. *Man's Quest for God*. NY: Scribner's, 1954.

———. *God in Search of Man*. NY: Farrar, Strauss, Giroux, 1976.

———. *The Prophets*. San Francisco: Harper & Row, 1969.

Kealy, Sean. *The Apocalypse of John*. Wilmington, DL: Michael Glazier, Inc., 1987.

Laffey, Alice L. *An Introduction to the Old Testament: A Feminist Perspective*. Philadelphia: Fortress, 1988.

Lawler, Ronald, *et al. The Teaching of Christ: A Catholic Catechism for Adults*. Huntington: Our Sunday Visitor, 1976.

John Paul II. *Redemptoria Mater*. Washington, DC: U.S. Catholic Conference, 1979.

Lynch, William. *Images of Hope*. Notre Dame: University of Notre Dame, 1965.

O'Connor, Kathleen. *The Wisdom Literature*. Wilmington, DL: Michael Glazier, Inc., 1988.

Pritchard, James B. *The Ancient Near East: An Anthology of Texts and Pictures*. 3d ed. Princeton, NJ: Princeton University Press, 1969.

Sawicki, Marianne. *The Gospel in History*. Mahwah, NJ: Paulist, 1988.

Stuhlmeuller, Carrol. *Psalms 1*. Wilmington, DL: Michael Glazier, Inc., 1983.

Scott, R. B. Y. *The Relevance of the Prophets*. NY: Macmillan, 1967.

U.S. Bishops. *Economic Justice for All*. 1986.

Vawter, Bruce. *On Genesis*. Garden City, NY: Doubleday, 1977.

Vatican Council II. *Dogmatic Constitution on Divine Revelation*. Northport, NY: Costello Publishing, 1987.

_____. *Declaration on the Relation of the Church to Non-Christian Religions*. Northport, NY: Costello Publishing, 1987.

_____. *Constitution on the Church in the Modern World*. Northport, NY: Costello Publishing, 1987.

_____. *General Instruction of the Liturgy of the Hours*. Northport, NY: Costello Publishing, 1987.